THE CONTEMPORARY CONGRESS

Third Edition

Burdett A. Loomis

UNIVERSITY OF KANSAS

BEDFORD/ST. MARTIN'S
BOSTON • NEW YORK

For Charlie Tidmarch and John Lee:
Good friends, gone too soon.

For Bedford/St. Martin's
Political Science Editor: James R. Headley
Senior Editor, Publishing Services: Douglas Bell
Production Supervisor: Joseph Volpe
Project Management: Stratford Publishing Services, Inc.
Cover Design: Lucy Krikorian
Cover Photo: Diana Walker/Liaison Agency, Inc.
Composition: Stratford Publishing Services, Inc.
Printing and Binding: Haddon Craftsmen, an R. R. Donnelley & Sons Company

President: Charles H. Christensen
Editorial Director: Joan E. Feinberg
Director of Editing, Design, and Production: Marcia Cohen
Manager, Publishing Services: Emily Berleth

Library of Congress Catalog Card Number: 99-62346

Manufactured in the United States of America

5 4 3 2 1 0
f e d c b a

For information, write: Bedford/St. Martin's, 75 Arlington Street, Boston, MA 02116
(617-426-7440)

ISBN: 0-312-20861-8

Preface

In developing *The Contemporary Congress,* we anticipated updating it every two years. As the wild rise of the Republican House in 1995 has given way to budget confrontations, hotly contested elections, leadership shake-ups, and, finally, the impeachment and trial of a president, this has proven a useful strategy. The 106th Congress, with Speaker Dennis Hastert (R-Ill.), is a lot different than that of Speaker Newt Gingrich. Likewise, the politics of budgetary surpluses is a very different politics than that of continuing budget deficits.

Nor does the future look any more certain on Capitol Hill. The election of the year 2000 is arguably the first since 1952 in which both houses of Congress and the presidency are up for grabs. Such a circumstance will probably induce the national parties to spend record amounts on campaigning. The nationalization of congressional elections has become well established, even as the number of competitive races have decreased.

Congress has scarcely become a highly adaptable institution, fast on its "1,070 feet" in Nelson Polsby's memorable words. Still, the scholarship of congressional parties, elections, committees, voting, and relations with the president do evolve, year to year.

I would like to thank several reviewers whose suggestions led to improvements in the manuscript as it developed through three editions: Cary R. Covington, University of Iowa; Hulen Davis, Prairie View A&M University; Marjorie Randon Hershey, Indiana University, Bloomington; G. Calvin Mackenzie, Colby College; Michael J. Malbin, State University of New York, Albany; Ronald M. Peters, Jr., University of Oklahoma, Norman; Harold W. Stanley, University of Rochester; Randall W. Strahan, Emory University; and Shirley Anne Warshaw, Gettysburg College.

As with the first two editions of *The Contemporary Congress,* Bedford/ St. Martin's has proven a supportive partner. Beth Gillett and James Headley have been most encouraging, as have Doug Bell and Leslie Connor on the production end. I look forward to future editions, and future Congresses, as the process of representation continues past the millennium.

Burdett A. Loomis

Contents

About the Author

Burdett A. Loomis is a professor of political science at the University of Kansas. He received his Ph.D. from the University of Wisconsin, Madison, in 1974, served as an American Political Science Congressional Fellow in 1975–1976, and has taught at the University of Kansas since 1979.

He has written on a variety of topics, including Congress, interest groups, state legislatures, and public policy. Among his books are *The New American Politician* (Basic, 1988), *Time, Politics, and Policy: A Legislative Year* (University Press of Kansas, 1994), and *The Sound of Money,* with Darrell West (Norton, 1999). In addition, he has coedited five editions of *Interest Group Politics* (CQ Press), the leading reader in the interest group field.

In 1984, Loomis directed the Congressional Management Project, which produced the first of many editions of *Setting Course: A Congressional Management Guide,* a book that helps newly elected legislators in organizing their offices and activities on Capitol Hill. Aside from teaching courses on congressional politics, interest groups, and policy making, since 1983 Loomis has directed public internship programs in Washington and Topeka. He currently serves as Interim Director of the Robert J. Dole Institute for Public Service and Public Policy at the University of Kansas.

Loomis won a Kemper Teaching Award in 1996, in part for his work in establishing the University of Kansas' Washington Semester Program. He lives in Lawrence, Kansas, with his wife Michel and son Dakota.

One

THE DRAMA OF REPRESENTATION

E very two years, in 435 congressional districts, candidates conduct locally based campaigns to determine who will make national policy decisions. Portuguese-speaking fishermen in Massachusetts, Chicago suburbanites, and rural Oregonians, among others, must sort out who can represent their interests, and those of the nation. The U.S. Congress is, to be sure, a national political institution. But its roots are planted in 435 constituencies, each of which engages in its own biennial electoral drama. Our examination of the Congress begins with one district where the politics of the 1990s has played out in a series of dramatic episodes.

NATIONAL POLITICS COMES HOME: PENNSYLVANIA'S THIRTEENTH DISTRICT, 1992–1999

Although this Philadelphia-area congressional district does include some pockets of black voters, its core population is "overwhelmingly white and Republican" — with many residents living along the historic and affluent "Main Line" corridor.[1] Despite its traditional Republicanism, the district has proven unpredictable in recent elections; for example, its voters supported George Bush for president in 1988 by a twenty-point margin, yet it narrowly opted for Bill Clinton four years later. In the 1990s, neither party could take the allegiance of the Thirteenth District's electorate for granted, and the congressional elections of 1992, 1994, 1996, and 1998 demonstrated how national and local forces combine to produce a complex and sometimes contradictory representational linkage between legislator and constituency.

---

[1]Philip B. Duncan and Christine C. Lawrence, eds., *Politics in America, 1996* (Washington, DC: Congressional Quarterly, Inc., 1995), p. 1146. The "Main Line" refers to a railroad line that has long served its upscale commuters.

Act I

August 5, 1993. The vote was at hand on the most important proposal of President Bill Clinton's initial year in office — a five-year, $492-billion deficit reduction package. The top House Democratic leaders and the party's extensive whip organization had worked relentlessly to round up every available vote in support of the deficit reduction proposals that had resulted from endless hours of negotiations in House–Senate conference committee meetings. Almost every representative had come to the floor, eager to witness the concluding scene of this extended struggle. For those who remained undecided, there was no place to run, no place to hide.

As the fifteen minutes formally allowed for voting expired, almost all members had cast their ballots, but the electronic tally board showed the result was still in doubt. President Clinton's fellow Democrats would have to provide the margin of victory; no Republican had broken party ranks. Unanimously, the 174 minority-party legislators had voted against the Clinton package, with its combination of spending cuts and tax increases. Four Democratic members remained in the well of the House, waiting to cast their votes. Representative David Minge, a conservative first-term Minnesotan, wanted considerably more in spending cuts. Representative David Thornton, from the president's own state of Arkansas, and Representative Pat Williams, from Montana's wide-open spaces and ordinarily a staunch party loyalist, objected to the 4.3-cent gas tax increase. The president called Williams and pleaded, "I can't win this without you. My presidency is at stake."[2] Williams agreed to support the package, despite his desire to cast a "no" vote that would please his constituents, who often drove long distances across Big Sky Country.

Representatives Thornton and Minge refused to budge, and both voted against the Clinton budget. For Thornton, to oppose his fellow Arkansan was an especially difficult decision. In the end, however, he observed, "My job is to represent the people of the Second Congressional District."[3]

That left the House's verdict on the Clinton budget proposal in the hands of first-term Representative Marjorie Margolies-Mezvinsky (D-Pa.), who had previously announced her opposition to the plan and had steadfastly resisted all tax increases. Although Bill Clinton had received 46 percent of the vote — a bit above his average across the nation — in her upscale, suburban Philadelphia district, Margolies-Mezvinsky won her seat, held by Republicans for the previous seventy-six years, with the extremely narrow margin of 1,373 votes out of 254,000 cast. She had triumphed, she argued, because of her stand "on two basic principles: deficit reduction and holding the line on taxes."[4] True to

---

[2]Clifford Krauss, "Whips Use Soft Touch to Succeed," *New York Times,* August 7, 1993, p. 29.

[3]Krauss, "Whips Use Soft Touch."

[4]Richard E. Cohen, "Baptism by Fire for House Newcomers," *National Journal,* June 5, 1993, p. 1366.

nominated Joseph Hoeffel, a well-qualified, well-funded candidate. The question at hand was whether Representative Fox could win enough local support to offset the apparent distaste of many of his constituents for the style and substance of the Republican House in the 104th Congress. With moderation on environmental issues and a willingness to oppose his own leaders, the congressman hoped to convey that he was responding to local concerns on national issues.

In the end, Jon Fox retained his seat by a razor-thin margin (less than one hundred votes) that symbolized the national competitiveness of the 1996 elections. Representative Fox would head into the 105th Congress with a very different message from his constituents than he received two years earlier. His attempt to distance himself from some elements of the Republican Congress had succeeded, but just barely. At least in Pennsylvania's Thirteenth District, the 1994 and 1996 elections demonstrated that attentive constituents can insist that their representatives be responsive or face the real threat of enforced retirement. Looking forward to the election of 1998, Representative Fox could scarcely take his support for granted.

Act IV

The neverending drama of Pennsylvania's Thirteenth District continued apace in 1997–1998. Representative Jon Fox had scarcely a moment's rest after his eighty-four–vote landslide in 1996. Seeking to position himself as a moderate, Fox remained under attack from both the right wing of his own party and the impending opposition of Democrat Joe Hoeffel in the general election. Fox compiled a reasonably moderate voting record over the course of the 105th Congress (he was among the twenty-five most moderate Republicans in the *National Journal*'s rankings for 1997–1998), but this did little to ward off strong challengers in either the Republican primary or the general election. Not only did Hoeffel challenge him again, this time with better funding, but the incumbent was forced to defeat three challengers in the Republican primary.

Hoeffel built on his 1996 base to raise $1.27 million in 1998 — as opposed to $704,000 two years earlier. Fox also raised more money — from $1.4 million in 1996 to more than $2 million in 1998 — but his primary election campaign expenses reduced the amount he could spend against Hoeffel. More generally, Fox found himself pulled by much the same forces that brought down Representative Margolies-Mezvinsky four years earlier. The congressional Republican party remained to the right of the moderate voters in Pennsylvania's Thirteenth District. Fox found himself caught between factions of the Republican party in the primary, and then had to face a well-prepared, well-financed moderate Democrat in the general election. The ultimate result was not a complete surprise; Fox lost by more than 9,000 votes of 175,000 cast. The Thirteenth District remained a battleground — defined both by local and national forces. And the future looks no less indeterminate, as Republicans and

Democrats scramble both to raise funds for the 2000 race and to affect the redistricting that will occur after the 2000 census.[7]

THE CENTRIFUGAL CONGRESS

Each year 435 separate House electorates and 33 or 34 state electorates (only a third of the Senate seats are contested in any given election) make their separate decisions and create a new Congress. Following the Framers' outline, the Congress brings together a remarkable variety of legislators, especially in an era of increasing representation of minorities and women. Party leaders and presidents consistently face difficulties in building coherent majorities that can pass legislation. Why is this so?

For the Congress, at least, the answer seems deceptively simple. In responding to 50 state electorates, 435 separate House constituencies, and thousands of distinct interests, the institution has organized itself in decentralized ways that impede the building of consistent majorities that can pass coherent legislation on difficult issues. This is not a recent phenomenon. Congress has traditionally been the "slow institution," emphasizing representation of interests rather than rapid, perhaps overly hasty, responses.[8] As recently as 1992, scholars could reach a rough consensus that in reflecting societal strains, the Congress had become "atomistic," even though some countering trends toward centralizing power could also be observed.[9]

Although members of Congress adopt party labels, express their support or opposition to presidential policies, and seek to solve difficult societywide problems, they must ultimately answer to 435 distinct constituencies in the House and 50 separate state electorates in the Senate. For the most part, American legislators are on their own as they seek election and reelection. They must raise the funds to finance their own campaigns, although parties and presidents will offer some assistance. Moreover, they must often survive primary elections within their own party, just to claim the Democratic or Republican label that they will carry into the November general election.[10]

Coming to Capitol Hill, legislators will seek the help of party leaders and the president, especially if they share a party label, but they will also react to the pressures of interest groups, the pull of the committees to which they

---

[7]Steven A. Holmes, "The Big Census Issue: Using Sampling in Redistricting," *New York Times*, February 14, 1999, p. 22.

[8]Richard F. Fenno, Jr., "Strengthening a Congressional Strength," in Norman J. Ornstein, ed., *Congress in Change* (New York: Praeger, 1975).

[9]Allen D. Hertzke and Ronald M. Peters, "Introduction: Interpreting the Atomistic Congress," in Allen D. Hertzke and Ronald M. Peters, eds., *The Atomistic Congress* (Armonk, NY: M. E. Sharpe, 1992), chap. 1.

[10]Alaska, Washington, and Louisiana hold blanket primaries: If no candidate wins a majority, the top two vote-getters run off, regardless of party.

have been assigned, pleas of the bureaucracy that provides seemingly limitless information, and, of course, the often-inconsistent communications from their own constituents. They will be — as Representative Margolies-Mezvinsky was — pushed and pulled from all directions. This struggle is both mystifying and off-putting to those who seek to understand congressional politics. However, Congress is not entirely without order as it seeks to represent constituents and make coherent national policies.

Indeed, the Republicans' success in capturing the Congress in 1994, pressing forward with a highly partisan agenda in 1995, and retaining control of both houses in 1996 and 1998 demonstrates that a reasonably homogeneous party can overcome many of the decentralizing tendencies of Capitol Hill politics. Republican House members willingly accorded Speaker Gingrich and the party leadership substantial power; most notably, the GOP membership chose — at least for the 104th Congress — to embrace the order imposed by a centralized party leadership, as opposed to that of a strong committee system. As Republicans reflect on the requirements of governing, they have begun to find more merits in the decentralized order of the committee system, in which expertise may temper ideology in the framing of policy change. The longer Republicans make up the congressional majority (after being out of power for forty years prior to 1995), the more likely they will devise a representational scheme that will combine a serious partisan agenda with the strong committee system that has served the institution since the early 1800s.

REPRESENTATION AND COLLECTIVE CHOICE

The U.S. Congress is a representative institution comprising two bodies that must make a series of collective, authoritative decisions — laws.[11] Ordinarily, this occurs by majority vote or, more accurately, a series of majority votes. Representatives and senators, although sporting party labels and owing much to their respective parties within the Congress, are still beholden to their own distinct district and statewide electorates. Political scientists Roger Davidson and Walter Oleszek distinguish between two different, if overlapping, visions of the U.S. Congress. On one hand, the legislators constitute a "Congress of Ambassadors," who congregate in Washington to pursue the interests of the individual states and districts. On the other hand, they meet together as a single "deliberative assembly" to address issues and reach accords that roughly serve the broad, collective interest of the nation as a whole.[12]

This sounds straightforward, but from its founding, the United States has embraced an independent, powerful legislature that has often been at odds with the two other branches of government — the presidency and the

---

[11]David Vogler, *The Politics of Congress*, 6th ed. (Madison, WI: Brown & Benchmark, 1993).

[12]Roger Davidson and Walter Oleszek, *Congress and Its Members*, 6th ed. (Washington, DC: CQ Press, 1998).

Supreme Court. Without direct, formal ties to the executive (in contrast to a parliamentary system[13] in which cabinet ministers are drawn from the legislature), the individual lawmakers have prospered by representing their own constituents, districts, states, regions, and specific interests, often at the expense of ill-defined or chimerical national interests. Legislative structures and practices have evolved that facilitate this tendency toward representation of particular interests, thereby making it difficult to construct majorities. The rules of the Senate, for example, have long protected the rights of minorities, most notably by requiring supermajorities (usually sixty votes, but sometimes two-thirds of the members) to shut off debate on a bill. Indeed, extended debate — the filibuster — may be the most distinctive feature of the highly individualistic U.S. Senate.[14]

Although protecting the rights of individual legislators has forged the nature of the U.S. Senate, it is the decentralization of the committee system that has historically marked the operation of the House of Representatives. With its large membership, the chamber has used committees to conduct much of its legislative business. Writing in 1885, Woodrow Wilson observed that the entire House "sits, not for serious discussion, but to sanction the conclusions of its committees as rapidly as possible."[15] Even in 1885 this statement was hyperbole, but it does convey the House's organizational tendency toward decentralization through subunits, as opposed to a highly centralized party structure (as, for example, in the British Parliament). Although the relative power of committees has varied since 1789, it is the standing committee system, as much as any other characteristic, that has defined the operation of the House of Representatives.

Representation as Responsiveness

Legislators take representation very seriously. Although one common, negative view of the Congress depicts it as frequently immobilized by its ties to individual constituencies and interests, such a perspective may largely reflect the highly representative nature of the institution. Political theorist Hannah Pitkin has argued that political representation means "acting in the interest of the represented, in a manner responsive to them."[16] But knowing the wishes of one's constituents across a wide range of complex issues is difficult at best, given most citizens' low levels of knowledge and interest in most policy con-

---

[13]In parliamentary systems, the executive (e.g., the prime minister) is often the leader of the majority party (or coalition among parties) *within* the chamber. The distinction between legislature and executive is thus blurred, especially when compared with the United States's separation of powers.

[14]Sarah A. Binder and Steven S. Smith, *Politics or Principle?* (Washington, DC: Brookings Institution, 1997).

[15]Woodrow Wilson, *Congressional Government* (Boston: Houghton Mifflin, 1885).

[16]Hannah Pitkin, *The Concept of Representation* (Berkeley: University of California Press, 1967), p. 209.

troversies. Nonetheless, motivated by their desire to win reelection, members of Congress seek to represent their constituents as best they can, often trying to anticipate their desires.[17] In this context, representation may be best viewed as a set of overlapping attempts to respond to "a number of targets" within a legislator's environment.[18]

Indeed, Eulau and Karps advance our understanding of representation by specifying it not in terms of mere agreement on policy preferences between legislators and their constituents. Rather, they outline four kinds of responsiveness that, taken together, constitute representation. These are, respectively, service responsiveness, allocation responsiveness, symbolic responsiveness, and policy responsiveness.[19]

Put in slightly different terms, on some issues representatives act as delegates of their constituents, especially when their interests and preferences are clear.[20] Conversely, on other issues, such as the budget, they act more like trustees, who have to sort through complex policy options and decide what is most "in the interest of the represented," to use Pitkin's language. After making such a policy choice, they then have to explain their actions to their constituents. This after-the-fact explanatory behavior is central to representation, in that it allows constituents to assess their legislators' broad policy decisions, which are often made with only a vague sense of district opinion. Members of Congress must anticipate their constituents' reactions and subsequently educate them in terms of the merits of a vote or policy position. If a legislator has acted responsively on the dimensions of service, allocation, and symbolism, he or she may well have more latitude in convincing district constituents to accept the less popular policy choices made on their behalf.[21]

Deliberation

The focus on individual legislators and their attention to their own districts has often obscured the role of the Congress as a deliberative body capable of engaging in productive debates on policy issues, large and small.[22] Such

---

[17]See Douglas Arnold, *The Logic of Congressional Action* (New Haven, CT: Yale University Press, 1990).

[18]Heinz Eulau and Paul D. Karps, "The Puzzle of Representation: Specifying Components of Responsiveness," *Legislative Studies Quarterly* 2 (August 1977): p. 241. Much of the following relies on the line of argument in this article.

[19]Eulau and Karps, "The Puzzle of Representation."

[20]The trustee-delegate distinction between representative styles has its roots in Edmund Burke's speech to his Bristol parliamentary constituents in the eighteenth century. The modern discussion derives from Warren E. Miller and Donald E. Stokes, "Constituency Influence in Congress," *American Political Science Review* 57 (March 1963): pp. 45–57.

[21]For more extensive development of this theme, see Richard F. Fenno, Jr., *Home Style* (Boston: Little, Brown, 1978); and Douglas Arnold, *The Logic of Congressional Action.*

[22]Joseph M. Bessette has produced the most cogent examination of congressional deliberation in *The Mild Voice of Reason* (Chicago: University of Chicago Press, 1994).

discussions do not always occur. For example, the extended congressional consideration of health care reform in 1993–1994 produced little reasoned give and take. Rather, deliberation simply disappeared under a deluge of highly publicized claims, counterclaims, and appeals to emotion.[23] More generally, meaningful deliberation is often missing in congressional debates.[24] As David Vogler and Sidney Waldman point out, reaching decisions on difficult issues is more than simply producing a majority that carries the day. They conclude that

> the democratic legitimacy of Congress rests on both the legislative process and the resulting policies. The value of unitary democracy [that emphasizes face-to-face deliberation] is found not simply in widespread agreement or consensus *but in the creative nature of the process itself.*[25]

The potential for creative solutions to difficult problems continues to reside within the Congress, and there is ample opportunity for deliberation, although much more so in committees, within informal task forces, and perhaps in the House gym than on the floor of either chamber. Only rarely can one tune in C-SPAN and observe substantive deliberation among legislators who are seeking to exercise their creative powers. Rather, one is treated to legislative position-taking par excellence, in which almost all senators and representatives represent some specific point of view. Effective deliberation, to the extent that it occurs at all, takes place offstage, where legislators need not worry that their constituents and campaign contributors are watching intently.

Ironically, when Congress does rise to the occasion and acts either as a decisive policy-making body or as a deliberative assembly, the normally skeptical, even cynical, public embraces the congressional actions. The Congress that worked with Lyndon Johnson to enact his expansive Great Society programs achieved widespread popularity among the public; twenty-five years later, another Congress won accolades for its cogent deliberations over the merits of the Persian Gulf war. But public support dipped to new lows for the Congress that cobbled together a highly symbolic crime bill in 1994 and found itself unable to engage in much useful debate over health care reform. As a rule, individual legislators can act in their *own* interests, but Congress as a collective finds it most difficult to act for the *whole*.

What, then, are we to make of the rush of legislation through the House of Representatives in the wake of the 1994 elections? The Republicans followed

---

[23]See, for example, James Fallows, "A Triumph of Misinformation," *The Atlantic* 275 (January 1995), pp. 26–37.

[24]See, for example, the arguments put forth by Representative Gerald Soloman (R-N.Y.) and Donald R. Wolfensberger, "The Decline of Deliberative Democracy in the House and Proposals for Change," *Harvard Journal of Legislation* 31 (1993): pp. 320–370.

[25]David J. Vogler and Sidney R. Waldman, *Congress and Democracy* (Washington, DC: CQ Press, 1984), p. 166. More generally on deliberation, see Joseph Bessette, *The Mild Voice of Reason.*

their historic electoral sweep with a legislative whirlwind in the House that was without parallel in this century. Speaker Gingrich and the House GOP captured the agenda and brought the ten Contract with America items to a vote. An initial analysis would give them high marks for responsiveness and, perhaps, representation and low scores for deliberation. By effectively nationalizing the 1994 congressional elections, using the Contract as a legislative agenda, and setting up their individual House offices, Republicans demonstrated all four kinds of responsiveness:

1. By refusing to cut back on office staff, they retained the ability to provide high levels of service to their constituents.
2. By supporting a tax cut, they sought to allocate funds back to their constituents.
3. By passing the balanced budget constitutional amendment, they adopted a policy that was backed by the public at large.
4. By voting in favor of a term limits amendment, but by less than the required two-thirds majority, they proved themselves symbolically responsive to a popular public position without endangering their own seats.

More generally, the Contract allowed House Republicans to claim that they were acting in response to an overall mandate from the electorate, even if the Contract was at best a minor element of their triumph.

At the same time, the first few months of Speaker Gingrich's tenure in the House proved almost completely devoid of deliberation. Proposed constitutional amendments were pushed through committees in a few days, as were tax cuts. When the first one hundred days came to a close, the Senate found itself with a huge backlog of major policy initiatives that had gone essentially without deliberation in the House. Indeed, many House Republicans assumed, even hoped, that the Senate's slower, deliberative style would temper the energy and partisanship of the House actions.

In the short term, the Senate and the president did either block or modify the House's actions. As Rules Committee Chairman Gerald Solomon (R-N.Y.) concluded, after serving on the front lines throughout the 104th Congress, "There are things we don't need to bring up, knowing we can't get it through the Senate or get the president to sign it. We ought to concentrate on balancing the budget and [easing] the regulatory burden . . . not take on the controversial issues [e.g., repealing gun control laws or rolling back environmental regulations] that we can't win."[26]

---

[26]Jonathan D. Salant, "Some Republicans Turned away from Leadership," *Congressional Quarterly Weekly Report,* December 7, 1996, p. 3352.

THE CONTEMPORARY CONGRESS

This book addresses the tension between the constituency-oriented, individualistic Congress that emphasizes the representation of particular interests and the Congress that can, on occasion, act coherently to pursue some broader representative goals, perhaps achieving this through creative deliberation. Much of this tension is expressed in organizational terms, with overall tendencies toward decentralization and individualism being countered by the centralizing forces of party and presidential leadership. Even the most centrifugal of forces, such as locally oriented congressional elections, sometimes reflect the unifying pull of national trends, as demonstrated by the elections of 1964, 1974, 1980, and, most recently, 1994.

This book provides a series of related pictures of the Congress that builds on the three aspects of legislative life:

1. The strong element of fragmentation, or decentralization, which reflects centrifugal forces on the Congress. These forces result from the pull of district constituencies, congressional committees, reelection campaigns, individual member offices, and the effects of interests outside the institution.

2. The corresponding centralizing (or centripetal) forces, such as the party leadership, the president, and, on occasion, landmark elections, clear trends in public opinion, national crises, and broad coalitions of interests.

3. The continuing tensions between the ever present centrifugal and centripetal forces within the Congress. Even in the extremely decentralized, fragmented period of the late 1970s, there were many forces pushing the Congress toward greater centralization. Indeed, far more interesting and important than merely categorizing different elements of the Congress as centrifugal or centripetal is examining the interplay between these forces, which simply never ends — and which was dramatically illustrated by Representative Margolies-Mezvinsky's wrenching either-or vote choice between the pressures of Democratic leaders and her constituents. In the post-1994 era, the most important source of tension has been the struggle to balance strong leadership with the traditionally powerful committee system. As of the 106th Congress (1999–2001), that struggle continues.

The next chapter traces the evolution of the modern Congress across two centuries of representation. Chapter 3 focuses on the congressional context, especially the growth of organized interests and the explosion of national policy, which create hundreds upon hundreds of new constituencies for members to represent. At the same time, the Congress is increasingly made up of relatively young and conservative Republicans who express skepticism toward many federal programs, but may well discover virtues in those that benefit their districts.

Chapters 4, 5, and 6 emphasize the foundations of congressional decentralization: elections, committees, and the "enterprises" that surround each senator and representative.[27] Individual legislators mount their own campaigns, operate within the specialized environments of committees, and control substantial resources that afford them great flexibility of action. Should we be surprised that they are hard to organize into working majorities?

Chapters 7 and 8 offer insights into the usual channels of coordination and centralization on Capitol Hill, direction from congressional party leaders and the president. Strangely enough, as the House grew more fragmented in the 1970s with the expansion of subcommittees and the sharp increase in individual office resources, party leaders also won substantial powers. By the mid-1980s, House Democratic leaders harnessed many of these procedural and appointive powers, and Speaker Jim Wright (D-Tex.), backed by the Democratic Caucus, was briefly able to wield great influence. Beset by ethics problems and a restive membership, Wright surrendered the Speakership and his House seat, and the Democratic leadership found itself faced with various minor scandals and a general loss of public confidence. The 1992 election of Bill Clinton brought with it the promise of single-party control of the executive and legislative branches for the first time in twelve years, yet President Clinton found it difficult to muster party-based majorities, especially in light of Senate delaying tactics that often required sixty votes to overcome. Then, in 1995, the Speakership of Representative Newt Gingrich demonstrated strikingly how strong a contemporary House leader could become, although the individualistic Senate remained a much less malleable institution.

Chapter 9 focuses on the formal and informal elements of congressional decision making. The formal rules and procedures of the Congress can determine the outcomes of legislative initiatives and may allow party leaders to dominate the proceedings, especially in the House. At the same time, informal rules of the game, or "folkways," provide an interpersonal context for legislative actions, as lawmakers observe (or don't) norms that encourage civil behavior even as they disagree. The increase in partisanship on Capitol Hill has challenged the civility of congressional behavior, as witnessed by the politicization of the ethics process, both in the ousting of Speaker Jim Wright (1989) and the reprimand issued to Speaker Gingrich (1997), to say nothing of Gingrich's forced resignation as Speaker in 1998.

Chapter 10 provides two extended case studies: (1) the defeat of the Clinton health care reform bill in 1993–1994 and the subsequent success of modest health care legislation in 1996; and (2) the passage of the Contract with America through the House in 1995 and the delays and defeats it encountered as its items moved through the legislative process. The richness and scope of these examples offer detailed illustrations of many of the general observations made

---

[27]Robert Salisbury and Kenneth Shepsle, "The U.S. Congressman as Enterprise," *Legislative Studies Quarterly* 6 (November 1981): pp. 559–576.

in Chapters 3 through 9. In addition, the cases and the post–104th Congress extension of Republican majorities in both houses provide fodder for some concluding thoughts on the continuing tensions between centrifugal and centripetal forces on Capitol Hill — tensions well recognized by the Framers and thoroughly incorporated into our political life by the Constitution and more than two hundred years of legislative practice.

Two

CONGRESSIONAL DECENTRALIZATION IN DESIGN AND EVOLUTION

T he Framers of the Constitution faced a dilemma: how to create a strong national government that would not use its powers in arbitrary or antidemocratic ways. Within the republican construct of federalism and a separation of powers, the powers of the Congress were spelled out in far more detail than were those of the executive or judicial branches. The contradictory concerns of how to concentrate power and simultaneously limit it led the Framers to design a potentially powerful Congress that is capable of acting quickly and decisively, but is ordinarily slow and cautious in struggling to represent the disparate interests of its widely varied constituencies. The Framers might have a difficult time recognizing the size and scope of the modern presidency or the policy reach of the Supreme Court (for example, the *Roe v. Wade* abortion decision based on the "right to privacy," which is nowhere detailed in the Constitution), but most would have been at home in the 1993 congressional debate on the North America Free Trade Agreement, in which national benefits (increased exports through lower tariffs) were juxtaposed with potential local costs (the loss of jobs to cheaper foreign labor).

THE FRAMERS CONSTRUCT A CONGRESS

Although they recognized the need for a strong, effective central government, the Framers worried greatly over the potential for abuse that comes with any concentration of power. After all, they had fought a revolution to rid themselves of the British monarchy. By providing the Congress with large grants of well-defined authority, most notably the powers to tax and spend, they placed the largest share of national power in legislative hands. At the same time, "the Framers regarded [the Congress as likely] to succeed in deceiving and dominating the people."[1] They thus engineered a number of design features into

---

[1]For an extended discussion, see Martin Diamond, Winston M. Fish, and Herbert Garfinkle, *The Democratic Republic* (Chicago: Rand McNally, 1966), pp. 75ff.

the Constitution to reduce the possibility of systematic abuse by willful congressional majorities. Its three basic elements were

1. The representation of "a multiplicity of interests" within an "extended republic."[2]
2. The separation of powers at the national level into the legislative, judicial, and executive branches.
3. The creation of a bicameral (two-chamber) legislative body.

These provisions defined a decentralized congressional structure in three distinct ways. First, the representational nature of the legislature would work against the concentration of power. The Framers knew from firsthand experience how difficult it was to build majority positions from the diverse views harbored by legislators with differing state and regional backgrounds. Even so, vigorous representation of various interests and constituencies was scarcely enough to check a determined congressional majority. Curbing the potential for tyranny required permanent structural barriers to legislative dominance. This was accomplished by constructing both external and internal limitations on the congressional majorities — the separation of powers and bicameralism, respectively.

Second, the separation of powers provides both independence for each of the three branches and the capacity for each branch to retain that independence by checking the actions of the others.[3] This elemental decentralizing feature of American government has produced legendary intragovernmental confrontations ranging from the congressional censure of President Andrew Jackson in 1834 to the Supreme Court's unanimous 1974 decision requiring President Richard Nixon to hand over the Watergate tapes to the Congress. The 1998–1999 impeachment drama only reemphasized the potential for destructive confrontation.[4]

At the same time, interbranch cooperation is crucial, especially between the executive and legislative branches, for the power of the national government to be effectively mustered. Thus, the president must continually act to promote his legislative agenda, while the Congress presses its own oversight of the executive branch and government bureaucracy. In addition, the judicial branch imposes its own constraints on congressional actions, given its powers to rule laws unconstitutional and to interpret their applications. A substantial

---

[2]Diamond, Fish, and Garfinkle, *The Democratic Republic,* pp. 75ff.

[3]See Louis Fisher, *The Politics of Shared Power,* 2nd ed. (Washington, DC: CQ Press, 1987), pp. 4ff.

[4]On the Jackson episode, see Senator Robert C. Byrd, "The Senate Censures Andrew Jackson," in his *The Senate 1789–1989: Addresses on the History of the United States Senate* (Washington, DC: Government Printing Office, 1988), pp. 127–141. Among many sources on Nixon and the White House tapes, see Louis Fisher, *Constitutional Conflicts between Congress and the President* (Princeton, NJ: Princeton University Press, 1985), pp. 213ff.

amount of legislative activity lies in Congress's responses to judicial decisions (for example, abortion policy in the wake of *Roe v. Wade* and subsequent cases).

Third, not content to rely on external checks on the Congress, the Framers created formidable internal restraints as well. Most of these derive from the adoption of a bicameral structure with distinctive bases of power for each legislative chamber. Given the tendency of legislative authority to dominate in a representative government, James Madison concluded that "the remedy for this inconvenience is, to divide the legislature into different branches; and to render them, by different modes of election, and different principles of action, as little connected with each other, as the nature of their common functions and their common dependence on society, will admit."[5]

The Constitutional Convention's fundamental compromise was to create a two-chamber structure in which only members of the lower body, the House of Representatives, would be elected directly by the people. Senators would be selected by state legislatures, and each state would be represented by two senators, regardless of its population.[6] Senate terms would stretch for six years, as opposed to the two years given representatives. The Senate would be accorded the power to ratify treaties and confirm executive branch appointments, and the House would be granted the sole authority to originate revenue bills.

Among their myriad accomplishments, the Framers of the Constitution succeeded in laying the groundwork for a strong national government. This potential for centralized power — realized in fits and starts over the past two hundred years — was simultaneously checked by representation of diverse interests, the separation of powers, and a bicameralism that roughly balanced the strengths of the two chambers. Even before the first Congress met or before George Washington assumed the presidency, the stage had been set for the tensions between centrifugal and centripetal forces that have characterized American legislative politics since 1789.

What follows is in no way a complete history, even in outline form, of the U.S. Congress. Rather, laying out a succession of congressional eras offers a series of sketches on how the legislature has developed since its inception and how the initial tensions over representation and structural experiments, such as bicameralism, have shaped the nature of the institution. Indeed, even as Republicans won control of both houses of Congress in 1994 for the first time in forty years, Speaker Gingrich and his unified band of 230 GOP Representatives were forced to contend with a Senate that was slow to act, especially in passing a House-generated agenda, and a Democratic president who exercised his constitutional powers, both by actually vetoing legislation and, more often, by threatening further vetoes.

---

[5]From *Federalist*, No. 51.

[6]This practice was ended by the 1913 ratification of the Seventeenth Amendment, which provided for the popular election of senators, although such elections had been adopted widely, if informally, in many states.

THE EARLY CONGRESS: ORGANIZATION AND TENSIONS

Despite defining congressional powers more clearly, and at much greater length, than the other national branches of government, the Constitution did little to dictate how the two houses would be organized.[7] No mention is ever made of committees or political parties; only the offices of Speaker, president of the senate (the vice president), and the Senate's president pro tempore are noted, although without any demarcation of their duties. The larger size of the House (65 members in 1789 and 181 by 1813, in contrast to 26 and 36 senators for the same years, respectively) led to the development of a more complex structure to conduct its business. To take advantage of its numbers, the House soon developed the decentralized standing committee system that remains an organizational hallmark of the body. Concurrently, however, the House's size also fostered the growth of political parties that served to pull together the diverse interests of their members, who had begun to feel the centrifugal pull of their committees as well as that of their constituencies.

For the first ten Congresses, most committees operated as ad hoc bodies to "perfect" the work done by the Committee of the Whole House,[8] but gradually — especially after 1825 — standing committees, which continued from one Congress to the next, took on the major tasks of writing and revising legislation.[9] Reliance on growing numbers of committees illustrates the increased decentralization of the House. This organizational style benefited the average representative by allowing each committee to become expert in its own policy area and to share that knowledge with the rest of the members.[10] Moreover, by facilitating a division of labor, the House could take advantage of the very condition — its large number of members — that rendered it most unwieldy.

As committees were beginning to develop the specialized expertise essential to address particular issues, the House also needed some way to build consistent majorities. As with committees, congressional leaders turned to a structural answer. American politicians of the 1790s to 1830s gradually

---

[7]Elaine Swift argues that the Senate, in particular, consumed much of the Framers' attention. See her *The Making of an American Senate* (Ann Arbor: University of Michigan Press, 1997).

[8]George Galloway, *History of the House of Representatives* (New York: Thomas Crowell, 1961), p. 70. The Committee of the Whole House is the organizational format in which the House conducts almost all of its business. Rules are somewhat more permissive in this circumstance, and the legislative process is expedited. See Walter Oleszek, *Congressional Procedures and the Policy Process,* 3rd ed. (Washington, DC: CQ Press, 1989), pp. 144ff.

[9]Joseph Cooper, perhaps the leading scholar of congressional organization, concludes that a standing committee system was established by Jackson's presidency. See his *Origins of the Standing Committees and the Development of the Modern House* (Houston: Rice University Press, 1970). Galloway, *History of the House,* puts the date at 1816, although he notes that "by 1825, with the appointment of their chairmen by the Speaker . . . so far as its organization was concerned the House of Representatives had assumed its present form," p. 99.

[10]The contribution of committees to both particularism and the beneficial sharing of expertise is explored at some length in Chapter 5.

invented a new organization designed for a republican form of government — the political party.[11] Although scholars disagree about the extent of partisanship and party organization in the first two decades of constitutional government, there were distinct factions that opposed each other in elections and within the legislature. As early as the Second Congress (1791), even though parties had not become formalized, "common ideas and concerns were fast binding men together, and when Congress met, many individuals in both houses became more or less firmly aligned into two voting groups — Federalists on one side and republican-minded [a Madison-Jefferson faction] on the other."[12]

The central figure in establishing strong parties and leadership in the House was Representative Henry Clay of Kentucky, who energized the Speakership during his three periods of service in that chamber. By 1814, Clay and his colleagues "had succeeded in erecting a new system, based on the party caucus, in which legislative leadership was now the prerogative of a group of prominent men in the House of Representatives."[13]

Party divisions and organizational strength would vary over the next four decades, but by 1825 the beginnings of a stable party system with regular leaders and consistent voting patterns had taken firm hold as a centralizing force within the House. Indeed, by this time, both committees and parties were established to the point that a scholar could write in 1917, "so far as its organization was concerned, the House of Representatives had assumed its present form."[14] This is a significant observation for contemporary legislative politics because the House of the 1825 and 1917 eras contained both strong committee systems and powerful party leaderships, much like that of the Democratic House of Speaker Jim Wright (1987–1989) and the Republican chamber under Speaker Newt Gingrich (1995–1999).

Through the early 1820s the House, with its emerging structure and growing numbers, was accorded more weight than the Senate largely because of the direct election of its members.[15] The Senate, however, was also changing, if more through evolution than through the impatient leadership of Clay. By 1830, the Senate had moved from being an elitist imitation of the English House of Lords to a strongly American institution. Commenting on the evolution of the chamber, Elaine Swift observes that the Senate began to respond

---

[11]The scholarship here is extensive. In relation to Congress, see, for example, James S. Young, *The Washington Community: 1800–1828* (New York: Columbia University Press, 1966); Allan G. Bogue and Mark Marlaire, "Of Mess and Men: The Boardinghouse and Congressional Voting, 1821–1842," *American Journal of Political Science* 19 (May 1975): pp. 207–230; and John F. Hoadley, *Origins of American Political Parties* (Lexington: University of Kentucky Press, 1986).

[12]Alvin M. Josephy, Jr., *On the Hill* (New York: Touchstone, 1979), p. 79.

[13]Galloway, *History of the House*, p. 99.

[14]Ralph V. Harlow, *The History of Legislative Methods in the Period before 1825* (New Haven, CT: Yale University Press, 1917), pp. 176–177.

[15]Ross K. Baker, *House and Senate*, 2nd ed. (New York: Norton, 1995), pp. 37–38.

more to citizen voters than to the state legislatures that formally elected its members, and it became increasingly active in developing its own legislation. The Senate thus "came to be more like the House . . . [and] the executive could no longer bank on its all-but-certain support."[16]

SENATE INDIVIDUALISM AND
HOUSE FRAGMENTATION: 1830–1860

By the beginning of the Jackson administration in 1829, the Senate had begun to attract the most formidable leaders of the day, such as Kentucky's Henry Clay. Clay had instituted vigorous party leadership in the House before serving as secretary of state and continued his illustrious, meandering career by returning to Congress in 1831 as a Whig senator. There he would join such notables as Daniel Webster (Whig-Mass.), John Calhoun (D-S.C.), and Thomas Hart Benton (D-Mo.) in a chamber composed of the most notable men of the era. The French observer Alexis de Tocqueville contrasted the "vulgarity" he found in the House with the Senate, which he described as being filled with "eloquent advocates, distinguished generals, wise magistrates, and statesmen of note."[17]

Although many senators operated skillfully behind the scenes, this was a time of great individual oratory and sweeping attempts to hold the Union together. Setting the stage for the era's politics was the legendary Webster-Hayne debate of 1829, which defined the slavery issue in terms of the survival of the Union as a whole. Several other subthemes also ran through the Senate of the 1830s, most of them revolving around the roles of the states and the national government, slavery, the populistic aims of Jackson and the Democratic Party, and the sectional split within the Democrats' ranks between New York's Martin Van Buren and John Calhoun.[18] The freedom of individual action within the still-small Senate (forty-eight members in 1831) meant that coalitions could form and reform as these able legislators jockeyed for advantage over a wide range of issues. All the while, they understood that their fundamental division over slavery might destroy the very system of government that allowed them to flourish.

In contrast, the House found it difficult to organize itself coherently in the 1830–1860 period. With a larger, less stable membership than the Senate, the House could not rely as easily on the leadership of strong individual legislators. Nor could it count on its party factions and sectional interests to provide

---

[16]Swift, *The Making of an American Senate*, p. 140.

[17]From *Democracy in America*, quoted in *Origins and Development of Congress*, 2nd ed. (Washington, DC: Congressional Quarterly, Inc., 1982), p. 215.

[18]Byrd, *The Senate: 1789–1989*, p. 107.

the organizational coherence demanded by the fractious body. Extended, bitter contests for the Speakership became commonplace. In 1849, for example, five major groupings vied for control, and a Speaker was finally elected on the sixty-third ballot after the members agreed that the office could be awarded to the candidate who won a plurality, not a majority, of the votes. In 1855, a mix of Whigs, Republicans (a newly formed party), Democrats, and various minor parties went 133 ballots before selecting (again by plurality) antislavery Representative Nathaniel Banks (Mass.) of the nativist American (Know-Nothing) Party.

Finally, in the Thirty-sixth Congress (1859–1861), which again harbored no clear party majority, forty-four ballots over three months were required to elect the most unlikely of Speakers: William Pennington (R-N.J.), who was serving his first (and last!) term in the House. His election to this post matched Henry Clay's 1811 victory as a first-term representative, but Clay had won the Speakership because of his strong personality and forceful leadership qualities; conversely, Pennington was the lowest common denominator in a highly fragmented chamber of a nation that was about to burst apart.

THE RISE OF THE MODERN CONGRESS: 1860–1920

Between the Civil War years and the end of World War I, the U.S. Congress underwent a series of organizational restructurings that culminated in what can be called its modern form by about 1920. The combination of a growing national industrial base and an increasing U.S. role in world affairs required the legislative branch to adapt to a very different environment than that of the pre-1860 United States, in which an agrarian nation had wrestled with the fundamental, highly divisive slavery issue.

Over the 1860–1920 period, the Congress experimented with strong party leadership in both chambers, created and then limited a separate committee for appropriations, first dominated a series of weak presidents and later looked to the president for coherent leadership initiatives, and eventually moved toward the mixture of standing committee decentralization and oligarchy that would characterize the institution until the mid-1960s. Why such a flurry of activity? As a representative body, the Congress adapts to its environment; new members enter the body, new issues come before it, and new party alignments arise. In the course of adapting to broad societal changes (such as industrialization in the late 1800s and early 1900s) the Congress has often restructured itself internally to consolidate power and regularize procedure.[19]

---

[19]See Roger Davidson and Walter Oleszek, "Adaptation and Consolidation: Structured Innovation in the U.S. House of Representatives," *Legislature Studies Quarterly* 1 (1977): pp. 37ff.

The House

For more than a quarter-century after the Civil War, Congress stood astride national politics and policy making, but battles raged over the control of both chambers. Standing committees dominated the legislative process, especially after the House stripped the upstart Appropriations Committee (established in 1865) of much of its authority. At the same time, a number of strong Speakers increased the power of their office; in particular, the Speaker could appoint all committee members and could aggressively employ his power to recognize members who wished to speak. Still, Davidson and Oleszek conclude that in the 1880s, "despite growth in the Speaker's prerogatives, centrifugal forces in the House remained strong, even dominant."[20] Although committees contributed to this dominance, even more significant was the almost total inability of House majorities to work their will, largely because of delaying tactics that allowed any member to slow actions of the chamber to a crawl.

Enter Speaker Thomas Brackett Reed (R-Maine), elected to lead the House in 1889. In his first three months as Speaker he rewrote the House rules from his position as chair of the Rules Committee and — on the House floor — revised the rules for recognition of a quorum (a majority of all members). Since the 1830s the House had operated under the odd, but powerful, precedent of not recognizing the presence of those who sat mute in the chamber, refusing to answer a quorum call.[21] As Representative Benjamin Butterworth (R-Ohio) put it, a member may, "while present, arise in his place and assert that he is absent, and we must take his word for it. What an absurdity on the face of it. . . . It is the weapon of anarchy."[22] A unanimous, if slender, Republican majority upheld Reed's decision that all members physically present would be counted as present in constituting a quorum. This ruling was reconfirmed by the Democrats when they took control of the House in the early 1890s.

Reed's quorum ruling and other rules that consolidated organizational power opened the way for twenty years of great centralization in the House.[23] Speakers Reed, Charles Crisp (D-Ga.), and, most notably, Joseph Cannon (R-Ill.) increasingly employed the formidable weapons that the position had

---

[20]Davidson and Oleszek, "Adaptation and Consolidation," p. 23.

[21]Davidson and Oleszek note that the "disappearing quorum appears to have originated with [former President] John Quincy Adams, . . . who served with distinction in the House after leaving the White House." Adams refused to vote on a proslavery measure in 1832, and enough fellow members joined him so that a quorum was not present. The House could not conduct business absent a quorum (a majority of its members). "Armed with this precedent, obstructionist minorities for more than fifty years could bring the work of the House to a halt." *Congress Against Itself* (Bloomington: University of Indiana Press, 1977), p. 23.

[22]Quoted in Samuel W. McCall, *The Life of Thomas Brackett Reed* (Boston: Houghton Mifflin, 1914), p. 170.

[23]Randall Strahan, "Thomas Brackett Reed and the Rise of Party Government," in *Master of the House,* Roger H. Davidson, Susan Webb Hammond, and Raymond W. Smock, eds. (Boulder, CO: Westview Press, 1998), pp. 33–62.

accumulated. From 1903 to 1909, "Uncle Joe" Cannon steadily became more dictatorial (the word is not too strong) in his command of the House.[24] Finally, a coalition of minority Democrats and insurgent Republic reformers (many from the Midwest) broke the Speaker's hold over the combination of power levers that permitted him to dominate the process and outcomes of House decision-making. As we shall see later in more detail, Cannon had lost control of the majority that allowed him to function as an autocrat. The support of his fellow Republicans, which was crucial to his dominance, had crumbled. Cannon remained as Speaker for the rest of the term, but both his personal power and that of the office were greatly diminished.

For a few years, the Democratic party caucus and the presidential leadership of Woodrow Wilson combined to retain some relatively strong centripetal momentum in the House, but this dissipated with increasing disagreement over international policies surrounding World War I.[25] By 1920, strong party leadership had given way to a decentralized committee system as the principal means of organizing the House — a condition not to change for more than half a century.

The Senate

In his classic account of the nineteenth-century Senate, historian David Rothman concludes that

> the Senate of 1869 was very much like its predecessors; by 1901 it had come to resemble its successors. . . . Senators in the 1870s . . . were free to go about their business more or less as they pleased. By 1900 all this had changed. The party caucus and its chieftains determined who would sit on which committees and looked after the business calendar in detail. Members were forced to seek their favors or remain without influence in the chamber. At the same time, both organizations imposed unprecedented discipline on roll calls.[26]

Though the House could consolidate power around the constitutional office of the Speaker, the Senate had no similar touchstone. Ironically, strong political parties at the state and local levels formed the context from which centripetal forces flowed into the Senate, where party ties rose in importance through the 1880s and 1890s. Most members of this then-sizeable body (ninety

---

[24]A compact summary of Cannon's actions can be found in Davidson and Oleszek, *Congress against Itself*, pp. 25ff. See also, Ronald Peters, *The American Speakership* (Washington, DC: CQ Press, 1990).

[25]James S. Fleming, "Oscar W. Underwood: The First Modern House Leader, 1911–1915," in *Master of the House*, pp. 91–118.

[26]David J. Rothman, *Politics and Power* (New York: Atheneum, 1969), p. 4. Some of the arguments in the following paragraphs are drawn from Rothman's work.

lawmakers in 1901) functioned as party loyalists, who provided the votes for the policy positions endorsed by the leadership-dominated party caucus.[27]

Occupying the central positions within the Republican caucus of the 1890s were the chair, Iowa's William Allison, and New York's Nelson Aldrich, perhaps the most talented and influential member of the chamber. They dominated Senate policy making through a combination of formal and informal linkages. The Allison-Aldrich faction gained control of overlapping party committees and standing committee positions to dominate the chamber's agenda and its policy outcomes. For example, controlling the Republican Steering Committee "confirmed the power of the Allison-Aldrich faction over the Senate business. Arranging the legislative schedule in detail, week by week, the committee extended the party leaders' authority unimpaired from the caucus to the chamber. Senators knew they had to consult the committee before attempting to raise even minor matters."[28]

Remnants of the traditional Senate individualism remained, but those Republicans who refused to cooperate with the Allison-Aldrich group found themselves without influence. As Rothman notes, "Anyone could use the chamber as a forum and address the nation. Senators willing to abandon the opportunity to increase their own authority could act freely, following their own inclinations. . . . But barring a take-over of the party offices, they could hardly affect the exercise of power. The country might honor their names but the Senate barely felt their presence."[29]

Given the underlying differences among senators, based on region, party, interests, and ideology, the Senate's centralization could not hold for long, and the Republican caucus's domination eroded over the 1901–1912 period. The individualistic, centrifugal forces of the chamber came to the fore in caucus challenges to Aldrich, the growing strength of Progressive senators (often supported by President Theodore Roosevelt), and the election of a Democratic Senate to complement the presidential victory of Democrat Woodrow Wilson in the 1912 election. In addition to the partisan turnover of 1912 came the 1913 adoption of the Seventeenth Amendment to the Constitution, which provided for the direct election of senators. No longer would state legislatures and state party machines formally dominate the selection process, although by the time of the amendment's ratification, most states already selected Senate candidates through the primary election process.[30]

---

[27]Over the years Republicans have often called their caucus the Republican Conference. The term *caucus* is used here as a generic description of all the members of one party in one legislative chamber.

[28]Rothman, *Politics and Power,* pp. 58–59.

[29]Rothman, *Politics and Power,* p. 60.

[30]Congressional Quarterly's *Origins and Development of Congress,* 2nd ed., cites congressional scholar George Galloway, who notes "that more than half [the senators] chosen by legislative caucuses [in the states] were subsequently approved [through reelection to their office] by the people."

Finally, the Senate did change one further fundamental element of its procedure. From its inception, the Senate had allowed unlimited debate on any subject; the filibuster — or its threat — had proved a powerful tool for many Senate giants of the past. This was one of the strongest decentralizing elements within the entire legislative process. An individual senator (or, more likely, a band of legislators with similar, intense feelings) could indefinitely delay consideration of a crucial bill. This occurred in 1917, when, in President Wilson's words, "a little group of willful men" blocked his armed neutrality bill, which had the public support of seventy-five of ninety-six senators.[31]

In the aftermath of this inability to act, the Senate adopted cloture, the first measure that provided a mechanism to shut off debate; cloture could be imposed by a two-thirds vote of those present and voting. Although this procedure was employed in 1919 to end a filibuster on ratification of the Versailles Treaty, until the late 1970s the Senate rarely approved cloture, save in extraordinary cases such as the 1964 Civil Rights Bill. The filibuster remained a potent weapon, both in its occasional implementation and in its frequent use as threat.[32]

The Drift toward Decentralization

Allied with the Republican presidencies of William McKinley (1897–1901) and Theodore Roosevelt (1901–1908), the House's strong Speakership and the Senate's dominant Allison-Aldrich faction served to concentrate legislative power in the congressional parties at the turn of the century. The ability of legislative party leaders to set the nation's policy agenda became increasingly important, in that the industrializing U.S. society was placing rising numbers of demands on government.[33] In the Fortieth Congress (1867–1869), lawmakers introduced a total of 3,003 bills; by the Fifty-second Congress (1891–1893) that number had grown to 14,518, and the Sixtieth Congress (1907–1909) witnessed the introduction of almost 38,000 bills, more than a twelvefold increase in forty years.[34] This volume of legislation eventually benefited those restive representatives and senators who desired to reduce the power of their party leaders.

Some mechanism was needed to handle this immense flow of prospective legislation. The committee system offered the most obvious organizational response for the Congress. In fact, the number of standing committees had proliferated in both chambers, to the point that in 1918 the House had sixty such units and the Senate a staggering seventy-four. The very number of

---

[31]Congressional Quarterly, *Origins and Development of Congress*, p. 244.

[32]Sarah A. Binder and Steven S. Smith, *Politics or Principle?* (Washington, DC: Brookings Institution, 1997), pp. 114–115.

[33]See Stephen Skowronek, *Building the New American State* (New York: Cambridge University Press, 1982).

[34]Roger Davidson and Walter Oleszek, *Congress and Its Members,* 3rd ed. (Washington, DC: CQ Press, 1990), p. 30.

committees might imply the development of a highly decentralized Congress, but through 1910 party leaders combined their leadership roles with those of key committees to produce strongly centralized operations in both chambers.[35] With Speaker Cannon's defeat, the subsequent waning of Democratic caucus unity in the House after 1914, and the Senate's growing fragmentation in the period from 1901 to 1919, congressional party organizations could no longer move bills through the legislative process in a predictable, timely manner. Relying on committees would be essential for the sake of coherence. Such reliance dictated that both chambers reform their committee systems, which they did in 1919 and again, more meaningfully, in 1946.

THE DEVELOPMENT AND DECLINE OF THE TEXTBOOK CONGRESS: 1920-1970

Although Woodrow Wilson could celebrate the work of congressional committees in the 1880s, their great ascendancy did not come until fifty years later and lasted well into the 1960s. Gradually, over the 1920s, 1930s, and 1940s, committee strength grew, and members almost universally advanced on the basis of their seniority — the length of their consecutive tenure on a given committee. The 1946 Legislative Reorganization Act sharply reduced the number of committees in both chambers and thus sharply increased the value of the remaining standing committee chairmanships — nineteen in the House, fifteen in the Senate.

The committee-dominated Congress of the 1950s coincided with the first systematic analysis of the Congress by political scientists trained in behavioral methods.[36] Scholars and students received a much fuller picture of the Congress of the period from the late 1950s to 1970 than of any previous era. The Congress of this time was relatively stable, which allowed for well-documented, detailed analyses to capture the essence of an increasingly complex institution. There is no question that this generation of congressional scholars "got it right." The strength of their analyses was so great that the cumulative picture, circa 1970, was so clear and detailed that it dominated conventional views of the Congress long after the institution changed profoundly in the 1970s and 1980s.

With his term *the textbook Congress,* political scientist Kenneth Shepsle has captured the extent to which the studies made up a received wisdom that still shapes many perceptions of legislative politics.[37] In representing their con-

---

[35]Steven S. Smith and Christopher J. Deering, *Committees in Congress,* 2nd ed. (Washington, DC: CQ Press, 1990), p. 34.

[36]Although many careful scholars had described and analyzed the Congress before the 1950s, never before was there such a systematic examination of the institution. The American Political Science Association's Study of Congress project sponsored much of the work by such scholars as Richard F. Fenno, Jr., Robert Peabody, John Manley, and Charles Jones.

[37]Kenneth A. Shepsle, "The Changing Textbook Congress," in John E. Chubb and Paul E. Peterson, eds., *Can the Government Govern?* (Washington, DC: Brookings Institution, 1989), pp. 238–266.

stituencies and making national policy, legislators confront tensions that "derive from three competing imperatives — geographical, jurisdictional, and partisan. . . . Congress is [thus] an arena for constituencies, committees, and [party-based] coalitions. The textbook Congress of the 1950s represented an equilibrium among these imperatives involving an institutional bargain that gave prominence to committees."[38] Although legendary party leaders such as Speaker Sam Rayburn (D-Tex.) and Senate Majority Leader Lyndon Johnson (D-Tex.) wielded substantial personal power in the 1950s, the Congress of these years emphasized the work of autonomous committees as directed by a set of senior chairmen.[39] The textbook Congress was both decentralized and oligarchic: decentralized in that committee chairs dominated their own policy domains; oligarchic in that top party leaders, committee chairs, and chairs of the thirteen Appropriations Committee subcommittees in each chamber all benefited from their joint control of the domestic policy agenda. Although the House relied more heavily on committee work than did the Senate, the same general committee-based equilibrium existed in both chambers.

The organizationally stable Congress of the 1950s did not bend easily to the winds of change. Popular pressure for more educational spending fell victim to procedural wrangling. In the face of filibusters and a hostile bloc of southern senators, civil rights legislation proceeded slowly in the aftermath of the Supreme Court's 1954 *Brown v. Board of Education* school desegregation ruling. Nor was medical care for the elderly allowed to wend its way through the legislative process. The committee-dominated system proved superb at slowing the pace of policy change in a narrowly Democratic Congress that faced the moderate-to-conservative Republican presidency of Dwight Eisenhower.[40] Indeed, the title of Robert Bendiner's study of educational policy making, *Obstacle Course on Capitol Hill,* would have been equally apt in describing the limited progress of many other policy initiatives.[41]

The congressional equilibrium began to change with the Democratic landslide in the 1958 congressional elections, which greatly increased the size of the party's majorities in both chambers. More important, many of the newly elected legislators were relatively liberal and committed to policy changes. Six years later another surge of Democratic legislators ascended Capitol Hill, brought there in part by Lyndon Johnson's sweeping presidential victory over Senator Barry Goldwater (R-Ariz.). Despite coming in disproportionate numbers from Republican districts, these rank-and-file Democratic legislators proved

---

[38]Shepsle, "The Changing Textbook Congress," p. 239.

[39]In the 1950s, with the exception of Representative Leonor Sullivan (D-Mo.), chair of the Merchant Marine and Fisheries Committee, committee chairs were men, and Congress was a bastion of white, middle-aged (and older) men. On Johnson, among many others, see Ralph Huitt, "Democratic Party Leadership in the Senate," *American Political Science Review* 60 (1961): pp. 331–344; on Rayburn, see D. B. Hardeman and Donald C. Bacon, *Rayburn* (Lanham, MD: Madison Books, 1987).

[40]James Sundquist's *Politics and Policy* (Washington, DC: Brookings Institution, 1968) provides an excellent guide to the obstructionism of the 1950s as well as the policy changes of the 1960s.

[41]Robert Bendiner, *Obstacle Course on Capitol Hill* (New York: McGraw-Hill, 1964).

crucial to the passage of several of Johnson's ambitious domestic programs.[42] Liberal voting records denied many first-termers a chance for reelection; those who survived, however, felt entitled to a real voice within the legislative process. The major outlet for this voice came in positions taken by the Democratic Study Group, a body of progressive Democrat House members formed after the 1958 elections.[43] This unofficial, but well-organized, group consistently pressed for a reform agenda, which included reducing the power of committee chairmen.

The standing committee oligarchy was thus ripe for challenge by the late 1960s. Party leaders had begun to chip away at the chairs' powers, while reformist junior members hungered for responsibility within the committee structure. Both leaders and backbenchers stood to gain from reining in the chairs; change was inevitable, but with it came great disruption that lasted for a decade.

REFORMING THE CONGRESS: THE 1970s

> *It is the members who run Congress. And we will get pretty much the kind of Congress they want. We shall get a different kind of Congress when we elect different kinds of congressmen.*
>
> Richard E. Fenno, Jr.

Beginning in 1958, continuing through the 1960s, and culminating in the 1974 and 1976 elections for Democrats and the 1978 and 1980 elections for Republicans, we did get different kinds of new members. Subsequently, we got a different kind of Congress. Fenno's deceptively simple statement captures the essential ability of lawmakers to determine the nature of their institution.[44] More indirectly, voters can roughly determine the direction and extent of change, even if they are unaware of the specific mechanics.

In general, the newly elected legislators were impatient, eager to use their expertise, and unconcerned if they ruffled some senior members' feathers.[45] In the House, subcommittees gained a measure of independent authority; members sought and received many more resources for their offices; most votes on the floor were recorded and thus open to public scrutiny; and the Democratic Caucus provided enhanced powers for the Speaker and the top party leaders.

---

[42]See, in particular, Jeff Fishel, *Party and Opposition* (New York: David McKay, 1973), pp. 161ff.

[43]Arthur G. Stevens, Jr., Arthur H. Miller, and Thomas E. Mann, "Mobilization of Liberal Strength in the House, 1955–1970: The Democratic Study Group," *American Political Science Review* 68 (1974): pp. 667–681.

[44]Richard F. Fenno, Jr., "If, as Ralph Nader Says, Congress Is the 'Broken Branch,' How Come We Love Our Congressmen So Much?" in Norman J. Ornstein, ed., *Congress in Change* (New York: Praeger, 1975), p. 287.

[45]See Burdett Loomis, *The New American Politician* (New York: Basic Books, 1988), chap. 1.

Shepsle summarizes: "The revolt of the 1970s thus strengthened four power centers. It liberated members and subcommittees, restored to the Speakership an authority it had not known since the days of Joe Cannon, and invigorated the party caucus. Some of the reforms had a decentralizing effect, some a recentralizing effect. Standing committees and their chairs were caught in the middle. Geography and party benefited; the division-of-labor jurisdictions were its victims."[46]

The powerful, but relatively brief, reform era of the late 1960s–1970s produced a highly unstable political environment on Capitol Hill, especially in the House. Even though they held the presidency under Jimmy Carter and enjoyed comfortable numerical advantages over the Republicans in both chambers, Democrats could not generate consistent congressional majorities to pass major policy initiatives. Leaders and backbenchers alike struggled to understand what their reforms had wrought.[47]

THE DEMOCRATIC POSTREFORM CONGRESS: 1980–1994

Many analyses of the Congress of the late 1970s emphasized, with good reason, the proliferation of subcommittees, the growth of individual members' resources, and the apparent weakness of both the Carter presidency and the Democratic legislative leadership. In 1980, Republicans ran a pointed national campaign advertisement that depicted Democratic Speaker Tip O'Neill as unresponsive and woefully out of touch on important, pressing issues.[48] Building on substantial public dissatisfaction, Republican candidates ran strongly in 1980, capturing the Senate and narrowing the Democrats' majority in the House to the point that President Reagan's initial tax and budget proposals won speedy congressional approval as conservative Democrats joined with Republicans to provide majority support.

Speaker O'Neill and his fellow House Democrats were not quite dead, however. Their rejuvenation over the next few years derived in part from the Speaker's winning personality; by the time he retired from the House in 1986, he could claim that his popularity levels had surpassed those of Ronald Reagan. O'Neill, a great listener, could find grounds to bring together the different strands of the legislative party. Equally important, however, were the aggressive use of party-strengthening reforms adopted in the 1970s and the

---

[46]Shepsle, "The Changing Textbook Congress," p. 256.

[47]A good collection of articles by leading scholars that captures the difficulties of the reform era can be found in Frank Mackaman, ed., *Understanding Congressional Leadership* (Washington, DC: CQ Press, 1981).

[48]The commercial portrayed O'Neill as driving a car and ignoring the pleas of a young aide, who warned him that they were running out of gas. Although effective, the ad focused great attention on the Speaker, increased his stature as a national figure, and encouraged him to take a more aggressive stance toward the Reagan programs in 1981 and beyond.

consistent reduction of ideological disagreements among House Democrats.[49] Thus, the personally popular O'Neill could lead an increasingly homogeneous group of partisans with a combination of carrots, such as including many members within the leadership, and sticks, such as controlling the process of appointing members to committee seats.

By the 1980s, majority party members — most elected since 1974 — decided that they did indeed want, in Fenno's words, a "different kind of Congress." When these members judged, finally, that the "legislative process was no longer producing the legislation they needed, the costs of maintaining the legislative status quo [embodied in the committee-dominated 'textbook Congress'] became very high." At the same time, continues congressional scholar Barbara Sinclair, "the costs of change in the direction of stronger party leadership declined," as House Democrats grew more similar in their ideologies.[50]

If the reforms of the House produced large-scale changes in the 1970s and 1980s, with fragmentation giving way to Speaker Jim Wright's consolidation of leadership powers in 1987–1988, the Senate of the same period underwent a less striking, more evolutionary transformation.[51] By 1989, both Senate parties had strong, partisan floor leaders in place (Senators Bob Dole [R-Kans.] and George Mitchell [D-Maine]), but the chamber continued to respect the almost sacred status of the individual member. A lone senator could often tie the institution in knots, as the whole deferred to the "rights" of a single willful legislator. Senators like Jesse Helms (R-N.C.) and Howard Metzenbaum (D-Ohio) gained notoriety and power as they proved willing, time and again, to bring the business of the Senate to a halt if their desires were not accommodated.[52] Senators chose not to limit their colleagues' excesses, and the chamber has become steadily less collegial since the 1960s. Indeed, when compared with the sharp partisanship of the House in the 1980s and 1990s, complete with competing visions of the role of government, the contemporary Senate has often seemed less focused and less sure of its step. This may be an "identity crisis" of a highly individualistic body, but it may also reflect the traditional Senate role of addressing issues in a leisurely and frustratingly repetitive manner.[53]

---

[49]These issues will be considered at greater length later in this book (in Chapter 7, especially). A minimal list of key sources includes David Rohde, *Parties and Leaders in the Postreform House* (Chicago: University of Chicago Press, 1991); Barbara Sinclair, *Legislators, Leaders, and Lawmaking* (Baltimore: Johns Hopkins University Press, 1995); and Roger H. Davidson, ed., *The Postreform Congress* (New York: St. Martin's, 1992).

[50]Sinclair, *Legislators, Leaders, and Lawmaking,* p. 301. See also, Sinclair, "Tip O'Neill and Contemporary House Leadership," in *Masters of the House,* pp. 289–318.

[51]See, especially, Barbara Sinclair, *The Transformation of the U.S. Senate* (Baltimore: Johns Hopkins University Press, 1989).

[52]Why this is so requires some detailed untangling; see Chapter 9.

[53]See Norman J. Ornstein, Robert L. Peabody, and David W. Rohde, "The U.S. Senate in an Era of Change," in Lawrence Dodd and Bruce I. Oppenheimer, eds., *Congress Reconsidered,* 5th ed. (Washington, DC: CQ Press, 1993), pp. 13–40.

Finally, the development of the Democratic postreform Congress coincided with an era of divided government. From 1969 to 1993, the same party controlled both houses of Congress and the presidency for only four years (1977–1981). Until the onset of the Clinton Administration, the Democrat-dominated postreform legislature had functioned only with Republican presidents. Despite the constitutional need to cooperate, the interbranch relationship was often adversarial. In 1993–1994, despite the eagerness of many Democratic legislators to serve with a Democratic president, single-party control of the national government scarcely eliminated interbranch wrangling.[54]

THE REPUBLICAN ERA, 1994–

After forty years of Democratic control of the House (the longest continual stretch of partisan control in the American experience), Republicans won a majority of seats in 1994, and retained their majority, albeit diminished, in 1996. Likewise, Democrats lost control of the Senate in 1994, by a 47-53 margin, and surrendered two more seats in 1996. Even as Bill Clinton won reelection, with a margin of 8 million votes over former Senate Majority Leader Bob Dole, the Republican House and Senate performance offered reasonable evidence that a new Republican era of congressional control was at hand.

The results of the 1998 elections demonstrated the tenuous nature of party control in the Republican era. Although Republicans did hold on to majorities in both chambers for a third consecutive Congress, their margin remained the same (55-45) in the Senate and actually declined (to 223-211) in the House, as Democrats picked up five seats. Although Republicans could push through impeachment of President Clinton on a series of party-line votes in the House, the partisan balance worked against his conviction in the Senate. Ironically, the first victim of the Republicans' reduced majority was Speaker Newt Gingrich — the individual most responsible for creating his party's triumph in 1994. Indeed, Gingrich was pushed out of the Speakership when six Republican representatives announced that they would not vote for him as Speaker when the House organized itself in January 1999. This opened up the real possibility that a Democrat could be elected Speaker — an unthinkable result for a Republican-majority chamber.

Narrow margins offer the potential for disproportionate power to groupings of even a few members, especially on the majority side. Republicans thus sought a leader who would represent the conservatism of their members without alienating more moderate, more institutionally oriented legislators. Strangely enough, they had to make this choice twice — first selecting Appropriations Committee chair Robert Livingston (R-La.), only to have him resign in

---

[54]President Clinton compiled a strong overall success record in 1993–1994, as he won on more than 86 percent of the votes on which he took a position. On major issues, however, especially health care, he was much less effective.

the wake of an impeachment-related admission of extramarital affairs. Subsequently, the party turned to little known Representative Dennis Hastert (R-Ill.), a widely respected conservative who had maintained cordial relations with all wings of his own party — and many Democrats as well. As Hastert proclaimed in an early speech, "I will meet you [Democrats] halfway, maybe more so on occasion. I expect you to meet me halfway, too."[55]

With a thin majority in the House and increasingly assertive committee chairmen, the Republican leadership allowed centrifugal forces considerable leeway. Still, the leadership retained substantial powers in committee appointments and agenda control; committee chairmen remained subject to term limits on their positions. Less dramatically, the Senate has also become more partisan under Republican control, both in terms of voting patterns and the importance accorded party caucuses in developing legislation.[56]

Regardless of which party holds majorities on Capitol Hill, the postreform Congress has evolved from the constitutional and organizational elements that have shaped the institution in previous eras. It remains highly responsive to constituency interests, even as it addresses national issues such as health care and welfare reform. The separation of powers continues to affect its operations. Committees and party leaders are still central to congressional organization. Henry Clay and John C. Calhoun would recognize the ins and outs of politics on Capitol Hill 150 years after their salad days.

At the same time, there have been great changes, both within the Congress and in its relations with its environment. This chapter has traced some continuities and changes on Capitol Hill. Before considering these in more detail, we will examine some external forces that affect the capacity of Congress to act. In particular, we will look at the growth of special interests and organized groups and the related expansion in the role of government. Clay and Calhoun may have faced the slavery question, the single most divisive issue in the American experience, but they did not have to parcel out a $1.7 trillion annual budget and respond to tens of thousands of special interests and lobbyists seeking to influence thousands of separate federal programs. In many ways, the seeds of fragmentation and individualism on Capitol Hill are sown by interests from across the country (and beyond) whose lobbyists congregate in committee rooms and whose fax messages pile high on 535 legislators' desks. The politics of Congress remains a politics of representation.

---

[55]Richard E. Cohen and Marilyn Werber Serafini, "In the Eye of the House Hurricane," *National Journal,* January 2 and 9, 1999, p. 49.

[56]Senate Party Unit Scores, *Congressional Quarterly Weekly Report,* December 21, 1996, p. 3461; and discussion on C-SPAN, January 19, 1997, between former senators Bennett Johnston (D-La.) and Alan Simpson (R-Wyo.)

Three

THE CHANGING
ENVIRONMENT OF
CONGRESSIONAL POLITICS

Many of the centrifugal forces affecting Congress originate outside the institution. Indeed, as a representative body, Congress was designed to offer easy access to those interests and individuals who sought to influence policy. To a greater or lesser extent, it has always fulfilled this goal. Until the mid-twentieth century, save in extraordinary circumstances (war, the Depression), Congress met for about half the year. From July through January, members would live at home, among their constituents. With the New Deal, World War II, and the growth of government, to say nothing of the widespread installation of air conditioning in Washington, congressional sessions have come to run virtually year-round. At the same time, air travel has afforded almost all members the possibility of living in their districts and joining the "Tuesday through Thursday" club of those spending three days a week in Washington. Although many recently elected legislators have made this choice, the sight of members of the California delegation stumbling into committee hearings after returning on the Tuesday morning "red-eye" flight scarcely offers much encouragement for coherent lawmaking. In addition, large increases in staff allotments, the growth of district offices, and advances in communication mean that almost all members are well informed about their districts, regardless of their formal place of residence. Indeed, for all the talk of legislators being out of touch with their constituents, a strong case exists that they know altogether too much about the preferences of their most vocal and visible local district interests.

CONGRESS: THE PERMEABLE BRANCH

In Washington, members of Congress can almost always carve a few minutes from their busy schedules to chat with visitors from their districts. Moreover, responding to constituent mail receives priority attention from legislative offices. After all, it is the home folks who have sent the representatives to Capitol Hill. However, access to Congress is scarcely limited to members' constituents. Traditionally, interest groups have found lawmakers hospitable to their requests for time and attention. The ease of obtaining a legislative audience contrasts markedly with the lengthy process of obtaining a hearing in the judiciary or the difficulty of gaining an audience with top-level executive-branch officials. In its 1997–1998 session, for example, the Supreme Court agreed to hear fewer than one hundred oral arguments from among the thousands of appeals filed before it. Likewise, the presidency and the top rungs of the bureaucracy are highly insulated from most citizens (electronic mail and town hall–style meetings notwithstanding). Conversely, the Congress — especially the House — has always opened its doors to complaints and requests from citizens and organized interests. Over the years, as the national government has grown larger and made increasingly important decisions, the demands on Congress have risen in number and intensity, but even before the policy explosions of the New Deal and the Great Society there were many instances of intense, sophisticated, and frequently successful lobbying efforts by organized interests.

As industry expanded and flourished in the 1870s, interests swarmed around the Congress, often directly and corruptly influencing individual legislators. For example, in the years following World War I, the farm lobby, led by the American Farm Bureau Federation (AFBF) demonstrated its worth — in terms of information and support — for dozens of legislators, who repaid the agriculture interests with increasing access to the process of lawmaking.[1] More subtle than most interests from the pre-1900 era, the farm lobby often worked through farmers back in the legislators' home districts. The political and policy information provided to members of Congress by the farm groups gave them good reason to listen to these organizations. Legislators face great uncertainties in understanding both the policy and political effects of their actions; well-informed groups such as the AFBF could offer information that would make members a bit less uncertain, especially in terms of their constituents' opinions and the positions of the farm community. Providing regular access to the Farm Bureau thus benefited both the lawmakers and the interest group.

The "textbook Congress" that emerged by the 1950s dictated a committee orientation for interests in search of access. In the 1950s many committees served as one corner of close-knit triangular relationships, variously labeled "cozy" or "iron" triangles, that linked them to key outside interests and, as the third corner, to particular agencies within the federal bureaucracy.[2] For example, sugar interests worked with the appropriate Agriculture Committee sub-committees in the House and Senate and the relevant U.S. Department of Agriculture officials to maintain domestic sugar prices that were consistently several times higher than those in world markets. By the 1960s, various interests began to challenge the tidy, profitable sugar subsystem. Consumer and

---

[1]See John Mark Hansen, *Gaining Access* (Chicago: University of Chicago Press, 1991), pp. 57–58.

[2]There is a very large literature here. For a contemporary summary, see James A. Thurber, "Dynamics of Policy Subsystems in American Politics," in Allan Cigler and Burdett Loomis, eds., *Interest Group Politics,* 3rd ed. (Washington, DC: CQ Press, 1991), pp. 319–344.

environmental groups, among others, began to influence agriculture policies. In 1974, the sugar triangle broke apart, as the subcommittee could not maintain control over the price support policies.[3] Subsequently, however, sugar interests succeeded in lobbying a broad mix of legislators to reconstruct a similar marketing system that continues to fix U.S. prices at a considerably higher level than elsewhere in the world.

More generally, while the Congress changed greatly from 1960 into the 1980s, so too did its environment. In parallel, related developments, more interests became politically active and more governmental policies prompted them to action.[4] Environmental groups, for example, possessed almost no political clout in the 1950s; either they emphasized traditional conservation issues or they remained outside the policy debate. By 1970, both traditional and newly formed environmental organizations had become major players in policymaking on issues that ranged from pesticide levels to air quality standards to toxic waste disposal. As a result, many old policy assumptions, such as maximizing returns for domestic sugar producers, were open to question.[5]

Not only did interest groups serve as effective advocates on behalf of specific programs, but new policies engendered new agencies, even whole new departments (for example, Energy and Education), each with its own turf to protect. As the federal budget rose from $100 billion in 1969 to $1.7 trillion in 1997, many interests had become entrenched within government as well as outside it. Legislative consideration of issues thus has proceeded within a complicated, dense environment of complex policies and numerous organized interests.[6]

Equally important, in the 1960s presidents like John F. Kennedy and Lyndon Johnson could promise new programs for particular constituencies, such as the poor and the elderly, that would simply distribute new benefits.[7] Indeed, the impulse to distribute benefits to specific constituents and interests operates as a key centrifugal force within the Congress.[8] Lawmakers seek to deliver concentrated benefits (such as a dam or farm support payments) paid

---

[3]The "three pillars" of the sugar program include loans for the sugar industry, import restrictions, and regulations, at times, of domestic sugar allotments for planting. See David Hosansley, "Florida Sugar Growers Edgy as Farm Bill Nears," *Congressional Quarterly Weekly Report,* May 13, 1995, pp. 1311–1315.

[4]Kay Lehman Schlozman and John T. Tierney, *Organized Interests and American Democracy* (New York: Harper & Row, 1986).

[5]David Vogel, *Fluctuating Fortunes* (New York: Basic Books, 1989).

[6]Lawrence Brown, *New Policies, New Politics* (Washington, DC: Brookings Institution, 1983); see also, Paul Light, *Thickening Government* (Washington, DC: Brookings Institution, 1995).

[7]James Sundquist, *Politics and Policies* (Washington, DC: Brookings Institution, 1968).

[8]Congressional scholars differ as to how effective legislators are in distributing their largesse to their geographic constituencies. In *Congress and the Bureaucracy* (New Haven, CT: Yale University Press, 1979) Douglas Arnold, summarizing several works, sees as too simplistic just addressing the variations in programs and policies as they affect members' districts (pp. 15–16). See also Robert M. Stein and Kenneth M. Bickers, *Perpetuating the Pork Barrel* (New York: Cambridge, 1995).

for by widely dispersed costs (a few cents of every tax dollar). But as both federal programs and budget deficits have grown, distributive politics has proven an increasingly difficult game to play.

From the 1990s on, for every policy winner there have often been many policy losers. Given huge budget deficits, new programs must compare against established policies. Entitlement programs such as Medicaid or farm price support payments often require increased funding; the expenditures must increase the deficit or come from someplace else. But where? Such redistributive questions continually bedevil members of Congress, who cannot endlessly distribute benefits when the government consistently spends more than it takes in. Redistributive policies — which reallocate funds from one sector of society to another, as in welfare — ordinarily produce sharp conflicts on Capitol Hill.[9] The contentious partisan battles over budgets in the 1980s and 1990s have done little to increase public confidence in the Congress, largely because individual legislators have continued to provide benefits to their constituencies and their favored interests. At the same time, the Congress has placed restrictive caps on overall spending, which pose difficulties in responding to new priorities, such as increased defense allocations, even when there is a federal budget surplus.

This chapter explores four major changes in the congressional environment: the advocacy explosion, as the number and specialization of interests have grown steadily since the 1960s; the policy explosion and the impact of sixty years of an activist federal government; the overwhelming attention given to budgetary considerations since the early 1980s — the so-called *fiscalization* of policy making; and declining respect for Congress. The growing numbers of interests and policies have exerted significant decentralizing pressures on the Congress, whereas the fiscalization of policy has operated to centralize congressional actions, as budgetary concerns dominate decision making. And the low public standing of Congress may make it all the more difficult for its members to address divisive, and potentially unpopular, policies.

Related to these developments, several other external changes also have occurred; these range from the gradual weakening of political parties to the growing political sophistication of business interests to major transformations in the media and in information technology. In short, the Congress of the 1950s did its work in a very different context than did the Congress of the 1980s and 1990s. Overall, the contemporary Congress has grown both highly responsive to particular interests and remarkably insular within the hothouse environment of Washington policy making and Capitol Hill politics.

The Advocacy Explosion

In the early 1960s political scientists, if not journalists, often discounted the impact of interest groups on most policymaking. Lobbyists plied their

---

[9]Randall B. Ripley and Grace A. Franklin, *Congress, the Bureaucracy, and Public Policy*, 5th ed. (Pacific Grove, CA: Brooks/Cole, 1991).

trade, of course, but many interests lacked the resources and sophistication to wield much influence.[10] Between 1960 and 1990, the number of active organized interests and their use of a wide range of techniques for influencing policymakers rose sharply. Simply put, more lobbyists have been working for more interests and have been employing more tactics to affect policy outcomes. Although much popular attention has been directed toward the tremendous post-1974 growth of political action committees (from 608 PACs in 1974 to 4,009 in 1984, with a slight rise to 4,528 for the 1996 campaign),[11] organized interests have expanded their actions across the board. The number of Washington-based interest representatives grew from 4,000 in 1977 to more than 14,500 in 1991; registered lobbyists rose in numbers from around 1,000 in the 1960s to almost 6,000 in 1981 and an astonishing 23,000 in 1989; trade associations relocated their offices in Washington in great numbers during the 1980s; and between 1973 and 1983, the District of Columbia Bar increased its membership from around 11,000 lawyers to more than 37,000.[12] As of the mid-1990s, the best estimate of the number of individuals who earn their living from Washington-based attempts to influence policies stood at an astounding 91,000.[13]

The advocacy explosion has not affected all sectors of the Washington community with equal force. Most notable, perhaps, have been the declining role of labor unions, the growing presence of corporate and professional interests, and the increasing importance of large-scale citizens groups, ranging from Common Cause to the Sierra Club to the American Association of Retired Persons and its 33 million members.[14] In addition, American states, cities, and other governmental units came to Washington in droves during the 1970s era of revenue sharing, stayed to press their cases during the leaner years of the Reagan administration, and have remained to lobby against unfunded federal

[10]See Raymond A. Bauer, Ithiel de sola Pool, and Lewis Anthony Dexter, *American Business and Public Policy* (Chicago: Aldine, 1963); and Lester Milbrath, *The Washington Lobbyists* (Chicago: Rand McNally, 1963).

[11]Indeed, the number of active PACs has always been less than the total. As of 1992, there were 1,677 inactive PACs that made no contributions, of which 910 were defunct as organizations. See Paul Herrnson, *Congressional Elections* (Washington, DC: CQ Press, 1994), p. 109.

[12]The preceding figures are cited in Mark Petracca, "The Rediscovery of Interest Group Politics," Mark Petracca, ed., *The Politics of Interests* (Boulder, CO: Westview Press, 1992), pp. 14–15.

[13]Kevin Phillips, *Arrogant Capital* (Boston: Back Bay Books/Little, Brown, 1995, p. 43), cites James Thurber on the above figure. Thurber estimated a total of 80,000 in 1991, "off the top of [his] head," and Phillips provides data to demonstrate that this estimate was conservative.

[14]Schlozman and Tierney present data that demonstrate the rise of individual corporate representation, the decline of trade groups (as a percentage of all groups), and the decline of the percentage of citizens groups. At the same time, the overall number of groups with Washington representation had shot up, so that even labor unions, whose presence had decreased from 11 percent of all interests in 1960 to 2–3 percent in 1980, still increased in absolute numbers, from about 55 groups in 1960 to more than 100 in 1980. Individual corporate representation, in contrast, rose from about 80 firms in 1960 to approximately 3,000 in 1980. Given differences among data, these comparisons may be a little loose, but the overall trends are clear. See Schlozman and Tierney, *Organized Interests and American Democracy,* p. 77.

mandates.[15] In addition, foreign governments and private interests, often acting through sophisticated Washington lobbying and public relations firms, have become important players in the complex politics of trade, foreign aid, and international business.[16]

From the 1960s through the early 1990s the thousands of interests actively seeking to influence congressional decisions multiplied several times over. Equally important, however, has been the wide variety of strategies and tactics that organized interests have employed in their efforts to gain advantage. By the end of the 1980s a majority of Washington-based organizations reported using more than twenty different techniques for exercising influence; these ranged from testifying at legislative hearings to joining coalitions to mounting grassroots lobbying efforts.[17] At the same time, these groups have used most of these techniques considerably more often than they had in the past. For example, two-thirds of the organizations noted that they paid increased attention to press relations, worked harder at building coalitions, and spent more time contacting governmental officials.[18]

In the end, the advocacy explosion encompasses at least three distinct elements. First, there are more groups and interests in the fray. Second, there are many new techniques available to all interests; computers and enhanced communication capacities allow groups to serve as linking agents between the public — or specific sectors of the public — and legislators. Third, both well-established groups and new entries are employing a more extensive range of techniques to influence policy decisions.[19] As a result, more messages from more interests than ever before are aimed at legislators. Whether they hear those messages remains an open question.

Lobbying: Information, Access, and Influence

Members of Congress continually find it difficult to inform themselves adequately on a wide range of policies. There is a great deal to know, and time pressures are often intense. This does not mean that they do not have enough information on most issues. Quite the contrary. Capitol Hill is awash in information: from congressional staff (see Chapter 6), from think tanks, from the

---

[15]See, in particular, Donald Haider's *When Governments Come to Washington: Governors, Mayors, and Intergovernmental Lobbying* (New York: Free Press, 1974) for the 1970s era and Beverly Cigler's "Not Just Another Special Interest: Intergovernmental Representation," in Allan Cigler and Burdett Loomis, eds., *Interest Group Politics*, 4th ed. (Washington, DC: CQ Press, 1995), pp. 131–153, for a perspective on the 1980s and 1990s.

[16]Eric Uslaner, "All Politics Is Global," in Cigler and Loomis, *Interest Group Politics*, 4th ed.

[17]Schlozman and Tierney, *Organized Interests and American Democracy*, p. 180.

[18]Schlozman and Tierney, *Organized Interests and American Democracy*, p. 155.

[19]Schlozman and Tierney, *Organized Interests and American Democracy*, p. 169. See also, Allan J. Cigler and Burdett A. Loomis, "From Big Bird to Bill Gates: Organized Interests and the Emergence of Hyperpolitics," in Cigler and Loomis, eds., *Interest Group Politics*, 5th ed. (Washington, DC: CQ Press, 1998), pp. 389–403.

media, and, of course, from organized interests and lobbyists. But truly useful information is often in short supply. Legislators operate under highly uncertain conditions much of the time, and they must frequently act with less than perfect information on a given subject. Useful information comes in three general types: (1) political intelligence that lays out the reelection consequences of their actions; (2) process-oriented details that allow for assessing the chances that a bill will make it through the legislative process; and (3) policy data that spell out the impact of a proposal.[20] As one insider account puts it:

> Lobbyists see it as their job to persuade legislators that voters are on the lobbyists' side. . . . [They] know that the best way to guarantee that their point of view will be heard is to take the constituents with them when they go to speak to members of Congress. Lobbyists also function as unpaid staff to the decision-makers . . . [and] provide information about both policy and process that [legislators] cannot get. . . .[21]

Although lobbyists are important sources of information, they must first gather bits and pieces of relevant data that will be of use to legislators and then they must have access to those they desire to influence. Thus, much of lobbying resides in accumulating useful (that is, not widely known) information and finding ways to get the material to relevant legislators. Lobbyists gain access in various ways, including socializing (subject to some reductions in the wake of 1995 reforms[22]), making campaign contributions, and developing reputations for providing accurate and useful information.

Once access has been obtained, however, two questions remain: Whom does one seek to lobby? And under what conditions does access allow for influence? Despite the intriguing first steps of some congressional scholars, there is no clear answer concerning who becomes the target of lobbying.[23] Although hard-boiled foes are rarely sought out, both allies and the undecided (and even nondogmatic opponents) are frequently the objects of attention. As for influence, lobbying most often succeeds when it focuses on low-profile issues and legislation, as opposed to matters that stir the public's interest. It is no accident that highly complex issues such as telecommunications reform and tax law generate tremendous amounts of lobbying, in that the

---

[20]Various scholars note these different forms of education. John Wright provides a good summary in his *Interest Groups and Congress* (Boston: Allyn & Bacon, 1996), pp. 88ff.

[21]Jeffery Birnbaum, *The Lobbyists* (New York: Times Books, 1993), p. 6.

[22]For a battlefield report, see Karen De Witt, "In Washington, Giving Is Now Art of Making Gifts Pass through the Eye of the Needle," *New York Times,* January 5, 1997, p. 10.

[23]There is a burgeoning literature here that is both useful and oversimplified. See, for example, Frank R. Baumgartner and Beth L. Leech, "The Multiple Ambiguities of Counteractive Lobbying" and David Austen-Smith and John R. Wright, "Theory and Evidence of Counteractive Lobbying," both in *American Journal of Political Science,* 40 (May 1996): pp. 521–542; 543–565, respectively. Also, Marie Hojnacki and David C. Kimball, "Organized Interests and the Decision of Whom to Lobby in Congress," *American Political Science Review* 92 (December, 1998): pp. 775–790.

complexities of both policies and procedures offer great opportunities for advocates to turn access into influence as they shape arguments that favor their causes, often on an obscure procedural point or some dense wording, buried deep inside a comprehensive piece of legislation.

Public Lobbying: International Trade, 1993–1999

Increasingly, even when conflict over legislation becomes highly publicized, organized interests can still affect decisions on Capitol Hill. The continuing struggles over U.S. trade policy illustrate how the interest group environment can affect congressional actions. The Congress was faced with implementing the North American Free Trade Agreement (NAFTA) and ratifying the General Agreement on Tariffs and Trade (GATT). Given that both agreements were supported strongly by Presidents Reagan, Bush, and Clinton, the Congress represented the logical venue for opponents to mount their attacks, which emphasized the loss of American jobs (with NAFTA) and sovereignty (with GATT), in that international tribunals could rule against some practices of U.S. businesses.

Opponents of NAFTA included an unlikely coalition of organized labor, consumer advocates (particularly Ralph Nader), some environmental groups, and, perhaps most importantly, 1992 independent presidential candidate Ross Perot. Perot brought both his own constituents and his highly public tactics to the battle. Indeed, Nader, the environmentalists, and Perot combined to produce an effective outside attack on the trade accord; they could direct their own supporters to lobby hundreds of members of Congress while they simultaneously advertised extensively against the pact. Only late in the day did NAFTA backers, often prompted by President Clinton, counter the public arguments of Perot, Nader, and their allies.

NAFTA opponents did not have to rely solely on sophisticated grassroots lobbying techniques, clever public relations, and considerable paid advertising; they enjoyed the support of key Democratic legislators near the core of the party leadership. House Democratic Whip David Bonoir (D-Mich.) proved inexhaustible in his coordination of opposing forces within the House. Less public, to reduce the embarrassment of his own party's president, was the firm opposition of House Majority Leader Richard Gephardt (D-Mo.). As a highly representative body (both Bonoir's and Gephardt's districts included large numbers of union members), the House encourages interests to seek out powerful champions to provide inside leadership on key issues. NAFTA foes could scarcely have done better than to enlist two of the three top leaders in the House. Only after the Clinton White House made some eleventh-hour pleas, agreed to a few modest concessions, and issued several specific policy clarifications did NAFTA win House approval. The opponents had set the terms of the debate, mounted impressive grassroots campaigns by constituents, and benefited from advertising purchased by Perot and others.

Many of the same interests came together to oppose GATT's approval in late 1994. Obscured by the debate over health care reform, GATT provides a somewhat different illustration of the ways in which organized groups and the Congress can serve each other's needs. Although some business interests opposed NAFTA, virtually all major corporate bodies expressed strong support for the lower tariffs promised by GATT.[24] GATT induced considerably less public opposition than did NAFTA. Nonetheless, congressional consideration of the treaty offered an attractive opportunity for foes of the trade pact. Under the rules of the Senate, Senator Ernest Hollings (D-S.C.), whose state's textile industry desired protection from the competition of cheap foreign labor, was able to hold up a vote on GATT for forty-five days — from early October until after the 1994 congressional elections. Given the delay, opponents hoped to mount a vigorous and public challenge to GATT, with Ross Perot again playing a major role. The Senate's individualism, like the House's sensitivity to district concerns, provided an opening for groups to delay or defeat trade legislation.

Helped by generally supportive Republican leaders, the Clinton administration won approval for the treaty, but only after vigorous debate; given a design that usually discourages speedy or efficient decision making, Congress offered organized interests, with their increased numbers and capacities to mobilize key constituents, an inviting opportunity to take advantage of the very openness that defines the institution.[25]

In 1998, the House decisively defeated (243-180) a bill that would have granted President Clinton the same "fast track" authority that every president since Gerald Ford had enjoyed.[26] Such authority is crucial to passing a trade bill through the Congress, in that it allows a single up-or-down vote on the legislation. By denying Clinton fast track power, the House essentially killed trade legislation by opening it up to dozens, even hundreds, of special interest provisions.

The Policy Explosion

Tied directly to the growth of interests is the great increase in the volume of national policy established since the 1930s, especially since the 1960s. In 1930, the reach of the federal government did not extend very far in terms of expenditures, taxation, or regulation. Congressional committee chairs may have been gaining independent power at this time, but they had very little to control.

Political analyst Michael Barone writes that "macroeconomic fiscal policy, redistribution of wealth, and government spending programs were not major issues [because] the federal government neither raised nor spent . . . much money in the late 1920s."[27] Most federal spending went to pay for the military,

---

[24]Keith Bradsher, "Foes Set for Battle on GATT," *New York Times,* October 3, 1994.

[25]In *Home Style* (Boston: Little, Brown, 1978), Richard F. Fenno, Jr., concludes that the representativeness of the Congress makes it, at least most of the time, "the slow institution" (p. 245) — a description that should not be taken as criticism.

[26]David Hosansky, "How Two Fervent Free-Traders Helped Set Back 'Fast Track'," *Congressional Quarterly Weekly,* October 3, 1998, p. 2675.

[27]Michael Barone, *Our Country* (New York: Free Press, 1990), p. 31.

TABLE 3-1
Federal Spending, 1940-1995 (in billions, not adjusted for inflation)

Year	National Defense	Nondefense	Total (including interest on debt)
1940	$ 1.7	$7.8	$ 9.5
1950	13.7	28.8	42.6
1960	48.1	44.1	92.2
1970	81.7	114.0	195.6
1980	134.0	456.9	590.9
1990	299.0	848.9	1,151.8
1995	271.0	1,034.7	1,518.9
2000 (est.)	274.0	1,492.0	1,766.0

Sources: Harold W. Stanley and Richard G. Niemi, eds., *Visual Statistics on American Politics,* 2nd ed. (Washington, DC: CQ Press, 1990), pp. 385–386; and Allen Schick, *The Federal Budget: Politics, Policy, Process* (Washington, DC: Brookings Institution, 1995), pp. 8, 33; *Congressional Quarterly Weekly Report,* February 11, 1995, p. 429; President's FY 2000 Budget Proposal, <www.access.gpo.gov/usbudget>.

either in the form of current expenses, interest on the national debt incurred by borrowing to pay for past wars, or veterans' benefits. Of the $3.3 billion budget for 1930, less than $1 billion went to fund all other governmental activities.[28]

Even after the increased spending commitments of the New Deal, domestic expenditures stood at just $7.8 billion in 1940 and $12.6 billion in 1946, the first post–World War II year. As late as 1954, domestic spending amounted to only $21.6 billion, a figure that almost doubled by 1960, the last year of the Eisenhower administration. Defense costs averaged $47 billion between 1952 and 1960; by 1960, the year of John F. Kennedy's election, total federal spending totaled $92 billion — a substantial increase since 1930, to be sure, but a figure that did not provide for much in the way of ambitious social programs.

The pent-up demand for more federal domestic intervention (such as Medicare) and more regulation (for example, the Environmental Protection Agency), along with continued requirements for high levels of Cold War defense spending (including Vietnam), produced great increases in both domestic and military spending during the 1960s (see Table 3–1). Still, the major story told in Table 3–1 is that of the great escalation in governmental expenditures during the 1970s and 1980s, when Republicans controlled the presidency for all but Jimmy Carter's 1977–1981 term.

No single explanation adequately accounts for burgeoning federal budgets, but the very existence of new programs in the 1960s and 1970s helped to create great pressures, both inside and outside the government, to increase spending levels. For example, the adoption of Medicare in 1965 produced a continuing rise in federal health-related costs over the next decade — from $9.9 billion in 1965 to $41.5 billion in 1975. More important than the mere cost,

---

[28]Barone, *Our Country,* p. 31.

TABLE 3-2
The Growth of Federal Regulation

Year	Number of Pages in *Federal Register*
1940	5,307
1950	9,562
1960	14,479
1970	20,032
1980	87,012
1990	53,618
1998	70,203

Sources: Harold W. Stanley and Richard G. Niemi, *Vital Statistics on American Politics,* 2nd ed. (Washington, DC: CQ Press, 1990), p. 248; Ornstein, et al., *Visual Statistics on Congress,* 1995–1996, p. 165, *Federal Register,* 1998.

however, was the fundamental redefinition of health care as an issue in American politics. As one scholar notes, "By nationalizing a large portion of the bill, Medicare made health care inflation a public-sector problem and placed it on the policy agenda."[29] In 1996, the government's own estimates that Medicare would go broke by 2001 both made the issue central to congressional campaigns and placed it on the top of the agenda for the 105th Congress.

Although the new policy commitments of the 1960s and 1970s often required more spending in such areas as health, education, and nutrition (in the form of food stamps), the reach of federal regulatory programs was at least as long. As shown in Table 3–2, from 1940 to 1980 the length of one year's body of regulations, printed in the *Federal Register,* grew almost twentyfold, although the 1980 figure is artificially high; the Reagan administration cut back substantially on regulations but still managed to average 54,000 pages of *Federal Register* material per year. More importantly, most regulations stayed on the books, thus producing an overwhelmingly dense policy environment by the 1980s.

Even before the Reagan era, Theodore Lowi had described a national government that had fundamentally changed the nature of American political life. He saw the results as a "two-part model" of highly institutionalized politics, in which

▶ "The national government by some formal action monopolizes a given area of private activity." This may be accomplished through spending, regulation, or other means.

▶ "Following that, a program is authorized and an administrative agency is put into operation to work without legal guidelines through an elaborate, sponsored bargaining process [between governmental agencies and specific interests]."[30]

[29]James A. Morone, *The Democratic Wish* (New York: Basic Books, 1990), p. 266.
[30]Theodore Lowi, *The End of Liberalism,* 2nd ed. (New York: Norton, 1979), p. 278.

In the end, tens of thousands of governmental units and interests have large stakes in countless discretionary decisions made within the bureaucracy, inside the presidency, by the judiciary, and on Capitol Hill. Lowi argues that there is virtually no accountability for most decisions; instead of clear policy and well-defined procedure, there is only process.[31]

This "process" has become the heart and soul of relations between organized interests, the bureaucracy, and the Congress. Robert Salisbury observes that much activity by groups and other interests emphasizes the monitoring of capital information sources: "Washington is, after all, the main source of what governmental officials are doing or planning to do. To get that information in a timely way, a continuous and alert presence . . . is vital."[32] Moreover, it is accurate information on political contingencies, not on policy alternatives, that is often most at a premium. Given its size and diversity, the Congress is ideally suited to provide such knowledge. Individual members and their staffs are well positioned to convey valuable political information to particular interests; in turn, these interests will have good reason to support their reelection bids. Through the 1980s, ideology played little role in the game. Rather, majority House Democrats became the vehicles for many business interests that wanted to "invest" in careerist legislators who would, it seemed, control the Congress, and especially the House, for the foreseeable future.[33] Of course, once Republicans won a majority of the House seats in 1994, such an arrangement lost much of its luster for many corporate and professional interests, whose support for the GOP increased dramatically, as we shall see in Chapter 4.

The Budget: Taming an 800-Pound Gorilla

The growth of organized interests and the extended reach of national policies are developments that have reinforced each other. For the most part, both trends reflect an increased fragmentation of the decision-making context. Historically, the way the Congress appropriated funds also contributed to this decentralization. After the president proposed a unified budget, the Congress, through the appropriations committees in both House and Senate, would

---

[31]Lowi, *The End of Liberalism,* p. 63.

[32]Robert H. Salisbury, "The Paradox of Interest Groups in Washington—More Groups, Less Clout," in Anthony King, ed., *The New American Political System,* rev. ed. (Washington, DC: American Enterprise Institute, 1990), p. 203.

[33]The key figure for congressional Democrats was Representative Tony Coelho, first in his role as chair of the Democratic Congressional Campaign Committee and then as Democratic Whip. Coelho brought Democratic House members and various business interests together to their mutual benefit. In 1989, Coelho resigned from the House after reports surfaced of his favored treatment in the purchase of bonds, although no charges were ever brought against him. In the 1990s, Coelho, as a managing partner of a New York investment firm, maintained contacts with the Democrats and emerged as a key adviser to President Clinton. See Brooks Jackson, *Honest Graft,* rev. ed. (Washington, DC: Farragut, 1990), and Ruth Shalit, "The Undertaker," *New Republic,* January 2, 1995, pp. 17–25.

break up the spending proposals into thirteen separate pieces, each initially considered by one House appropriations subcommittee. Only at the end of the legislative process, with the passage of thirteen distinct bills, would the Congress and the president know how much had actually been appropriated. This decentralized format worked reasonably well into the 1960s,[34] but by the early 1970s pressures began to mount for a more coherent congressional approach to the entire budget.

Legislators began to face major budgetary problems as a result of enacting numerous policies and having many groups capable of competing to influence them; policies cost money (obtained from taxes) in addition to conferring benefits. During the 1950s and 1960s, the appropriations committees could maintain a check on overall spending by the Congress, but by the early 1970s, this informal constraint had weakened substantially.[35] In the 1970s, the Congress provided itself with the staff and committee structure to increase its role in constructing annual budgets, which had been almost totally the province of the president and the well-staffed Office of Management and Budget.[36] After 1974, when Senate and House Budget Committees and the Congressional Budget Office were established, members of Congress could fight their "budget wars" with the executive branch on roughly equal footing.[37] This legislative capacity became especially important during the Reagan administration, when 1981 tax cuts meant that every succeeding budget would include a large deficit and result in great pressures on existing levels of spending.

Over the 1980s, a centralizing change that was implicit in the new budget arrangements modified the nature of congressional actions: the fiscalization of the policy process. In short, fiscalization simply means that the question of paying for services and programs has become the proverbial "800-pound gorilla," a beast that can sit wherever it wants. Within the contemporary Congress, this budgetary ape camps out in almost every committee room and leadership meeting. Controlling spending levels and the funding (or killing) of continuing programs have become the central issues of the postreform Congress. In sum, the budget has ceased to be an "empowering process," at least for federal initiatives. Rather, the contemporary budget "often appears to be a

---

[34]In his 1966 book, *The Power of the Purse* (Boston: Little, Brown), Richard F. Fenno, Jr., could characterize the appropriations process in the Congress as a system. Within a few years, that system had broken down in terms of controlling expenditures and priorities, and Congress was unable to limit presidential intervention, as Richard Nixon aggressively used his informal powers to withhold or "impound" funds as a means of altering congressional spending priorities. See James Pfiffner, *The President, the Budget, and Congress* (Boulder, CO: Westview Press, 1979).

[35]See various works by Allen Schick and later editions of Aaron Wildavsky's *The Politics of the Budgetary Process* (Boston: Little, Brown).

[36]There is a vast literature here. A good starting place is Allen Schick's *Congress and Money* (Washington, DC: Urban Institute, 1980).

[37]Allen Schick introduces the term *budget war* in reference to the 1966–1974 period, but there has scarcely been a peace after the adoption of the Budget Reform Act. See Schick, *Congress and Money*.

limiting process . . . [and it] crowds out genuine choice; it forces tomorrow's programs to give way to yesterday's decisions."[38]

With little ability to fund new programs, legislators sought to control the spending commitments that had already been enacted into law. The large annual deficits through the 1980s and into the 1990s demonstrate the difficulty of reducing expenditures; nonetheless, the post-1981 period has been dominated by budgetary politics. In several highly centralized budget summits from 1982 to 1993, congressional leaders negotiated with top executive-branch officials to arrive at acceptable spending and deficit levels. Thurber and Durst conclude that this will continue, in that "budget and party leaders will continue to build coalitions to formulate the budget and to negotiate with the president about spending priorities. [Current practices produce] a tighter zero-sum budget game with more control and with top-down, centralized budgeting by the congressional party leadership."[39]

This party-based, centralized process is what came crashing down on Democratic first-term Representative Marjorie Margolies-Mezvinsky, as she came under intense pressures from the party leadership and the Clinton administration to vote in favor of the 1993 budget agreement, whose taxation provisions she had consistently opposed. The context for such pressures is a budget process that regularly produces high-visibility votes on the entire set of spending and taxing commitments for an entire year. Every increase in funding for one program must be taken out of the spending for some other governmental activity. Debate over policies thus turns more and more on fiscal considerations. Put bluntly, how much will each program cost? In such an environment, it is those who can survey the entire budget — members of the budget and appropriations committees and the party leadership — who have the most leverage in determining outcomes. The very nature of redistributive, or zero-sum, decision making is to empower those whose reach facilitates negotiations and whose power can enforce agreements, as long as they can convince even a bare majority of members to agree. Short of voting against the entire budget agreement, rank-and-file members of both parties can exercise little influence over the budgets that their leaders construct.

Remarkably, however, the politics of budgets shifted dramatically in the second term of the Clinton administration. The budget deficit first narrowed, then disappeared in the late 1990s, buoyed by a strong economy and the results of the 1990 and 1993 budget deals that restricted spending levels. Legislators such as House Budget Committee chair John Kasich (R-Ohio), who had spent their entire careers railing against budget deficits, needed to address new questions surrounding a surplus that was predicted to reach $100 billion by fis-

[38]Allen Schick, *The Federal Budget* (Washington, DC: Brookings Institution, 1995), p. 2.

[39]James A. Thurber and Samantha L. Durst, "The 1990 Budget Enforcement Act: The Decline of Congressional Accountability," in Lawrence C. Dodd and Bruce I. Oppenheimer, eds., *Congress Reconsidered,* 5th ed. (Washington, DC: CQ Press, 1993), p. 391.

cal year 2000.[40] As President Clinton put it, "We have no permanent deficit anymore; the natural condition is a surplus. So the question is, what do we do with it?"[41] The prospective budget surplus demonstrates the extent to which the Congress can become a hothouse for the incubation of myriad policy proposals. As Representative John Spratt (D-S.C.) notes, while "a deficit discourages expectations, a surplus excites expectations. There are a lot of stakeholders in this process who are looking to cut different deals. We have our work cut out for us."[42]

As might be expected, many of the battle lines have formed around partisan proposals to "save" Social Security while allowing for some tax cuts or further spending. But the very programs that successfully capped spending in an era of deficits have made it difficult for legislators to act quickly on addressing the politics of budget surpluses. That may be all for the better, in that neither the public nor their representatives have fully grasped the implications of having trillions in budget surpluses projected for the next twenty years. It's a new game, and no one is quite sure how to play.

Can't Get No Respect: The Unpopular Congress

The very openness of the legislative process, which might otherwise be thought to endear Congress to the people, is much more likely to have the opposite effect. . . . Thus, while Congress is sometimes viewed by the public as an enemy, we wish to call attention to the fact that it is often viewed as an enemy because it is so public.

John Hibbing and Elizabeth Thiess-Morse, *Congress as Public Enemy*

Let there be no mistake about congressional popularity: The legislative branch, despite its putative ties to "the people," has never won great adulation from the public at large. Nor from editorial pages.[43] Historically, the Congress has been savaged by editorialists, much as it has been in more recent times. Most individual legislators do not help the situation, as they often

---

[40]The budget surplus reflects the merging of both regular income and Social Security income. Some analysts and members of Congress argued that Social Security surpluses unduly inflated income figures, but most legislators, the president, and both the Congresssional Budget Office (CBO) and the executive-branch Office of Management and Budget (OMB) operated under income definitions that produced substantial surpluses. Indeed, both CBO and OMB predicted that, absent tax cuts or disproportionate spending increases, the entire non–Social Security debt of the federal government could be erased by 2014.

[41]Quoted in Alexis Simendinger and David Baumann, "Let the Good Times Roll," *National Journal,* January 30, 1999, p. 248.

[42]Quoted in Simendinger and Baumann, "Let the Good Times Roll," p. 250.

[43]In the author's classes on Congress, he has a standing wager that no one will be able to bring in a post-1970 cartoon that depicts the institution in an unambiguously positive light. In more than ten years, no student has yet collected.

engage in the practice of seeking reelection by running vigorously against the institution.[44]

The percentage of the population viewing the Congress in favorable terms has remained a minority since the mid-1960s; on average, during this period one in three adults has had a favorable image of the Congress at the time.[45] Adding insult to injury, evaluations of the president and the Supreme Court have been consistently more positive than those of the legislative branch, although approval rates improved somewhat in the late 1990s. (See Figure 3–1.)[46] Why is this so, we might well ask, especially since most incumbent members of Congress regularly win reelection? The evidence points to two complementary culprits: first, the Congress itself, and second, the media.

THE INHERENT PROBLEMS OF A POWERFUL, PUBLIC, AND PROFESSIONAL LEGISLA-TURE   Two sets of scholars have concluded that the modern Congress is its own worst enemy. One study observes that "When Congress acts as it was constitutionally designed to act — passing major legislation and debating the issues of the day — it is rewarded by the public with lower levels of approval."[47] In effect, congressional disapproval is built into our constitutional structure of decision-making; to the extent that Congress does its prescribed job, it will remain unpopular. John Hibbing and Elizabeth Thiess-Morse flesh out this basic finding in *The Congress as Public Enemy*. Not only does the constitutional role of the Congress expose it to public criticism, the Congress has changed in various ways since the 1950s. They write:

> The elaborate institutional infrastructure, the committees, the subcommittees, the staffers, the partisanship, the nature of debate, the puffery, the boundaries, the sense of insularity, the lengthy careers, the perquisites, the salary, the maldistributed pork, and the special-interest representatives

---

[44]Of the many key findings in Fenno's *Home Style,* none was more important or more surprising than his conclusion that campaigning against the Congress was a ubiquitous strategy (p. 168). This contradicted the notion that members of Congress felt a strong sense of "institutional loyalty" to their body. Although this norm of loyalty may have had some continuing impact in Washington, it had virtually no impact on members' behavior back in their home districts.

[45]Among others, see Glenn Parker, *Characteristics of Congress* (Englewood Cliffs, NJ: Prentice-Hall, 1989), chap. 3; and Roger H. Davidson and Walter J. Oleszek, *Congress and Its Members,* 4th ed. (Washington, DC: CQ Press, 1994). Most recently, see John Hibbing and Elizabeth Thiess-Morse, *Congress as Public Enemy* (New York: Cambridge, 1995), chaps. 2 and 3.

[46]In 1993, the following percentage of respondents expressed a "great deal of confidence" in the three branches of government: the Supreme Court, 31 percent; the executive branch, 12 percent; and the Congress, 7 percent. In 1973, the Congress had received a 24 percent confidence rating in a similar survey. (*Source:* National Opinion Research Center surveys, cited in Karlyn Bowman and Everett Ladd, "Public Opinion toward Congress," in Thomas E. Mann and Norman J. Ornstein, eds., *Congress, the Press, and the Public* [Washington, DC: AEI/Brookings, 1994], p. 54.)

[47]Robert H. Durr, John B. Gilmour, and Christina Wolbrecht, "Explaining Congressional Approval," *American Journal of Political Science* 41 (January 1997): 199.

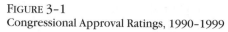

FIGURE 3-1
Congressional Approval Ratings, 1990-1999

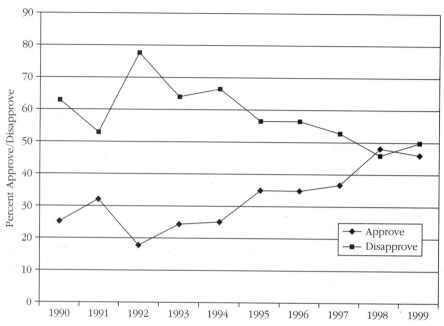

Source: Annual Gallup polls <www.gallup.com> and *Washington Post,* February 15, 1999.

attracted to Congress like bees to honey all serve as tremendous turn-offs for large portions of the citizenry.[48]

Indeed, the very professionalism of the contemporary Congress, which we will examine in some detail over the remainder of the book, stands at the core of the public's contempt for the legislature. Both professional legislators and professional interest-group representatives win the scorn of the public, but more generally, "a surprising number of people . . . dislike being exposed to processes endemic to democratic government." Citizens desire a sanitized politics, without disagreement without procedural wrangling — "in short . . . , a patently unrealistic form of democracy."[49]

The denigration of Congress as an institution has contrasted sharply with the highly positive evaluations given individual legislators by their constituencies, as witnessed both by polling data (see Table 3–3) and the overwhelming proportion of incumbents who win reelection. Individual legislators can usually present themselves in positive terms, whereas the Congress as whole

---

[48]Hibbing and Thiess-Morse, *Congress as Public Enemy,* p. 161.

[49]Hibbing and Thiess-Morse, *Congress as Public Enemy,* p. 147.

TABLE 3-3
High Approval for Members; Low Approval for Congress

Individual Members	Congress as an Institution
Serve constituents (usually done effectively).	Resolves national issues only with difficulty or not at all.
Run against Congress.	Has few defenders.
Emphasize personal style and outreach to constituents.	Operates as collegial body, difficult to understand.
Are reported on by local media in generally positive terms.	Is often reported on negatively by national media (scandals, etc.).
Respond quickly to most constituent needs/inquiries.	Moves slowly; cumbersome procedures limit rapid responses.
Are able to highlight personal goals and accomplishments.	Has many voices, but none can speak clearly for the Congress as a whole.

Source: Adapted from Davidson and Oleszek, *Congress and Its Members,* 4th ed., p. 444.

depends on the characterizations of others, especially those of the executive and the media. Although there are always interbranch tensions, the prevalence of divided government in the 1969–1993 era encouraged Republican presidents to issue regular attacks on an allegedly obstructionist and partisan Democratic Congress. The post-1994 situation, of course, has allowed similar claims to flow from a Democratic White House, although the Congress's standing has improved a bit (Figure 3-1).

THE MEDIA AS CRITIC AND CONDUIT OF CRITICISM   As much as interbranch bickering and congressional structure may contribute to disapproval, declining support for Congress may result from the nature of congressional press coverage in the post-Watergate era. "Over the years," concludes one recent study, "press coverage has moved from healthy skepticism to outright cynicism. . . . To believe the modern reporter or editor, legislators are egregiously overpaid, indulged, and indifferent to the problems of constituents who lack six-figure incomes and fantastic job perquisites."[50]

The press's relationship with Congress has become more complex over the years. In sheer numbers, the Washington press corps has grown steadily since about 1960, when it comprised fewer than one thousand reporters who predominantly represented newspapers and periodicals. By 1996, more than five thousand reporters were at work in the capital, with a slightly growing edge to those from television and radio.[51]

However significant the growth of the press corps and the rising importance of the electronic media, other developments have been equally telling. First, the nature of political reporting has changed since Watergate (c. 1973); the historically cozy relationships between Washington politicians and reporters, although

---

[50]Mark J. Rozell, "Press Coverage of Congress," in *Congress, the Press, and the Public,* pp. 109–110.

[51]Harold W. Stanley and Richard G. Niemi, *Vital Statistics on American Politics,* 2nd ed. (Washington, DC: CQ Press, 1990), p. 52; and Phillips, *Arrogant Capitol,* p. 45.

not disappearing, became more contentious, even adversarial — especially at the national level. Second, technical advances such as satellite linkages allow many members of Congress to communicate directly with their constituents, often through local television outlets that are far less critical than the national media.[52]

At the same time, the steady growth of cable television, which carries C-SPAN and its intense, unfiltered coverage of the Congress, and the popularity of talk radio, with its ability to generate thousands of letters and phone calls, have increased constituent pressures on members of Congress. Media sources are simply more varied and less subject to the control of any one voice, be it the president's or a legislative leader's. And many of the voices take a relentlessly negative approach to what they see as the needlessly complex and the insular context of Capitol Hill politics. The capacity of talk shows to affect the Congress became clear in 1993. Then-Representative James Inhofe (R-Okla.), an obscure minority-party congressman,[53] relentlessly traveled the talk-show circuit, pushing his proposal to open up the process of prying a bill out of committee through the use of a discharge petition, which, to succeed, requires a majority of members' signatures. His campaign turned on the highly technical point that members who signed the petition should have their names made public. The House leadership wanted to retain the cloak of anonymity on signees; such a practice allowed them privately to urge members not to sign, whereas public disclosure would increase pressures from outside interests to discharge a bill (and thus upset the leadership's control of legislative business). In a clever move, Inhofe constructed his own discharge petition to bring to the floor a bill that would open up the discharge process. Despite intense leadership opposition, this tactic succeeded, and the bill moved to floor debate and eventual approval.

Only within the legislative branch would such public intervention into an arcane intra-institutional conflict be easily available as a tactic. Representative Inhofe and his supporters could defeat the Democratic leadership by campaigning vigorously through radio talk shows against the way the Congress conducted its own business. Despite the occasional airing of divisions within the executive and judicial branches, only the highly permeable Congress would change its internal rules because of public pressures orchestrated through the media from within the institution itself.

---

[52]See Timothy Cook, *Making Laws and Making News* (Washington, DC: Brookings Institution, 1989), and his "PR on the Hill: The Evolution of Congressional Press Operations," in Christopher Deering, ed., *Congressional Politics* (Chicago: Dorsey, 1988), pp. 62–89.

[53]In something of an upset, Representative Inhofe won a Senate seat in 1994, but the Republican sweep was probably more responsible than any credit that he could claim from his discharge petition triumph.

CONGRESS IN CONTEXT

As a representative body, Congress necessarily responds to changes in its context, and we can best understand it within its contemporaneous environment. The strong state and local parties of the early 1900s helped produce well-disciplined legislative parties and the most powerful congressional leaders in the American experience (see Chapter 7). On regular occasions the electorate has modified its partisan preferences and thus changed the nature of Congress.[54] In such circumstances the usual condition of congressional elections as local contests is overwhelmed by national forces; the 1994 congressional elections reflect such an instance, even though the forty-year period of Republican minorities in the House does represent a historically unprecedented duration of such status. The 1994, 1996, and 1998 elections may indicate the emergence of a new, competitive congressional alignment, with Republicans winning narrow majorities. Even so, both centrifugal and centripetal forces will shape the practices and policies of the contemporary Congress.

For the most part, tendencies toward centralization and decentralization *within* the Congress flow from *outside* forces that continually affect the legislature and its members. For example, local economies place tremendous constituency-based pressures on legislators who seek emergency aid for drought-plagued farmers, assistance for unemployed steelworkers, or subsidized loans for a global firm like Boeing, which must compete against the European Airbus consortium. As public policies and organized interests have grown in number and scope, lawmakers face increased lobbying pressures that can pit constituency against constituency. In the 1970s, the Congress created more and more subcommittees to address these interests, but this fragmentation has been curbed in the 1990s (see Chapter 5).

As we shall see, congressional reapportionment and redistricting in the past twenty years (and especially in 1992, after the 1990 census) have created parties in the House whose members represent distinct constituencies — the core moderate base of the Democratic party and the increasingly conservative, both fiscally and socially, base of the Republicans. As the impeachment process demonstrated, House Republicans responded to their conservative constituents, even when it was almost certainly to the political disadvantage of the party. Enhanced partisanship has meant that both congressional parties have granted their leaders substantial powers, which has centralized the decision-making process.

The very responsiveness of individual members of Congress to specific constituencies may have rendered the Congress as an institution unresponsive to major societal concerns such as education, Social Security, Medicare, crime, and welfare. Members of Congress know best how to serve constituents and

---

[54]David Brady, *Critical Elections and Congressional Policy Making* (Stanford, CA: Stanford University Press, 1988).

groups with particular interests, even though they may desire to make large-scale changes to address broad societal problems. Given continuing budgetary restraints in either shaping new programs or eliminating old ones, legislators have contributed to a context that often breeds distrust and invites cynicism, a combination that makes coherent policy making all the more difficult. Into this breach has ridden an aggressive, ideological Republican party in the House and, increasingly, in the Senate. The continuing question is whether this centralizing element in national politics and on Capitol Hill can constrain the centrifugul forces that remain ingrained in American life. This, above all, has remained the task for Republican majorities between 1995 and 2000. As political scientist John Bader concludes after examining the agenda-setting powers of Congress: "A balance, however precarious and in need of adjustment, between heavy-handed leadership and fragmenting anarchy, should be maintained. . . . The ability to set priorities [by the Congress] fits into a larger set of factors that keep the system separated and in check."[55] Ironically, strong congressional leadership may contribute to an overall balance among the many contending powers in American politics. At the same time, Sinclair observes that the 1990s have found the president and the Congress to be at best "hostile partners" as they confronted each other, even before the highly partisan politics of impeachment intervened.[56]

---

[55]John Bader, *Taking the Initiative* (Washington, DC: Georgetown University Press, 1997), p. 223.

[56]Barbara Sinclair, "Hostile Partners: The President, Congress and Lawmaking in the Partisan 1990s" (paper presented at "Congress and the President in a Partisan Era," Texas A&M University, College Station, Februrary 5–6, 1999), p. 13.

Four

CONGRESSIONAL ELECTIONS: ROOTS OF THE CENTRIFUGAL CONGRESS

I n 1992, tremendous change rocked the U.S. House of Representatives. Extensive redistricting in the wake of the 1990 census and widespread abuse of check-cashing privileges at the House Bank induced many members to retire, led to nineteen primary election defeats and twenty-four general election losses by incumbents, and resulted in the largest turnover since 1948 — 110 newcomers (63 Democrats and 47 Republicans), more than a quarter of the chamber's 435 Representatives. Republicans did gain House seats, but, much to their dismay, Democrats continued to hold substantial majorities in both House and Senate.

Two years later, however, Republicans picked up fifty-two additional seats in the House and eight seats in the Senate to gain control of both bodies for the first time in forty years.[1] If the number of 110 new House members represented the most important aspect of the 1992 elections, in 1994 the central result was that all Republican incumbents in both houses waged successful bids for reelection (among Democrats, however, thirty-four Representatives and two senators were defeated[2]).

In sum, the 1992 and 1994 elections shook up much of the conventional wisdom about congressional elections in the postreform era, a conventional wisdom that emphasized stability, incumbency, and the insularity of sitting legislators from effective challenges. Moreover, few scholars or political professionals had viewed the Democratic House as vulnerable to a Republican takeover. Nonetheless, on January 3, 1995, Republican Newt Gingrich was sworn in as the presiding officer of the House — a House in which more than half the members had served for four years or less.

The 1996 and 1998 elections represented something of a return to the incumbency-dominated electoral politics that have become the norm for the U.S. Congress. Even though the Republicans maintained narrow majorities in

---

[1]A ninth Senate seat came to the Republicans through the November 1994 party switch of Alabama Democrat Richard Shelby. They added a tenth seat with Senator Ben Nighthorse Campbell's (Colo.) switch in March 1995.

[2]Beyond the thirty-four Democratic incumbents who lost in the general election, two more lost in Democratic primary contests.

the House and a 55-45 margin in the Senate, the electoral verdicts of 1996 and 1998 indicated no clear national trends. Rather, the local politics of congressional districts and individual states came to the fore, despite vast spending by independent groups and national political parties to influence results across the country.

This chapter explores a fundamental building block of the centrifugal Congress — the politics of congressional elections. In the postreform era, this has meant the politics of reelection, given that the vast majority of successful candidates are sitting representatives and senators. Indeed, the very success of these legislators represents part of a perplexing problem. Writing before the 1992 and 1994 elections, scholar Gary Jacobson observed that "political incapacity and stalemate are encouraged by a peculiar shortcoming of contemporary congressional election processes. They give us representatives and senators who are individually responsive but collectively irresponsible."[3]

Jacobson may have been correct, but the Congress does change — both in its membership and in its attitudes toward policies. Although most congressional results are determined by local issues and candidates, national trends also influence the electorate. The 1992 elections generated new concerns about the deficit, and legislators began to make efforts to reduce crime through enhanced funding for police and modest gun control policies. More definitively, the 1994 Republican triumph resulted from strong national forces that increased the vulnerability of many sitting House Democrats, and the electorate balanced the foreordained 1996 reelection of Bill Clinton with continued Republican control of Congress in both 1996 and, narrowly, 1998. Such broad interpretations do not mean that Americans pay a lot of attention to congressional races, either their own or the entire range of contests.

Ironically, the voters as a whole — the *electorate* — can succeed where *individual voters* may fail. As Erickson and Wright conclude:

> The average voter knows little about his or her representative and only a bit more about his or her senators. House challengers are almost invisible, and only a portion of the electorate has even a modest amount of information about senatorial challengers. Nevertheless, the electorates that candidates and parties face are smart and discerning, and they reward faithful representation. [In listening to and anticipating the electorate's wishes,] candidates . . . work to give them what they want. Elections bring about much higher levels of policy representation than most observers would expect based on the low levels of citizen awareness.[4]

---

[3]Gary Jacobson, *The Politics of Congressional Elections,* 3rd ed. (New York: HarperCollins, 1992), p. 2.

[4]Robert S. Erickson and Gerald C. Wright, "Voters, Candidates, and Issues in Congressional Elections," in Lawrence C. Dodd and Bruce I. Oppenheimer, eds., *Congress Reconsidered,* 6th ed. (Washington, DC: CQ Press, 1997) p. 156.

Why this is so requires some close scrutiny, in that local and national elements combine to forge a new Congress every two years. Local forces often seem to dominate congressional decision making, as lawmakers protect their constituents' particular interests, ranging from grazing rights for cattle to shipbuilding to the aerospace industry. At times, however, these centrifugal forces are offset by national issues and by increasingly heterogeneous congressional districts, where one or a few interests cannot dominate. Sometimes (most often after a high-visibility presidential election) the legislative and executive branches respond to the electorate by moving significant policy initiatives through the complex and slow legislative process. This occurred dramatically with the results of the election of 1994 and the initial months of the 104th Congress. Not only did Republicans win majorities, they proved themselves capable — at least in the House — of passing an impressive array of legislation, much of it drawn from a single campaign document, the Contract with America. Despite subsequent failures to push much of this program into law, House Republicans did succeed in shaping the terms of many national policy debates (e.g., welfare reform).

This chapter first examines the forces of fragmentation — localism, incumbency, and campaign finance — that have grown increasingly important in congressional elections since the 1970s. Then, more general forces are explored to see how much a Congress might reflect a "national verdict"[5] on hotly contested issues. If a national message is clear, congressional leaders and the president may well be able to overcome, or at least balance, the tendencies of members to look homeward in developing their policy positions.

LOCAL ELECTIONS FOR A NATIONAL OFFICE

All politics is local.

Former Speaker Thomas P. (Tip) O'Neill

Much of the fragmentation on Capitol Hill lies in the profoundly local nature of congressional elections, especially for representatives whose districts remain relatively homogeneous (even as they have become less dominated by a few interests over time). To be sure, a few constituencies cover immense areas such as the whole of Alaska, Montana, and Wyoming, each with a single representative. Other districts reflect highly diverse populations, such as those metropolitan seats that include substantial numbers of the urban poor, various racial and ethnic groups, small business owners, and wealthy suburbanites. Nonetheless, when compared with a presidential campaign or those for a few large-state U.S. Senate seats, most congressional races are fought within a well-defined local context.

---

[5]Erickson and Wright, "Voters, Candidates, and Issues in Congressional Elections," p. 91.

Members of Congress continually talk of their constituents, as if they know exactly who these individuals are. In fact, all legislators relate to several different, overlapping constituencies. Richard Fenno finds that "each member of Congress perceives four concentric constituencies: geographic, reelection, primary, and personal."[6] Roughly speaking, the geographic constituency reflects the physical boundaries of the district; the reelection constituency comprises the number of voters, and their preferences, that have provided (and will provide) electoral success; the primary constituency is that group that "each congressman believes would provide his last line of electoral defense in a primary";[7] and the personal constituency consists of those long-time intimates whom the legislator can trust to offer unvarnished advice and accurate political information.

Geographic Constituencies

In the wake of a series of key Supreme Court decisions and voting rights legislation in the 1960s, all congressional districts have had roughly equal populations;[8] post-1990 districts average about 570,000 as a result of the regular decennial apportionment, which allocated seats to states in accord with their populations. Thus, California's House delegation grew from forty-five in the 1980s to fifty-two in the 1990s, and each district has a total population of a little more than 571,000. In that congressional seats are awarded to states through a mathematical formula and districts cannot cross state lines, population variations from state to state can be much more substantial. For example, in 1991 the state of Montana filed an unsuccessful suit over the loss of one of its two congressional districts in the 1992 reapportionment process, which left the state with a single constituency of almost 800,000.[9] Conversely, Oklahoma districts consist of about 524,000 residents, about 8 percent less than the national average.

Members of the House all represent roughly the same number of constituents with roughly the same resources (see Chapter 6 on congressional enterprises). This ensures a substantial fragmentation within the House, given the great differences in culture, race, ethnicity, age, wealth, and so forth, across the nation, but recent judicial interpretations of the 1965 Voting Rights Act

---

[6]Richard F. Fenno, Jr., *Home Style* (Boston: Little, Brown, 1978), p. 27.

[7]Fenno, *Home Style,* p. 18.

[8]The Constitution mandates the reapportionment of House seats among the states every ten years, after the decennial census. Each state must then redraw its district lines to comply with equal representation requirements. For a good contemporary overview of the redistricting and reapportionment, see David Butler and Bruce Cain, *Congressional Redistricting* (New York: Macmillan, 1992).

[9]Given the increasing popularity of "Big Sky Country," it appears that Montana will regain its second House seat in the reapportionment that will follow the census of 2000.

(and its 1982 extension) have greatly increased the importance of racial representation.

The 1982 legislation mandated that redistricting — the actual redrawing of congressional districts, usually by state legislatures after reapportionment — not dilute minority voting strength. Minorities were explicitly defined as African Americans and Latinos. Congressional redistricting in 1991–1992 thus produced a slew of "minority-majority" districts that elected fifty-eight minority representatives in 1992, up from thirty-eight in 1990.[10] Minority populations were concentrated in districts by legal gerrymandering; that is, many odd-shaped districts were created specifically so that minority legislators would be elected. These expectations were fulfilled, in that "sixteen new black elected officials joined the 1992 Congress, each from a majority black district."[11]

In many ways, the emphasis on the racial composition of districts has turned the notion of gerrymandering on its head. Although gerrymandering — drawing political boundaries to benefit one candidate, party, or population grouping — has a long history in the United States, it has always been considered unethical.[12] The Voting Rights Act of 1965 and a series of important Supreme Court decisions in the mid-1960s established a "one-person, one-vote" rule that opened up the electoral system to minorities, but the impact of minority voters often appeared diluted. For example, in North Carolina, African Americans made up 22 percent of the population in 1990, but the state had elected no minority member to Congress in this century. The state's 1992 redistricting produced two districts designed to send an African American to Washington. Gerrymandering to concentrate minority voting strength had become an officially sanctioned policy.[13]

In fact, the most remarkable example of racial gerrymandering came in North Carolina's "I-85 district," so labeled "because it consists of a series of urban black areas, many of them poor, partially connected by a line sometimes no wider than I-85, splitting adjacent districts in two"[14] (see Figure 4–1). The government-sanctioned gerrymander worked; African-American candidates, both Democrats, won the seats that had been carved out for them.

Although the legal gerrymandering of North Carolina's First District had survived judicial scrutiny, the Supreme Court struck down the Twelfth District's lines as well as mandated the alteration of the racially based "majority-

[10]See Jon Meacham, "Voting Wrongs," *Washington Monthly* (March 1993), p. 28. Of the fifty-eight minority House members, fifty-two came from minority-majority districts.

[11]Lani Guinier, "Don't Scapegoat the Gerrymander," *New York Times Magazine,* January 8, 1995, pp. 36–37.

[12]See Butler and Cain, *Congressional Redistricting,* pp. 1ff.

[13]Several legal cases have challenged this policy; as of its 1997 session, the Supreme Court had approved maps in Louisiana and Georgia that reduced the role of race in redistricting.

[14]Michael Barone and Grant Ujifusa, *The Almanac of American Politics 1994* (Washington, DC: National Journal, 1993), p. 969.

FIGURE 4-1
North Carolina's Twelfth Congressional District — 1992 and 1998

| Congressional Plans — District 12 | 1992 Plan | 1998 Plan |

Source: State of North Carolina, <www.nega.state.nc.us>, January 20, 1999.

minority" seats in other Southern states (Georgia, Louisiana, Texas), where boundaries had reduced the emphasis on their racial composition.[15] In 1995, the Supreme Court reaffirmed its 1993 ruling (*Reno v. Shaw*) that cast doubt on any district lines drawn to take race into account as "the predominant factor."[16]

And in January 1999, the Supreme Court heard arguments on the constitutionality of the redrawn Twelfth District in North Carolina. Since 1992, as expected, the predominantly minority (African American or Latino) districts have elected Democrats in overwhelming numbers. At the same time, given the concentration of minority voters in a handful of districts, Republicans hoped to gain the remaining seats. Although estimates of the impact of racial gerrymandering vary considerably, Republicans have fared well in the South. In 1994, for example, GOP candidates gained sixteen seats in the eleven states

---

[15]Linda Greenhouse, "High Court Voids Race-Based Plans for Redistricting," *New York Times,* June 14, 1996, A1.

[16]Holly Idelson, "Court Takes a Harder Line on Minority Voting Blocs," *Congressional Quarterly Weekly Report,* July 1, 1995, p. 1944.

of the old Confederacy, and one estimate places the Republican gain at thirty seats, compared to earlier eras.[17]

Still, generalizations are difficult to reach when it comes to assessing the ultimate impact of making race a central criterion in drawing congressional districts. In 1996, despite court-mandated redistricting that witnessed a decline in the number of "minority-majority" House seats, all African-American incumbents won reelection, including a surprisingly convincing victory by Representative Cynthia McKinney (D-Ga.), who triumphed in a district that went from 64 to approximately 33 percent African American.

More generally, the emphasis on racial composition (and population equality) of congressional districts has reduced other important elements of representation as district lines are redrawn. In addition, save for single-seat states such as Delaware or Wyoming, congressional districts do not reflect other governmental units (e.g., cities and counties) or broad, nonracial community patterns (such as a large concentration of Italian Americans).

The Other Constituencies: Behavior and Perception

If the geographic constituency is unambiguous (if irregular) in its boundaries, the other constituencies identified by Fenno are more subjective. Even in the same district, no two incumbents would put together the same reelection constituency. Nor would we expect their primary supporters or their personal backers to be the same. In particular, personal constituencies are unique; Fenno recalls sitting in the living room of one member's top district staffer and best friend,

> watching an NFL game with the congressman, the district aide, the state assemblyman from the congressman's home county, and the district attorney of the same county. The last three were among the five people with whom the congressman had held his first strategy meeting four years earlier. . . . Between plays and at halftime, over beer and pretzels, the four discussed every aspect of the congressman's campaign. . . . Ostensibly they were watching the football game. Actually, the congressman was exchanging political advice, information, and perspectives with three of his oldest and closest political associates.[18]

Examining the evolution of constituencies within a single congressional district demonstrates both how the geographic boundaries can change through redistricting and how a series of incumbents construct their own unique bases of support. From 1971 through 1999, for example, Kansas's Second Congres-

---

[17]Gary C. Jacobson and Thomas P. Kim, "After 1994: The New Politics of Congressional Elections" (paper presented at 1996 Midwest Political Science Association meetings, Chicago, April 18–20), p. 8. See also Kevin A. Hill, "Congressional Redistricting: Does the Creation of Majority Black Districts Aid Republicans?" *Journal of Politics* 57 (May 1995): pp. 384–401.

[18]Fenno, *Home Style,* p. 25.

TABLE 4-1
Changing Constituencies in a Single Congressional District:
The Kansas Second, 1971-1999

Member/Term	Constituency Type			
	Geographic	*Reelection*	*Primary*	*Personal*
Bill Roy (D), 1971–1975	479K, NE 1/4 of KS, rural/urban	Democrats/ Independents/ Moderate Republicans	Kansas City, KS, Democrats; federal/state employees	State legislators' support, medical doctors
Martha Keys (D), 1975–1979	454K, NE 1/4 of KS, rural/urban	Democrats/ Independents/ Moderate Republicans	McGovern Democrats	Antiwar Democrats, 1972 campaign
Jim Jefferies (R) 1979–1983	454K, NE 1/4 of KS, rural/urban	Republicans/ Conservatives	Conservative Republicans	Reagan backers in 1976
Jim Slattery (D), 1983–1995	472K, NE 1/4 of KS, rural/urban	Democrats/ Independents/ Moderate Republicans	Topeka and Moderate Democrats	Loyalists from state legislature days
Sam Brownback (R) 1995–1996	619K, east 1/3 of KS, save suburban Kansas City	Republicans/ Perot supporters/ Reagan Democrats	Traditional Republicans	Agricultural community, Kansas State University, family media base
Jim Ryan (R) 1997–	619K, east 1/3 of KS, save suburban Kansas City	Most Republicans/ Christian Right	Christian Right	Personal friends with religious and athletic ties

Source: Almanac of American Politics, various editions.

sional District has changed its representative stripes as much as any seat in the country; six different individuals have held the seat in that period. Not only was the district redrawn in 1972, in 1982, and in 1992, but each of the incumbents developed his or her own set of personal, primary, and reelection constituencies (Table 4–1).

Over this twenty-eight-year period, the population of the Second District grew dramatically — from a low of 454,000 in the 1970s to well over 600,000 in the 1990s (Kansas lost one of its five House seats after the 1990 census) — and its geographic configuration changed as much. Historically, it had encompassed a relatively compact area of northeast Kansas; in 1992, however, it spread from the Nebraska border on the north to the Oklahoma line on the south.

Even more significant have been the changes in the reelection, primary, and personal constituencies represented by the six incumbents. A district with roughly the same geographic boundaries elected two fairly liberal Democrats, a moderate-to-conservative Democrat, a conservative Republican, and two extremely conservative Republicans — each with his or her own set of personal supporters and winning reelection coalition. Because their constituencies differed, so too did the ways in which they viewed the district. In addition, communication patterns from constituents changed; for example, many liberals considered conservative Representative Jim Jefferies a lost cause, and many Republicans viewed Representative Martha Keys, a liberal Democrat, unsympathetic to their concerns.

Incumbents also develop their own funding constituencies, often bringing in hundreds of thousands of dollars from *outside* the confines of their physical districts. With a seat on the powerful Energy and Commerce Committee, Representative Jim Slattery proved especially adept at obtaining substantial PAC funding from groups with little direct interest in Kansas's Second District. In his last two campaigns (1990 and 1992) he spent a total of $1,169,000, with $767,000 (or 66 percent) coming from PACs.

Careful cultivation of Fenno's four concentric constituencies (geographic, reelection, primary, personal), as well as maintaining a strong funding base, allows incumbents considerable latitude in deciding how to represent their districts, especially if they are skilled at explaining their positions. Nevertheless, there are real limits to this flexibility. As Democratic House members discovered in 1992 and 1994, incumbents can face problems as a result of unpopular votes, well-funded opponents, strong national trends, scandals of their own making, or some combination of the above. However successful members are at playing to their constituencies, they remain uncertain over their abilities to win reelection.[19] This uncertainty, in turn, represents a shaky base for building an extended congressional career. At the same time, many legislators have expressed support for term limits, and even if such limitations do not become the law of the land, some may feel obliged to end their service voluntarily after a promised number of terms. This may prove more difficult for members of Congress than they initially anticipated. For example, Representative George Nethercutt (R-Wash.), who upset sitting Speaker of the House Tom Foley in 1994, has expressed serious reservations about stepping down after three terms.

ELECTIONS IN A CAREERIST CONGRESS

> *If a group of planners sat down and tried to design a pair of American electoral assemblies with the goal of serving members' electoral needs year in and year out, they would be hard pressed to improve on what exists.*

David Mayhew, *Congress: The Electoral Connection*

Over the course of the past one hundred years, the Congress has developed into an institution that fosters long careers. In the 1990s this may be changing, as formal and informal pressures for term limits affect legislators' choice, but over the course of the twentieth century, extended careers have become the

---

[19]This is not new. For an earlier analysis of electoral uncertainty among House members, see Thomas Mann, *Unsafe at Any Margin* (Washington, DC: American Enterprise Institute, 1978).

norm. Between 1911 and 1971, the number of "careerists" (legislators serving ten or more terms) rose steadily, from 2.8 percent to 20 percent. After substantial turnover in the 1970s, the percentage of careerists stabilized at about 15 percent of the House for almost twenty years, then the post-1990 elections witnessed enough turnover (often through Democratic retirements and defeats) to reduce the careerist numbers to fifty-five, or 13 percent in the 105th Congress, but the number rebounded to sixty-eight (15.6 percent) in the 106th Congress. The average tenure of House members stands at five terms, and the typical senator's length of service is roughly similar — eleven years.[20]

Careerist legislators want to remain in office; thus, every two (or six) years they must win reelection. Unsurprisingly, with the careerist, professional Congress has come both increased incentives to run for reelection and enhanced capacities for incumbents to emerge victorious. Since 1950, 90 percent of House incumbents ordinarily run for reelection and well over 90 percent of them win.[21] Incumbency success rates rose to historic highs in the 1984–1990 period, when House members won a staggering 97 percent of their bids for reelection. Even in 1992, with anti-incumbency sentiment running at a fever pitch and the House Bank scandal in full bloom, almost nine in ten (88 percent) of those seeking reelection were returned to office. Sitting senators are more vulnerable than House incumbents, with the 1952–1992 period producing an overall reelection rate of 80 percent. From 1982 on, Senate incumbents have won more than 86 percent of their races, indicating a trend toward a greater safety that roughly mirrors that in the House. Indeed, in 1996, sitting senators won 95 percent of their reelection bids, slightly outpacing their House counterparts (94 percent success rate). In 1998, twenty-six of twenty-nine Senate incumbents who ran won reelection.

Why are incumbents so difficult to unseat? And what difference does it make that they remain relatively safe? The answers to both these questions are central to understanding the fragmentation, or atomization, of the U.S. Congress. Most of our attention will be directed at House elections, given the greater safety of House members and the extensive research that has focused on these contests.

House Incumbents and the Structure of Competition

Although House members have consistently won reelection at high rates, there have been major changes in how this has occurred in the past forty years, especially since the early 1970s. First, incumbents' margins rose substantially over this period; second, freshman members, who were historically more

---

[20]Charles S. Bullock III, "House Careerists: Changing Patterns of Longevity and Attrition," *American Political Science Review* 66 (1972): pp. 1295–1305. See also Donald Matthews, "Legislative Recruitment and Legislative Careers," in Gerhard Loewenberg, Samuel C. Patterson, and Malcolm E. Jewell, eds., *Handbook of Legislative Research* (Cambridge, MA: Harvard University Press, 1985), pp. 17–56. See also, seniority lists in *Congressional Quarterly Weekly Report,* various years.

[21]Jacobson, *The Politics of Congressional Elections,* 4th ed., pp. 19ff.

vulnerable than their more experienced colleagues, improved their success rates to match those of the chamber as a whole. Congressional campaigns have also changed tremendously in terms of their spending levels and funding patterns since the mid-1970s, and, as we shall see in Chapter 6, individual members voted themselves consistently higher levels of office resources in the 1960s and 1970s. With large numbers of staff and substantial travel budgets, Representatives could wage a "permanent campaign" if they chose.[22] Many did, even when no opponent emerged. For example, incumbents who ran unopposed in 1990 added to their safety by spending an average of more than $250,000 of campaign money for political purposes during the 1989–1990 period.[23]

Increasing Margins and the "Slurge"

In the 1960s and 1970s, fewer and fewer congressional races were won by narrow margins. By historical standards the "marginals," or closely contested seats in which the winning candidate receives no more than 55 or 60 percent of the vote, were vanishing.[24] This stark observation, illustrated in Figure 4–2, set off a scramble to find a "smoking gun" explanation for this phenomenon.

Political scientist Morris Fiorina concluded in 1977 that "the bureaucracy did it," as legislators created a series of programs to which they could subsequently control access (thus winning credit for their assistance in providing benefits).[25] Over the next decade, numerous scholars weighed in with their own assessments of the growing margins, as they looked at congressional redistricting, the growth of the congressional enterprise and its resources (such as staff, franking, and trips home), levels of casework, and patterns of campaign funding[26] (see Chapter 6).

This welter of research found no single cause for the sharply reduced number of marginal seats, but a rough consensus has formed to explain the trend toward reduced levels of congressional competition in the 1970–1990 era.[27] Findings include the following:

▶ *Redistricting has had little, if any, systematic effect.* Although some incumbents may have been protected, redrawing district lines after

---

[22]This term was popularized by Sidney Blumenthal's book *The Permanent Campaign* (New York: Touchstone, 1982).

[23]Sara Fritz and Dwight Morris, *Gold-Plated Politics* (Washington: CQ Press, 1992), pp. 14–15.

[24]David R. Mayhew, "Congressional Elections: The Case of the Vanishing Marginals," *Polity* 6 (1974): pp. 295–317.

[25]Morris P. Fiorina, "The Case of the Vanishing Marginals: The Bureaucracy Did It," *American Political Science Review* 71 (1977): pp. 177–181.

[26]Among an avalanche of studies, see the summary presented in Bruce Cain, John Ferejohn, and Morris Fiorina, *The Personal Vote* (Cambridge, MA: Harvard University Press, 1987), pp. 121ff.

[27]The best brief summary here can be found in Morris Fiorina, *Congress: Keystone of the Washington Establishment,* 2nd ed. (New Haven, CT: Yale University Press, 1989).

FIGURE 4-2
House Vote in Districts with Incumbents Running, 1948 and 1972

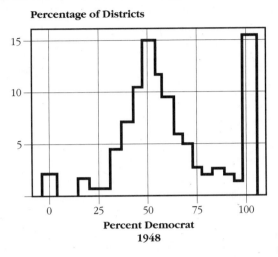

Percentage of Districts

Percent Democrat
1948

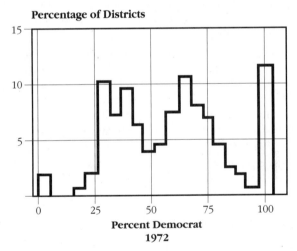

Percentage of Districts

Percent Democrat
1972

Source: Morris P. Fiorina, "The Decline of Collective Responsibility in American Politics,"
reprinted by permission of *Daedalus,* Journal of the American Academy of Arts and Sciences,
from the issue entitled "The End of Consensus?", Summer 1980, Volume 109, Number 3.

decennial censuses is not the cause of increasing margins.[28] The exception to this conclusion is the 1992 redistricting, which produced both heavily Democratic minority-majority districts and many new seats in which Republicans could and did compete effectively.

---

[28]Among others, see John Ferejohn, "On the Decline of Competition in Congressional Elections," *American Political Science Review* 71 (March 1977): pp. 166–176. More generally, see the discussion in Gary Jacobson, *Politics of Congressional Elections,* 4th ed. (New York: Longman, 1997), pp. 19ff.

▶ *The "personal vote" has grown.* That is, while broad partisan and national trend bases for voting in congressional elections have declined or remained minimal, the "personal" component has steadily increased.[29] Incumbency represents a large component of the personal vote, even without considering campaign spending or constituency service; incumbents are almost always better known than challengers. In campaigns during the 1980s, for example, almost half of the electorate (47 percent) recalled the name of their sitting member of Congress, but only one in five (19 percent) recalled the challenger's name.[30]

▶ *Constituency service is important, but there are 435 ways to do it.* In reviewing research on constituency service, various studies have found no relationship between electoral results and casework, federal spending in the district, travel back to the district, or size of staff. "The latest academic research," Fiorina incredulously wrote in 1989, "appears to show that members of Congress can close up their district offices, dismiss their staffs, spend weekends in Washington with their families, quit doing casework, abandon their quest for federal funds, discontinue their newsletters . . . and *nothing will happen to them.*"[31] This is patently absurd, but the variety among districts, individual members' home styles, and the required levels of effort in safe and potentially marginal districts combine to deny incumbents any sure-fire formula to improve their percentage of the vote.

▶ *Campaign spending is important, but mainly for challengers.*[32] If a challenger can spend enough money to gain substantial recognition, the chances of a close race rise sharply. Over the 1974–1998 period, challengers to incumbents have been sorely underfunded. In the 1980s, a challenger needed about $400,000 simply to have a one-in-five chance of defeating an incumbent.[33] By 1998, successful challengers spent an average of $1,175,823.[34]

▶ *The incumbent's most effective electoral strategy is to discourage serious opposition.*[35] So-called high-quality challengers — state senators, mayors, previous losers who did reasonably well — start out with substantial name recognition and may well be able to raise funds more easily than a neophyte. Incumbents thus seek to maximize their victory margins, raise substantial sums of campaign funds, and provide excellent

---

[29]See Cain, Ferejohn, and Fiorina, *The Personal Vote.*

[30]Jacobson, *Politics of Congressional Elections,* 3rd ed. p. 118. The same tendency holds for name recognition: 92 percent for House incumbents; 54 percent for challengers.

[31]Fiorina, *Congress,* pp. 94–95.

[32]Jacobson, p. 50. For a differing view, see Donald P. Green and Jonathan S. Krasno, "Salvation for the Spendthrift Incumbents," *American Journal of Political Science* 32 (1988): pp. 844–907.

[33]Jacobson, *Politics of Congressional Elections,* 3rd ed., p. 50.

[34]Federal Election Commission (FEC), <www.fec.gov> February 11, 1999.

[35]Jacobson, *Politics of Congressional Elections,* 3rd ed., p. 55.

service at home in hopes of discouraging strong potential candidates from making what could prove to be a serious challenge.

▶ *Almost all of the rise in incumbents' margins derive from a combination of: (a) the "sophomore surge,"[36] the enhanced performance of House members running in their first reelection contest; and (b) the "retirement slump," the decline in the party's vote when an incumbent departs. Together, these effects produce a "slurge."[37]* Prior to the early 1970s, freshman Representatives provided the best opportunities for opposing candidates to capture a House seat, especially when the seat had changed parties in the previous election. For example, first-term Democrats from the large congressional class of 1964 accounted for most of the thirty-nine seats that changed to Republican control with the 1966 elections. But in 1976, of the forty-nine Democrats who had won a Republican-controlled seat in 1974, only one lost; this pattern was repeated with fairly large batches of freshmen in 1978, 1980, and 1984, as well as the smaller classes of the late 1980s. First-term representatives had learned how to use their large enterprises and raise substantial funds, to the point that their performance roughly equaled that of experienced legislators.[38]

Margins began to increase sharply in the late 1960s and even more so through the 1970s, but incumbents did not become much less likely to lose until the 1980s. By this time, only the occasional scandal provided a likely avenue for challenger success.[39] Incumbents continued to worry about their survival, however, as almost every election provided a vivid example of some seemingly safe member going down to an unexpected defeat.[40] Survey data demonstrated that increasing numbers of voters held their own representative, and not just the Congress as a whole, responsible for the ills of society, such as large budget deficits and high crime rates. For Democratic legislators, this posed a serious — and often insurmountable — challenge in the elections of 1992 and, especially, 1994. Still, incumbency remains a formidable asset, even in the 1990s, when both Republicans (especially in 1994) and Democrats (especially in 1996, in concert with labor unions) have sought to nationalize congressional elections. House members won reelection at a 94 percent rate in 1996, a figure exactly in line with the overall 1968–1994 average, and in 1998 just six (of 401) incumbents lost their seats, a success rate of 98.4 percent.

---

[36]Albert D. Cover and David R. Mayhew, "Congressional Dynamics and the Decline of Competitive Congressional Elections," in Lawrence Dodd and Bruce Oppenheimer, eds., *Congress Reconsidered* (New York: Praeger, 1977), pp. 54–74.

[37]Gary Jacobson, *Politics of Congressional Elections,* 4th ed., p. 24.

[38]In fact, experienced House members with long careers have become a bit more vulnerable. See Jacobson, *Politics of Congressional Elections,* 3rd ed., p. 29, on the "retirement slump."

[39]Jacobson, *Politics of Congressional Elections,* 3rd ed., p. 29.

[40]See Mann, *Unsafe at Any Margin.*

POLITICAL ACTION COMMITTEES, CAMPAIGN COSTS, AND INCUMBENCY

Along with the increasing official resources available to sitting members and the rising number of federal programs to which members could provide access and ombudsman services, the structure of campaign financing helped increase the margins and safety of House incumbents in the wake of 1974 campaign reform legislation. The 1974 amendments to the Federal Election Campaign Act, which had limited individual donations to $1,000 per campaign, and a 1976 Supreme Court decision (*Buckley v. Valeo*) that struck down limits on campaign spending combined to encourage the proliferation of political action committees (PACs), which could give congressional candidates up to $5,000 for each separate election (for example, a primary in August followed by the general election in November). Although labor unions and a few other groups had long given money to candidates through PACs, the 1974 legislation opened the door to businesses (such as oil companies[41]); trade associations (for example, realtors); and cause groups labeled nonconnected PACs[42] by the Federal Election Commission (such as the National Conservative Political Action Committee) to raise funds and make contributions to congressional campaigns.

In this context, two major changes have taken place in congressional campaign finance since 1974: (1) Campaigns have grown much more expensive; (2) increasing percentages of incumbents' funds, especially in the House, have come from PACs; and (3) national parties and interest groups have poured huge amounts of "soft money" and "independent" expenditures, respectively, into competitive congressional races. Although these broad trends encompass many specific decisions, they operated, at least until the sobering elections of 1994, to serve admirably the interests of incumbents, especially the majority-party House Democrats. In 1996 and 1998 Republicans benefitted in turn, and more money was added to the mix, although soft money and independent expenditures make results less predictable.

Rising Costs

Even with inflation pushing up campaign expenses in the post-1974 period, the growth in campaign expenditures has been striking. In 1976, the average House candidate spent $73,000 on his or her campaign; by 1982 that

---

[41]In particular, the Supreme Court ruled in 1976 that Sun Oil Company could absorb the administrative costs of its political action committee, and thus freeing virtually all the funds it raised to be distributed to candidates. This decision encouraged many corporations and trade associations to establish PACs. For a good overview of the first ten years of PAC activity, see Larry Sabato, *PAC Power* (New York: Norton, 1984).

[42]*Nonconnected* means literally not connected to any parent group such as a corporation or a trade association such as the American Medical Association or the American Trucking Association.

figure had tripled, to $228,000, and it almost doubled again in the next ten years, to $410,000 in 1992.[43] Looking at average expenditures is misleading, however, in that spending by incumbents has increased much more sharply than has that by challengers. To take the same three benchmark years, incumbents averaged $79,000 in 1976, $265,000 in 1982, and a whopping $595,000 in 1992. Challengers, on the other hand, struggled, as their mean expenditure rose from $51,000 in 1976 to $152,000 in 1982 to a relatively paltry $168,000 in 1992.[44] Between 1976 and 1982, challengers' total spending amounted to about 65 percent of what incumbents spent; by the 1988–1992 period, this proportion had decreased to just over 31 percent. Of all the obstacles facing a potential challenger, raising the roughly half-million dollars needed to compete effectively is perhaps the most daunting. Conversely, virtually every incumbent has the capacity to raise such a sum — and often much more. In 1996, the average incumbent's expenditures stood at $631,000, with no successful challenger spending less than half a million dollars,[45] and in 1998 the "cheapest" winning House challenger spent $822,511.[46]

Although some candidates — usually well-heeled challengers — personally finance their campaigns, most must solicit funds from friends, acquaintances, like-minded individuals, their party, and, especially, organized interests (through PACs). Incumbents and challengers alike need immense amounts of money, and such a requirement makes almost all serious candidates highly attentive to, if not beholden to, their contributors. In effect, these individuals and groups compose another constituency for a candidate, beyond those within his or her district. Much funding reinforces the local forces that shape representation (such as a tobacco PAC's funding of a North Carolina legislator), but many contributions come from interests far beyond the district's confines, as with the health care industry's $100,000-plus gifts to Representative Pete Stark (D-Calif.), the former health care subcommittee chair on the Ways and Means Committee. As campaigns have grown more expensive, members have turned to PACs as sources of campaign funds. On balance, this trend increases congressional fragmentation by creating a new set of influential constituents whose interests must be taken into account. In a study of campaign funding and its revolutionary practitioner Representative Tony Coelho (D-Calif.), who

---

[43]Norman Ornstein, Thomas Mann, and Michael Malbin, eds., *Vital Statistics on Congress,* 1995–1996 (Washington, DC: CQ Press, 1995), p. 75. All other figures and tables in this chapter come from the same source, pp. 75ff., save as noted.

[44]There is a seeming inconsistency here, which can be accounted for by taking open-seat campaigns into account. Thus, the average cost of all 1976 campaigns was $73,000, and incumbents and challengers spent $79,000 and $51,000, respectively. Open-seat candidates, however, averaged more than $124,000.

[45]Brigid Schulte and Jodi Enda, "Fund Raising Is Always on Political Agenda," *Lawrence* (Kansas) *Journal-World,* January 13, 1997, p. 3.

[46]FEC, <www.fec.gov>, April 17, 1999.

served as chairman of the Democratic Congressional Campaign Committee (DCCC) during the 1980s, journalist Brooks Jackson concluded that

> increasingly . . . House Members were acting as ombudsmen not only for their constituents but also for their donors. Those who gave money came to be [another] constituency, one not envisioned by the drafters of the Constitution. Coelho interceded for a donor from another state as naturally as he would have for a businessman from Modesto, in his district. One was entitled to help by virtue of residence, the other by virtue of his currency.[47]

At best such constituencies of contributors compete for a legislators' attention with their districts' voters. At worst, notes campaign reform advocate Senator Russ Feingold (D-Wis.), "the very notion of representative democracy [is lost]. Money cuts the link between the representative and the represented."[48]

Campaign Contributions and the Rise of PACs

In 1972, PACs contributed a bit more than $8.5 million to congressional candidates, about 17 percent of all House campaign spending in that year. Twenty years later, PACs gave more than $127 million to House candidates, a fifteenfold increase; PAC funds amounted to 38 percent of all campaign spending.[49] As dramatic as these changes appear, they mask even more significant patterns in PAC funding of congressional campaigns.

In the post-1974 era of campaign financing, PACs have always given disproportionately to incumbents and to Democrats, and in the 1980s these patterns became more pronounced. As many businesses and trade associations organized PACs in the 1970s, Republicans increased their reliance on PAC funds from 10 percent in 1974 to 30 percent in 1984, but the tendency of these groups to back incumbents has held overall Republican support from PACs to approximately the 30 percent level. Democrats, on the other hand, moved from 22 percent PAC support in 1974 (mostly from long-standing labor groups) to an average of 45 percent in 1990–1992. Indeed, House Democrats have proven the prime beneficiaries of PAC financing in the contemporary era of congressional electoral politics. Such a pattern has changed, however, in a post-1994 era of Republican majorities. In 1994, for example, PACs gave two-thirds of their contributions to House Democratic congressional candidates; after two years of Republican control, House Republicans received slightly

---

[47]Brooks Jackson, *Honest Graft* (Washington, DC: Farragut, 1990), p. 107.

[48]Quoted in Shulte and Enda, "Fund Raising Is Always on Political Agenda." Feingold tested this notion in 1998, as he limited his spending to $3.8 million and actively discouraged outside funding from the national Democratic party. His opponent, Rep. Mark Neumann, spent $4,316,928. Feingold won reelection, with just over 50 percent of the vote.

[49]These figures include general election candidates' spending in both the primary and the general elections. Defeated primary candidates are not included. These figures and others in this section are from Ornstein, Mann, and Malbin, *Vital Statistics on Congress,* chap. 3.

more than 50 percent of all PAC funding[50] and in 1998, this advantage rose to 52 percent.

Changing PAC Support Patterns: 1980–1998

In 1980, although incumbents received the lion's share (69 percent) of all PAC contributions, Republican challengers could realistically hope for some significant support from this source. Aside from labor groups, which funded only Democratic challengers, PACs provided substantial funds to the most viable Republican challengers and open-seat candidates (those with no incumbent to challenge). A decade later things had changed dramatically, as Table 4–2 illustrates. Total PAC contributions had tripled and 80 percent went to incumbents. A meager 6 percent of all funds went to challengers (in what was allegedly an anti-incumbent year), and only 2 percent found its way into the coffers of GOP challengers. Republican challengers had garnered $5.25 million in PAC contributions in 1980, compared with $2.17 million ten years later. Open-seat patterns witnessed a similar reversal, although it was not so dramatic. What happened in the 1980s?

Part of the explanation is idiosyncratic to the time: Republican challengers were generally seen as enjoying excellent prospects in 1980, given an unpopular Democratic presidential candidate (Carter) and a record of success in the 1978 elections. In 1990, however, Republicans ran with an incumbent president of their own party, which placed them in a more defensive position. Much more was at work, though, as PACs increasingly "invested" their funds with Democratic incumbents who had controlled the House since 1955. In particular, Representative Coelho and the DCCC succeeded in changing the contribution patterns of all nonlabor PACs.

The hard-driving, politically savvy Coelho became chair of the DCCC in 1981, after the Democrats had suffered serious losses in the congressional elections of 1978 and 1980.[51] Coelho not only possessed a gift for prying funds from contributors, he rapidly increased donations from PACs representing businesses and trade associations — the Republicans' natural allies. Coelho's job was to convince the business and trade PACs of two things: that Democrats would control the House for the foreseeable future and that business and trade interests could work effectively with Democratic party and committee leaders. Coelho and his lieutenants worked hard to reassure key PAC managers that this party would help them, while holding in reserve the real threat that House Democrats might well look unkindly toward interests that did not contribute.

Up to and including the election of 1992, the strategy of Coelho and his successors at the DCCC proved successful in retaining Democratic House majorities, weathering the Reagan-Bush period of Republican presidents, and

---

[50]"PAC Activity Increases in 1995–96 Election Cycle," Federal Election Commission news release, April 22, 1997, p. 2; 1998 data from <www.fec.gov>. See also Gary W. Cox and Eric Magar, "How Much Is Majority Status in the U.S. Congress Worth?" *American Political Science Review* 93 (June 1999): 299–310.

[51]For a fascinating account of Coelho and the DCCC, see Jackson, *Honest Graft*.

TABLE 4-2
Political Action Committee Contributions to House Candidates, 1980-1998

PAC Type	Amount Contributed (in millions)	Percentage of Contributions					
		Incumbent		Challenger		Open Seat	
		D	R	D	R	D	R
1980							
Corporate	11.7	36	32	1	20	1	9
Labor	8.9	69	4	16	0	10	0
Association*	11.2	39	32	2	17	3	8
Nonconnected†	2.8	21	15	5	41	4	12
Other	1.4	55	27	2	6	3	7
Total	36.0	45	24	5	15	4	7
1990							
Corporate	35.4	49	38	1	3	3	6
Labor	27.6	66	6	11	0	16	0
Association	32.5	52	33	2	2	3	8
Nonconnected	8.5	44	21	7	6	6	6
Other	4.4	61	27	1	2	4	5
Total	108.5	54	26	4	2	8	5
1994							
Corporate	44.3	50	33	<1	6	3	6
Labor	31.4	75	3	9	<1	13	<1
Association	37.1	50	30	2	5	5	8
Nonconnected	11.1	49	18	4	10	10	9
Other	4.7	60	26	2	4	4	4
Total	126.6	56	24	4	4	7	5
1996							
Corporate	53.2	30	59	1	3	3	6
Labor	40.2	49	7	29	0	15	<1
Association	45.4	27	51	4	4	5	8
Nonconnected	15.6	23	38	14	8	6	10
Other	5.4	24	46	4	4	4	6
Total*	159.9	32	41	10	3	7	6
1998							
Corporate	50.3	30	58	<1	3	2	6
Labor	37.3	62	8	14	<1	15	4
Association	48.3	32	50	2	4	4	7
Nonconnected	20.0	25	33	6	15	7	14
Other	2.9	39	43	2	6	4	7
Total*	158.8	38	40	5	4	6	6

* Percentages may not add to 100, due to rounding.

† Independent Committees.

Sources: Modified from data in Norman J. Ornstein, Thomas E. Mann, and Michael J. Malbin, eds., *Vital Statistics on Congress, 1995–1996* (Washington, DC: CQ Press, 1995), and "PAC Contributions to Federal Candidates, January 1, 1995–December 31, 1996," and January 1, 1997–December 31, 1998 from <www.fec.gov>.

maintaining expectations that the Democrats would control the House for years to come. Despite some indications that incumbents had grown increasingly vulnerable in 1990 and 1992, Democrats emerged from the 1992 elections with a seemingly healthy 258-176 margin in the House of Representatives.[52] Moreover, PACs remained steadfast in their support of Democratic incumbents, who received 56 percent of all PAC contributions (up from 54 percent in 1990; see Table 4–2). Even so, Democrats looked ahead to the 1994 congressional elections with some trepidation for the following reasons:

▶ Given control of the presidency, their party could be held responsible for the actions of the national government.

▶ President Bill Clinton received only 43 percent of the 1992 vote, while independent Ross Perot's antigovernment rhetoric helped him garner 19 percent.

▶ The president's party generally loses seats at midterm elections, and Democrats had already lost ten seats in 1992, despite the Clinton victory.

▶ As November 1994 approached, less than 40 percent of the electorate expressed the opinion that President Clinton was doing either an "excellent" or "good" job.

THE ELECTORAL EARTHQUAKE OF 1994 AND ITS AFTERSHOCKS IN 1996 AND 1998

Assessing the 1994 congressional elections, in which Republicans captured control of the Congress by gaining fifty-two House and eight Senate seats, various analysts reached for metaphors to communicate the breadth and depth of the change on Capitol Hill. One Washington editor likened the Republicans' victory to a "meteorite striking the American political landscape,"[53] and another editor, a Californian, viewed it as a "political earthquake that will send aftershocks rumbling through national politics for years to come."[54] The earthquake image seems all the more convincing in that it reflects the electoral tensions that have grown in an era of divided government and of heightened frustration within the electorate. The notion of aftershocks captures the political and policy implications of the Republicans' capture of the House for the first time in

---

[52]This margin was later trimmed, through special elections to fill vacant seats, to 256-178, with one independent.

[53]Robert W. Merry, "Voters' Demand for Change Puts Clinton on Defensive," *Congressional Quarterly Weekly Report,* November 12, 1994, p. 3207.

[54]Gary C. Jacobson, "The 1994 Midterm: Why the Models Missed It," *Extension of Remarks/Legislative Studies Section Newsletter,* Winter 1995, p. 2.

forty years. The narrow Republican majorities that emerged from the elections of 1996 and 1998 scarcely heralded a secure GOP era in the House. Rather, the 2000 elections offer Democrats a real chance to recapture the House.

Although the Republicans' 1994 Senate triumph, which produced a fifty-three–forty-seven-seat margin (gaining eight seats in the election and adding the partisan defection of Alabama Democrat Richard Shelby), was noteworthy, it was not a great surprise, in that Senate elections have proven much more competitive than House contests and the Republicans had controlled the upper chamber as recently as January 1987.[55] All observers predicted some gains for House Republicans, but almost none, save for GOP partisans, foresaw the Democrats losing their majority.[56] The House Republicans needed to win forty seats to gain control; their fifty-two-seat swing represented the largest shift since 1946, when Democrats suffered a fifty-five-seat loss. The Republicans' 1994 triumph was all the more significant because it came in an era of enhanced incumbent safety (despite some decline in 1990 and 1992) and it swept Democrats out of office all across the country. In 1994, at least, all politics was not local (see Figure 4–3).

The nationalization of the 1994 election was no random event. Rather, congressional Republicans — above all, Representative Newt Gingrich — made it a national election. Most obviously, in conjunction with political consultant and pollster Frank Luntz, Gingrich announced early in the year that on September 27, 1994, Republican House candidates would gather in Washington to offer their support for a ten-item "Contract with America," which would explicitly lay out the changes they would propose in the first one hundred days of the new Congress. Even though most voters had little understanding of the Contract's specifics, Gingrich's use of the document nationalized the voting decision to an extent and offered him, as Speaker, a useful vehicle to push a series of reforms. Most voters neither knew nor cared what was in the Contract; indeed, as the election grew near and Republican hopes soared, even Gingrich moved to distance himself from the Contract. In the end, however, all but three freshmen Republicans signed the document, which took on a life of its own in the wake of the GOP victory.

Beyond the Contract, Gingrich and his allies had other help in nationalizing the election, given that neither President Clinton nor the Democratic Congress enjoyed great popularity; the millions of voters who supported Ross Perot for president in 1992 saw little to like in the 103rd Congress (of 1993–1994). In two Tennessee races, Perot voters had "broke[n] for [the victo-

---

[55]The GOP lost control of the Senate in the 1986 elections, but they did not formally hand over the reins of power until January 3, 1987. In reality, Democratic control began in the wake of the 1986 elections, as did Republican control in 1994 after the final adjournment of the Senate in early December.

[56]Two weeks before the 1994 election, then-Minority Leader Gingrich put the odds at two to one that Republicans would win the House. Katharine Q. Seelye, "With Fiery Words, Gingrich Builds His Kingdom," *New York Times,* October 27, 1994, p. A1.

FIGURE 4-3
Partisan Change in Congressional Elections, 1992–1998

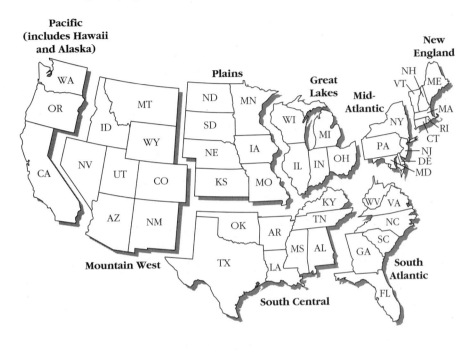

	House								Senate							
	103rd		*104th*		*105th*		*106th*		*103rd*		*104th*		*105th*		*106th*	
Region	D	R	D	R	D	R	D	R	D	R	D	R	D	R	D	R
New England	14[a]	8	14[a]	8	18[a]	4	18[a]	4	7	5	6	6	6	6	6	6
Mid-Atlantic	40	34	37	37	39	35	40	34	7	3	6	4	6	4	7	3
South Atlantic	38	28	27	39	28	38	27	39	6	6	6	6	6	6	7	5
South Central	48	26	40	34	30	44	31	43	10	6	6	10	4	12	3	13
Great Lakes	43	31	32	42	37	37	37	37	8	2	6	4	6	4	5	5
Plains	18	13	14	17	13	18	14	17	7	7	7	7	7	7	7	7
Mountain States	11	13	6	18	3	21	5	19	6	10	5	11	4	12	4	12
Pacific	44	25	34	35	38	31	39	30	5	5	5	5	6	4	6	4
Total	256[a]	178	204[a]	230	206	228	211	223	56	44	47	53[b]	45	55	45	55

[a]One member elected as independent.

[b]One Democratic senator subsequently switches party affiliation in the 104th Congress.

Sources: Adapted from *National Journal,* November 12, 1994, pp. 2628–2629, November 7, 1998, pp. 2656–2657, and *Congressional Quarterly Weekly Report,* June 7, 1997, 1333–1335.

rious] Republican Senate candidates by a margin of about 75 percent to 20 percent," and in California and Pennsylvania they had chosen Republicans for the Senate by two-to-one margins.[57]

Supplementing strong national trends, Gingrich, other top leaders, the National Republican Congressional Committee (NRCC), and like-minded PACs worked on behalf of Republican candidates on a district-by-district basis. Indeed, Gingrich helped recruit many members of the Republican majority, instructed them on key issues, campaigned for most of them, and raised money for their campaigns. Through GOPAC, a Gingrich-directed group, funds and campaign assistance flowed to Republican candidates, and the NRCC could guarantee the maximum allowable contribution of $25,000 to any seriously competitive candidate. Overall, Republicans spent more than half their funds (51 percent) on challengers in competitive races, a tactic that allowed them to counter the PAC receipts of Democratic incumbents.[58] From the perspective of many Republicans, their capture of the House came one district at a time, with each individual new member owing a great deal to the assistance provided by then-Minority Whip Gingrich. In the end, both the national themes and the leaders' expertise, funding, and energy contributed to a great unity among first-term members in particular and the entire Republican majority in general.

The 1996 and 1998 congressional elections proved important in their combining of continuity and change. The most obvious continuity (see Figure 4–3) came in the Republicans' control of both chambers; perhaps more interesting was how their candidates won — by departing from the nationalization of the electoral contest that helped them achieve majority status in 1994. As Jacobson notes, vulnerable GOP House members did much of what incumbent Democrats did for four decades: "run as independent champions of local district issues."[59] In particular, Republicans moved away from their initial emphases on revolutionary change by endorsing various policy and budgetary compromises (on education and welfare, for example) in the second session of the 104th Congress. At the same time, House Republicans aggressively used their status as majority-party incumbents to raise large sums of money, both to ward off powerful challengers and to conduct expensive campaigns. (See Table 4–2.) On the surface, the 1996 congressional elections, especially in the House, looked a good deal like previous elections, save that Republicans benefited from their position as members of the majority. But the mix of local and

---

[57]Merry, "Voters' Demand for Change Puts Clinton on Defensive," p. 3208.

[58]Paul Herrnson, "Money and Motives: Spending in House Elections," in Lawrence C. Dodd and Bruce I. Oppenheimer, eds., *Congress Reconsidered*, 6th ed. (Washington, DC: CQ Press, 1997), p. 101.

[59]Gary C. Jacobson, "The Congressional Elections of 1996," *Extension of Remarks/Legislative Studies Newsletter*, January 1997.

national forces, upset by the Gingrich-led assault of 1994, remained in flux as organized interests and the national political parties adjusted to increased partisanship on Capitol Hill. The 1998 elections further reduced the GOP majority, in part because a few strong Democratic candidates took advantage of both strong local campaigns and some modest national trends that favored them in the last few days of the campaign, as the public reacted against what was often seen as a partisan impeachment process.

LOCAL CAMPAIGNS FOR NATIONAL OFFICE: THE MIX OF FORCES

Buoyed both by Tip O'Neill's homey advice that "all politics is local" and by dozens of academic studies that explain or assume the power of incumbency, a strong conventional wisdom about the reduced competition in congressional elections emerged during the early 1970s and held sway for more than twenty years.[60] Bolstered by PAC funds and the contributions of interests and individuals who wanted to invest with the majority party, Democrats succeeded in sheltering their House members and, to a lesser extent, their senators from the winds of national politics that filled the sails of Republican presidential candidates in five of six elections between 1968 and 1988.[61]

As marginal seats vanished, less opportunity existed for powerful national forces to sweep large numbers of new members into office.[62] In part, however, this resistance to change had its foundation in the assumption of a continuing Democratic majority in the House of Representatives. Such an assumption no longer holds, and the underlying structure of competition has changed substantially.

In 1996, most House incumbents (94 percent, including 80 percent of the disproportionately vulnerable first-term Republicans) won reelection by focusing on *local issues* and by relying heavily on *nationalized sources of funding and expenditures*. First, a 1996 Supreme Court ruling largely freed political parties at the state and national levels from restrictions of spending so-called soft money directly on behalf of candidates' campaigns. For example, in the

---

[60]See the list in the previous section on the "slurge."

[61]Some voters may well have chosen to balance a Republican president with a Democratic Congress, and many have grown comfortable with it, but to see divided government as an explicit choice of rational voters may push the interpretation a bit too far. For a coherent discussion, see Gary Jacobson, *The Electoral Origins of Divided Government* (Boulder, CO: Westview Press, 1990), especially pp. 119–120.

[62]For a useful summary of the relative import of national and local forces, see James Campbell, *The Presidential Pulse of Congressional Elections* (Lexington: University Press of Kentucky, 1993).

weeks immediately prior to and following the 1996 general elections, Republicans and Democrats combined to raise more than $38 million, much of which went directly into advertising for congressional candidates.[63] In addition, many congressional leaders funneled money from their own campaigns or from their personal PACs into tight races. Second, organized interests spent enormous amounts of "independent expenditures" on behalf of individual candidates. The AFL-CIO embarked on the most visible campaign — at least $35 million spread across fewer than fifty districts. Other "soft money" expenses were equally substantial, if not so focused; at least thirty-four businesses, unions, and trade associations contributed more than $1 million in 1996, led by Philip Morris's $2.7 million plus.[64] In 1998, independent expenditures fell somewhat, as groups reduced their advertising spending, but many — especially unions — invested heavily in get-out-the-vote efforts. At the same time, party-based soft money funding rose sharply. With a maximum of about thirty House seats in play, parties could concentrate their resources on a small number of races. In 1994 (the previous off-year election), Democrats and Republicans raised $49 million and $53 million, respectively, in soft money; four years later the totals roughly doubled, to $89 million and $111 million.[65]

Democrats directed $22.5 million to their congressional candidates in 1998, and Republicans offered more than $18 million. If 1996 was the "year of the loophole" in which independent expenditures from interest groups affected a host of individual House races, 1998 was the "year of soft money," in which the parties took advantage of court rulings to pour funds into a handful of competitive races around the country. Despite the overwhelming strength of incumbents in both 1996 and 1998, national funds from groups and parties have been directed into a small number of key races. Even when competition levels are low and incumbents dominate, national funds from groups and parties can still play a great role in determining the balance of power in a Congress that continues to be closely divided.

In the waning days of the 1996 and 1998 elections, many close contests — especially in efficient and reasonably affordable media markets, such as Phoenix or Wichita — found the candidates themselves running a small minority of the advertisements that appeared on television (and radio, the venue of choice for the most malicious ads). The national parties and organized interests, who were often unidentifiable in the ads, dominated the airwaves, drowning out the messages of the individual candidates.

---

[63]Jonathon D. Salant, "Million-Dollar Campaigns Proliferate in 105th," *Congressional Quarterly Weekly Report,* December 21, 1996, p. 3449.

[64]David E. Rosenbaum, "In Political Money Game, the Year of Big Loopholes," *New York Times,* December 26, 1996, p. A11. "Soft money" represents funds meant ostensibly for so-called party-building activities.

[65]Federal Election Committee press release, January 26, 1999, via <www.fec.gov>.

Absent campaign reform, this combination of PAC financing, soft money, and independent expenditures is likely to continue. Incumbents will retain the advantage of providing services to their constituents, as well as their edge in fund-raising. At the same time, they may await the advertising barrage of an AFL-CIO or a business coalition that seeks to nationalize the traditionally local nature of congressional campaigns.

Five
CONGRESSIONAL COMMITTEES

> *The House sits, not for serious discussion, but to sanction the conclusions of
> its Committees as rapidly as possible. It legislates in its committee-rooms;
> not by the determination of majorities, but by the resolutions of its
> specially-commissioned minorities [the committees]; so that it is not far
> from the truth to say that Congress in session is Congress on public
> exhibition, whilst Congress in its committee-rooms is Congress at work.*

Woodrow Wilson, 1885

> *The future of the committee [system] is seriously in doubt.*

Representative John Boehner (R-Ohio), 1995

Wilson's words, most notably in the last two lines, have been quoted
ad infinitum, and like Tip O'Neill's dictum that "all politics is local,"
Wilson's phrase has become a cliché. Yet its essence remains true.[1]
The Congress, especially the House, performs the vast majority of work within
the confines of its committee rooms. Despite the enhanced powers of contemporary party leaders and the independence of individual members, committee
decisions and committee leadership dictate much of the pace and content
of congressional legislation. At the same time, Republican Conference Chair
Boehner articulates a position that, while extreme, reflects the attitudes of
many legislators who feel strongly that party majorities should be able to work
their will. In the Republican era (1995–   ) the decentralizing influence of committees has come under intense pressure.

Committees remain important and powerful because their existence makes
such good sense, both for individual legislators and for the Congress as a
whole. Acting on their own, 435 House members or 100 senators cannot reasonably be expected to hammer out coherent legislation across the entire
spectrum of issues on each year's congressional agenda. Like most large organizations, the Congress has profited from a division of labor among smaller
work groups. Committees specialize in particular policy areas ranging from the

---

[1]Woodrow Wilson, *Congressional Government* (Baltimore: Johns Hopkins University Press, 1981
[original publication date, 1885]), p. 69.

myriad issues taken up by the broadly inclusive Commerce Committee to the relatively narrow focus of the Small Business Committee. Committees are designed to serve their parent chambers, which has meant continuing changes over the years in the number, membership levels, and jurisdictions of the units. In 1995, for example, the House's Republican majority endorsed its leadership's proposal to eliminate three committees, to alter the jurisdictions of others, and to limit the number of subcommittees to five per committee. In the 104th Congress, the District of Columbia, the Post Office and Civil Service, and the Merchant Marine and Fisheries Committees all ceased to exist, and their responsibilities were farmed out to other panels (see Table 5–1). In the Senate, on the other hand, the new Republican majority initially proposed no major changes, but subsequently embraced some modest restraints on committee chairs.

Viewing committees as efficient sharers of information allows one to see how decentralization can benefit the Congress as a whole.[2] Given a $1.7 trillion annual budget and a federal government that regulates everything from trucking to toxic waste, congressional decentralization through the committee system allows lawmakers to specialize and make informed decisions on a wide range of complex, often conflicting proposals. In fact, by sharing information across committees, Congress as a whole may produce a relatively coherent, consistent set of policies.

Nevertheless, a fragmented committee system can and does serve more individualistic ends. Members often seek committee seats to serve their constituents' interests. Thus, most Merchant Marine and Fisheries members traditionally came from coastal areas, whereas the Resources Committee, which controls federal lands, has usually been dominated by legislators who represent districts west of the Mississippi River. Historically, the House Agriculture Committee's members have had rural constituencies.[3]

Most notably, perhaps, the Agriculture subcommittee responsible for tobacco policy has fought successfully to retain favored treatment for its crop in the face of a constant stream of attacks since the mid-1960s. And no wonder, given the subcommittee's membership over the past thirty years (see Table 5–2). Despite the growing number of subcommittee members and the expansion of their jurisdiction, the number of legislators from tobacco-growing states sitting on the subcommittee is far out of proportion to their overall numbers in the Congress. In 1973, with a single minority-party exception, all subcommittee members came from the South or border states. Ten years later, there was a bit more variation, but this region continued to dominate. By 1993, after some

[2]Keith Krehbiel, *Information and Legislative Organization* (Ann Arbor: University of Michigan Press, 1990).

[3]Theodore J. Lowi, "How the Farmers Get What They Want," *Reporter,* September 14, 1964, pp. 34–37; William Browne, *Cultivating Constituents* (Lawrence: University Press of Kansas, 1995); John Mark Hansen, *Gaining Access* (Chicago: University of Chicago Press, 1991).

TABLE 5-1

Standing Committees, 103rd, 104th, and 106th Congresses

House of Representatives

103rd Congress (1993-1994) *(22 Committees)*	*104th Congress (1995-1996)* *(19 Committees)*	*106th Congress (1999-2000)* *(19 Committees)*
Agriculture (27D/19R members)	Agriculture (27R/23D)	Agriculture (27R/24D)
Appropriations (37D/23R)	Appropriations (34R/26D)	Appropriations (34R/27D)
Armed Services (33D/22R)	National Security (30R/25D)	Armed Services (32R/28D)
Banking, Finance, and Urban Affairs (31D/20R)	Banking and Financial Services (29R/24D)	Banking and Financial Services (32R/28D*)
Budget (26D/17R)	Budget (24R/19D)	Budget (25R/19D)
District of Columbia (7D/5T)	—	—
Education and Labor (24D/15R)	Education and the Workforce (25R/20D)	Education and the Workforce (27R/22D)
Energy and Commerce (27D/17R)	Commerce (28R/23D)	Commerce (29R/24D)
Foreign Affairs (26D/15R)	International Relations (26R/21D)	International Relations (26R/23D)
Government Operations (26D/16R)	Government Reform and Oversight (24R/19D)	Government Reform (24R/20D*)
House Administration (12D/7R)	Oversight (5R/3D)	House Administration (6R/3D)
Judiciary (21D/14R)	Judiciary (20R/15D)	Judiciary (21R/16D)
Merchant Marine and Fisheries (29D/19R)	—	—
Natural Resources (33D/22R)	Resources (27R/23D)	Resources (27R/23D)
Post Office and Civil Service (14D/10R)	—	—
Public Works and Transportation (38D/25R)	Transportation and Infrastructure (36R/30D)	Transportation (35R/29D)
Rules (9D/4R)	Rules (9R/4D)	Rules (9R/4D)
Science, Space, and Technology (33D/22R)	Science (22R/18D)	Science (25R/22D)
Small Business (27D/18R)	Small Business (19R/16D)	—
Standards of Official Conduct (7D/7R)	Standards of Official Conduct (5R/5D)	Standards of Official Conduct (5R/5D)
Veterans' Affairs (21D/14R)	Veterans' Affairs (18R/15D)	Veterans (17R/14D)
Ways and Means (24D/14R)	Ways and Means (23R/16D)	Ways and Means (23R/16D)

Senate (17 Committees)

	103rd Congress	*104th Congress*	*106th Congress*
Agriculture, Nutrition, and Forestry	10D/8R	9R/8D	10R/8D
Appropriations	16D/13R	15R/13D	14R/12D
Armed Services	12D/10R	11R/10D	8R/7D
Banking, Housing, and Urban Affairs	11D/8R	9R/7D	8R/7D
Budget	12D/9R	12R/10D	10R/10D
Commerce, Science, and Transportation	11D/9R	10R/9D	11R/8D
Energy and Natural Resources	11D/9R	11R/7D	11R/7D
Environment and Public Works	10D/7R	9R/7D	9R/8D
Finance	11D/9R	11R/9D	10R/8D
Foreign Relations	11D/9R	10R/8D	10R/7D
Governmental Affairs	8D/6R	8R/7D	9R/6D
Indian Affairs	10D/8R	10R/7D	8R/6D
Judiciary	10D/8R	10R/8D	10R/8D
Labor and Human Relations	10D/7R	9R/7D	9R/8D
Rules and Administration	9D/7R	9R/7D	9R/6D
Small Business	12D/10R	10R/9D	8R/7D
Veterans' Affairs	7D/5R	8R/4D	7R/5D

*One independent is included in the Democratic committee membership.

Sources: Politics in America, 1994 and *1996, Congressional Quarterly Weekly Report,* February 1, 1997, pp. 310–316; the U.S. House of Representatives and Senate Web sites <www.house.gov> and <www.senate.gov>, see the committee membership lists.

TABLE 5–2

Membership on House Agriculture Committee Subcommittees Dealing with Tobacco Issues (chairmen in boldface)

Subcommittee on Tobacco, 1973	Subcommittee on Tobacco and Peanuts, 1983	Subcommittee on Specialty Crops and Natural Resources, 1993	Subcommittee on Risk Management and Specialty Crops, 1999
Stubblefield, D-Ky.	**Rose, D-N.C.**	**Rose, D-N.C.**	**Ewing, R-Ill.**
Jones, D-N.C.	Jones, D-N.C.	Baesler, D-Ky.	Barrett, R-Nebr.
Mathis, D-Ga.	Hatcher, D-Ga.	Bishop, D-Ga.	Smith, R-Mich.
Rose, D-N.C.	Thomas, D-Ga.	Brown, D-Calif.	Everett, R-Ala.
Litton, D-Mo.	Whitley, D-N.C.	Condit, D-Calif.	Lucas, R-Okla.
Mizell, R-N.C.	Tallon, D-S.C.	Clayton, D-N.C.	Chambliss, R-Ga.
Wampler, R-Va.	English, D-Okla.	Thurman, D-Fla.	LaHood, R-Ill.
Madigan, R-Ill.	Stenholm, D-Tex.	Minge, D-Minn.	Moran, R-Kans.
Young, R-S.C.	Hopkins, R-Ky.	Inslee, D-Wash.	Thune, R-S.D.
	Roberts, R-Kans.	Pomeroy, D-N.D.	Jenkins, R-Tenn.
	Skeen, R-N.M.	English, D-Okla.	Gutknecht, R-Minn.
	Franklin, R-Miss.	Stenholm, D-Tex.	Riley, R-Ala.
		Peterson, D-Minn.	Walden, R-Oreg.
		Lewis, R-Fla.	Simpson, R-Ind.
		Emerson, R-Mo.	Ose, R-Calif.
		Doolittle, R-Calif.	Hayes, R-N.C.
		Kingston, R-Ga.	Fletcher, R-Ky.
		Goodlatte, R-Va.	Condit, D-Calif.
		Dickey, R-Ark.	Brown, D-Calif.
		Pombo, R-Calif.	Dooley, D-Calif.
			Hilliard, D-Ala.
			Pomeroy, D-N.D.
			Bishop, D-N.D.
			Goode, D-Va.
			McIntyre, D-N.C.
			Stabenow, D-Mich.
			Etheridge, D-N.C.
			John, D-La.
			Boswell, D-Iowa
			Lucas, D-Ky.
			Thompson, D-Calif.

Sources: Almanac of American Politics, 1974; Politics in America, 1984 and 1994.

committee reshuffling,[4] the subcommittee on tobacco had ceased to exist as a separate entity, but the Specialty Crops subcommittee that handled tobacco policies was chaired by North Carolina's Representative Charlie Rose and remained firmly under the control of legislators from the leading tobacco-producing states. With the Republican takeover in 1995, tobacco interests

---

[4]As of the 103rd Congress (1993–1994), committees were limited to six subcommittees. The Agriculture Committee chose to eliminate all crop-specific committees, replacing them with three umbrella panels that dealt with general farm commodities, livestock, and specialty crops, respectively. More generally on the politics of jurisdiction, see David C. King, *Turf Wars* (Chicago: University of Chicago Press, 1997).

remained well protected, in that Virginia's Representative Thomas Bliley, an ardent defender of the crop and its related industry, became chairman of tobacco's chief nemesis, the Commerce Committee. In addition, as of the 106th Congress, Southerners served as both chair and ranking member of the full Agriculture Committee, and Virginia and North Carolina remained well represented on the Speciality Crops subcommittee.

In short, committees and subcommittees can and do serve the Congress *as a whole* by providing specialized information to the chamber at large. At the same time, though, the very decentralization of the committee system allows for *particular* interests to be well represented on very specific subjects where the stakes are high (and the visibility of committee actions is low). This dispersion of power and information serves both the whole Congress and its individual members, especially in the House of Representatives, where committee-based decentralization shapes how most bills advance and what comes out of legislative process.

Richard Fenno's simple statement that "we get the kind of Congress that the members give us,"[5] meshes seamlessly with his equally straightforward assertion that committees differ, one from another.[6] Their environments (including the range of their interests and the scope of their policies) differ, as do the motivations of their members. Not only do they differ from one another at any given time, but they have changed over time as the institution has adapted to its context in various political eras.[7] For example, between the mid-1980s and the mid-1990s, telecommunications policy has commanded increasing attention from the House Commerce Committee, whose members have responded to a mind-numbing onslaught of technological advances and intense competition between major players such as AT&T, the cable television industry, and the regional phone companies, among others.[8]

Members construct the kind of committee system they want, and they seek positions on these committees based on their districts' interests (such as agriculture), their own policy aims (such as those concerning science and technology), or a desire for power within the institution (such as a seat on the powerful Appropriations Committee). Some committee slots reflect a willingness to serve the Congress as a whole, but there are few, if any, volunteers for the Standards of Official Conduct panel, whose members must sit in judgment of their own colleagues. In fact, this committee's chairmanship proved dangerous to the political survival of its chair, moderate Republican Nancy Johnson

[5]Richard F. Fenno, Jr., "If, As Ralph Nader Says, Congress Is the 'Broken Branch,' How Come We Love Our Congressmen So Much?" in Norman Ornstein, ed., *Congress in Change* (New York: Praeger, 1975), p. 287.

[6]Richard F. Fenno, Jr., *Congressmen in Committees* (Boston: Little, Brown, 1973).

[7]See Steven S. Smith and Christopher Deering, *Committees in Congress,* 2nd ed. (Washington, DC: CQ Press, 1990), p. 18.

[8]See *The Information Arena,* a special issue of *Congressional Quarterly Weekly Report,* May 14, 1994.

(R-Conn.), who presided over the highly publicized investigation (1995–1997) of Speaker Gingrich. Perceptions that she was acting in a partisan manner allowed her 1996 Democratic challenger to come close to pulling a major upset. In the end, Representative Johnson won reelection and succeeded in producing a committee decision (reprimand and a $300,000 judgment) that won broad acceptance by the House. Having completed her term of service on the Standards of Official Conduct Committee, Representative Johnson gratefully, even eagerly, gave up her committee seat and removed herself from the line of fire. Her near-defeat experience scarcely made a seat on the committee any more attractive for future members. In 1998, she easily won reelection against the same opponent who nearly defeated her two years earlier.[9]

COMMITTEES OVER TIME

From the first days of the Republic, both the House and the Senate have used committees to process and draft legislation. Early on, most of these were ad hoc bodies that reported back to their chambers on the specific bills. By 1810, however, the 142-member House had organized ten standing committees, including familiar panels such as those on Interstate and Foreign Commerce and Ways and Means. Increasingly, legislation began its journey toward passage within committees, rather than following from an initial floor discussion, in which the House would constitute itself into the committee of the whole and conduct less formal consideration of the issue at hand.[10] In addition, the existence of standing committees produced greater continuity from one congress to the next, both in terms of organizational stability and members' ability to gain expertise on particular subject matters over time.

Between the early 1800s and the onset of the Civil War, committees slowly became integral to the legislative process, even though most key decisions were made on the floor. The number of standing committees grew steadily (see Figure 5–1), but their memberships changed substantially from congress to congress.

Ironically, the expanding numbers of congressional committees in the era between 1862 and 1919 did *not* lead to increased fragmentation. Rather, committees most often served the purposes of both chambers' party leaders, who controlled appointments and the capacity to move legislation on the floor.

---

[9]Diana Evans, "Johnson vs. Koskoff: The 1998 Campaign for the Connecticut 6th District" (paper presented at "Money, Media, and Madness: Inside the 1998 Elections," Center for Congressional and Presidential Studies conference, Washington, DC, December 4, 1998).

[10]Smith and Deering, *Committees in Congress,* 2nd ed., p. 26. The House ordinarily dissolves into the committee of the whole to conduct its legislative business under lenient rules that allow for the more efficient conduct of business. Decisions made in the committee of the whole are formalized in subsequent passage through the House.

FIGURE 5-1
Number of Congressional Standing Committees, 1789–2000

Source: Adapted from Steven S. Smith and Christopher Deering, *Committees in Congress,* 2nd ed. (Washington, DC: Congressional Quarterly Press, 1990), p. 25; and Norman J. Ornstein, Thomas E. Mann, and Michael J. Molbin, eds., *Vital Statistics on Congress: 1997–1998* (Washington, DC: American Enterprise Institute/Congressional Quarterly), pp. 120–121.

Nonetheless, committees became increasingly important elements of the legislative process, and their memberships grew more stable as lawmakers constructed careers inside the Congress — careers that were often based on the expertise they accumulated in specialized committees and subcommittees. In large part, such stability grew from the reliance on committee-based seniority in determining which veteran legislators would serve on given committees in each new congress, to the extent that "by the turn of the century, [seniority] had become such an 'iron-clad formula' that in both House and Senate party leaders' real discretion in committee assignments was limited primarily to new members."[11]

---

[11]Smith and Deering, *Committees in Congress,* 2nd ed., p. 35.

Although Representative Joseph Cannon (R-Ill.) would challenge the seniority basis for appointment during his speakership (1903–1911), the House's 1910 revolt against him and its decision to reduce the Speaker's powers meant that seniority would prevail on committee assignments; in turn, this meant that both committees and their chairmen would become increasingly powerful over the next fifty years. Davidson and Oleszek explain the workings and impact of a committee-based seniority system:

> The majority party member with the most years of consecutive service on a committee *automatically* became its chairman. *There were no other qualifications,* such as ability or party loyalty. As a result, committee chairmen owed little or nothing to party leaders and much less to presidents. This automatic selection process produced experienced, independent chairmen, but many members chafed under a system that concentrated authority in so few hands . . . [and] promoted the competent and incompetent alike. . . . [Moreover,] the system promoted members from "safe" one-party areas — especially conservative southern Democrats and midwestern Republicans — who could ignore party policies or national sentiments.[12]

Not only did the chambers accept the seniority system, they also steadily consolidated committee jurisdictions during the 1915–1965 period. The Legislative Reorganization Act of 1946 sharply reduced the number of committees in both House and Senate, to nineteen and fifteen, respectively (see Figure 5–1). Thus, most committee jurisdictions expanded tremendously, and the chairmen became even more powerful, leading the Congress into a relatively brief, but important, period of committee government (roughly 1947–1970).[13]

The generally conservative nature of the Congress and the modest goals of the Eisenhower administration (1953–1961) coexisted smoothly under the decentralized nature of committee government. Committee chairmen, drawn disproportionately from the states of the old Confederacy, generally represented the sentiments of the Southern Democrat–Republican conservative coalition that dominated the Congress. The presence of a pair of legendary congressional party leaders — Speaker Sam Rayburn (D-Tex.) and Senate Majority Leader Lyndon Johnson (D-Tex.) — did little to reduce the committee chairs' dominance. Both Rayburn and Johnson would consult closely with them, and neither pushed a legislative agenda that was unacceptable to the

---

[12]Roger Davidson and Walter Oleszek, *Congress and Its Members,* 4th ed. (Washington, DC: CQ Press, 1994), p. 207. Emphasis added.

[13]See Smith and Deering, *Committees in Congress,* 2nd ed., pp. 38ff. Why, one might ask, did many committee chairs allow their positions to be eliminated, especially in the House? Many chaired panels with modest jurisdictions, and the 1946 act provided benefits to those who were displaced and to those who had anticipated becoming chairs. Committees were granted several staff members, and their powers to oversee the executive branch were enhanced. In practice, committee chairs controlled many of these resources and opportunities, and consolidation of the number of committees worked hand in hand with the rise in resources to empower the chairs as individuals and as a group.

committee barons. Eventually, large numbers of new members, most notably the herd of young, activist Democrats who arrived after the 1958 elections, would begin to restrict the power of committee chairs. But through the 1950s, congressional decision making was dominated by an informal oligarchy of senior party and committee leaders, along with a few other key legislators.

At the very acme of their independent power, committee chairs generally agreed on a modest agenda and an incremental approach to policy making. Within their individual committee domains, they might well be considered masters of their own turf, but in the 1950s most chairmen acted more like brokers, largely content with making minor adjustments to the status quo.[14]

The Squeeze Play: Leaders and Members versus Committee Chairs

The combination of full-committee decentralization and leadership oligarchy served to benefit chairs, like-minded party leaders, and various entrenched interest groups that profited from the predictability of the actions within their areas of concern. For policy activists and impatient rank-and-file legislators, especially majority-party Democrats, government by strong committee was unresponsive and frustrating. Little change came immediately in the wake of the 1958 elections, even though Democratic majorities widened in both chambers.[15]

From 1959 though 1975, committees and their chairs faced dual threats to their independent influence — simultaneous efforts by party leaders to centralize their own authority and by junior members to win power by having more responsibilities delegated to subcommittees. By the mid-1970s, these movements had significantly weakened the authority of full committees and their chairs.[16] Nevertheless, the Congress, especially the House, continued to rely on its standing committees as fundamental building blocks for most of its actions.

In the twenty years after 1965, congressional reform reared its head in four special House initiatives, three similar Senate attempts, and two joint efforts.[17]

---

[14]Smith and Deering, *Committees in Congress,* 2nd ed., p. 45. More generally, see William S. White, *Citadel: The Story of the U.S. Senate* (New York: Harper & Row, 1956); Clem Miller, *Member of the House* (New York: Scribner's 1962); and various articles by Ralph K. Huitt, several contained in Huitt and Robert L. Peabody, eds., *Congress: Two Decades of Analysis* (New York: Harper & Row, 1969).

[15]For a detailed account of the obstacles to shifts in power, see James Sundquist, *Politics and Policy* (Washington, DC: Brookings Institution, 1968).

[16]For an excellent contemporaneous examination of these changes, see Norman Ornstein, "Causes and Consequences of Congressional Change: Subcommittee Reforms in the House of Representatives, 1970–73," in Ornstein, ed., *Congress in Change,* pp. 88 –114.

[17]Smith and Deering, *Committees in Congress,* 2nd ed., p. 47. See also, among others, Roger Davidson and Walter Oleszek, *Congress Against Itself* (Bloomington: Indiana University Press, 1977), and various works by Leroy N. Rieselbach, including most recently, *Congressional Reform: The Changing Modern Congress* (Washington, DC: CQ Press, 1994), which contains a comprehensive list of congressional reform efforts from 1970–1993.

In the House, making committees more responsive was a primary objective. But responsive to whom? Democratic party leaders wanted more control in moving legislation through the House, back-bench members of both parties wanted more responsibility and greater impact on the legislative process, and Republicans sought an effective voice on the legislative process. Between 1971 and 1975, the House acted consistently to reduce the authority and discretion of its full-committee chairs. The initial beneficiaries were clearly the junior Democrats, who gained both as individuals (and potential subcommittee chairs) and as members of the majority-party caucus, which gained substantial authority. Democratic party leaders also obtained a great deal of potential power, which they slowly began to exercise during the late 1970s.

Some key House changes came from reforms passed by the entire chamber, but the most profound developments emerged from the Democratic caucus, which effectively controlled the organization of the body. The two most important elements of reform focused on subcommittee rights and responsibilities and on the selection of committee chairs (and those of Appropriations Committee subcommittees). By 1974, the following limitations had been imposed on full committees and their chairs:

SUBCOMMITTEE REFORMS

Democrats could hold only one legislative subcommittee chair.

Subcommittee chairs could select one professional staff member for their panel.

A "Subcommittee Bill of Rights" guaranteed referral of legislation to subcommittees; bidding for subcommittee seats, which protects junior members; and fixed jurisdictions for subcommittees.

DEMOCRATIC CAUCUS/LEADERSHIP REFORMS

Automatic secret-ballot caucus votes would be held on the appointment of all committee chairs and Appropriations Committee subcommittee chairs at the beginning of each new Congress.

The Steering and Policy Committee was created and given committee appointment powers (stripped from Democratic membership of Ways and Means).

The Speaker would nominate Democratic members of the Rules Committee and also had the right to remove these members.

By the early 1970s, the number of subcommittees had grown sharply, and the number peaked in the mid-1970s. Despite the significant changes of the 1970s in subcommittee powers and authority (at least in the House) and the proliferation of these subunits, decentralization has not continued unabated. Indeed, the number of subcommittees has steadily declined, and both chambers moved toward consolidation in the 104th Congress (see Table 5–3). Republican consolidation in 1995 followed and strengthened the Democratic

TABLE 5-3
Number of House and Senate Subcommittees, Selected Congresses, 1955–2000

	84th ('55-'56)	90th ('67-'68)	94th ('75-'76)	100th ('87-'88)	104th ('95-'96)	105th ('97-'98)	106th ('99-'00)
House subcommittees	99	154	172	160	86	88	89
Senate subcommittees	105	126	174	93	70	68	68

Sources: Vital Statistics on Congress: 1993–1994; Congressional Quarterly's Players, Politics and Turf of the 104th Congress, special issue of *Congressional Quarterly,* March 25, 1995; *Politics in America: The 105th Congress, 1998* (Washington, DC: CQ Press, 1997), pp. 1607–1625; <www.capweb.net>, for the 106th Congress.

movement toward committee consolidation in the previous ten years. In the end, large numbers of subcommittees with highly specialized jurisdictions proved unwieldy for the parent chambers and for party leaders who struggled to provide coherent legislative decision making.

Although the powers of full committees and their chairs were limited in the 1970s, subcommittees did not become dominant. Rather, particularly in the House, they emerged as important units, whose decisions often set the agenda for subsequent full-committee and floor actions. Subcommittees have proven most significant on relatively routine, low-profile issues, where their specialized knowledge often helps to define problems and prospective legislative solutions. More controversial policies and more highly visible actions, such as health care reform or gun control proposals, move the locus of decision making to the full committee or to the House and Senate floors. In addition, chairs of House subcommittees are responsible to the party caucuses of their respective full committees, much as committee chairs must win approval of the party caucus as a whole, so individual chairs remain beholden to their party peers. To an extent, they must follow their colleagues' preferences, in order to lead them.[18]

The Republican Era: Reforming Committees and Controlling Them

Like the postreform Democrats, Republicans saw a need to limit the autonomy of committees. Unlike the Democrats, however, the House GOP did not engage in a pincer movement that squeezed committee chairs between strengthened subcommittees and stronger party leaders. Rather, under the direction of Speaker Gingrich, the Republicans sought to tilt the balance of power toward the party leadership and away from the committees/subcommittees. Despite some retrenchments after the 104th Congress, the Republican leadership, acting with the consent of the party's rank and file, succeeded at restraining the independent power of committees more than at any time since

---

[18]The classic study here is John Manley's analysis of Ways and Means Committee chairman Representative Wilbur Mills (D-Ark.): "Wilbur Mills: A Study of Congressional Influence," *American Political Science Review* 63 (1969): pp. 442–464.

the 1910–1920 era. In short, "committee leaders have been put on effective notice that they are expected to be servants of the party."[19] Although the Republican majority would pass a set of committee-oriented reforms (see page 90), the most important initial indications of the party leadership's ascendance came with the appointment of committee chairs in the 104th Congress Speaker Gingrich and the top leadership "simply asserted the right to choose committee chairs"[20] and in three instances ignored seniority to select chairs for the important Appropriations, Commerce, and Judiciary panels who would aggressively and effectively carry out the Republican agenda. Moreover, all committee chairs knew that they owed their appointment to the Speaker. Both in the rush of the hundred-day whirlwind consideration of the Contract with America in 1995 and during the remainder of the 104th Congress, Speaker Gingrich, Majority Leader Dick Armey (R-Tex.), and the rest of the leadership could legitimately consider the committee chairs as their agents as they moved bills on to the agenda and through the legislative process.

Specifically, the Republicans adopted various significant alterations in committee operations:[21]

Reduce committee staff by one-third and consolidate control of staff under full committee chair.

Limit full committee and subcommittee chairs to six-year terms.

Allow full committee chairs to appoint subcommittee chairs and to control subcommittee staffing and budgets at the full committee level.[22]

Limit most committees to five subcommittees.

Allow members to chair only one full committee or subcommittee.

Permit members to serve on only two full committees and four subcommittees, with exceptions granted by full party conference (Republicans) or caucus (Democrats)

Abolish proxy voting in committee and so-called rolling quorums (when votes are "held open" for absent members to cast their votes).

---

[19]Steven S. Smith, quoted in David S. Cloud, "Shakeup Time," *Congressional Quarterly's Players, Politics, and Turf of the 104th Congress,* supplement to *Congressional Quarterly Weekly Report,* March 25, 1995, p. 9. More generally, see Christopher Deering and Steven Smith, *Committees in Congress,* 3rd ed. (Washington, DC: CQ Press, 1997).

[20]John H. Aldrich and David W. Rohde, "Conditional Party Government Revisited: Majority Party Leadership and the Committee System in the 104th Congress," *Extension of Remarks/Legislative Studies Newsletter,* December 1995, p. 5.

[21]Some of these were incorporated into the Rules of the House, which are adopted at the start of each congress; others were adopted internally as practices of the Republican Conference. For a more extensive discussion, see Lawrence Evans and Walter Oleszek, *Congress Under Fire* (Boston: Houghton Mifflin, 1997), pp. 91–101.

[22]This set of practices effectively reversed the "Subcommittee Bill of Rights," adopted by the Democrats in 1973.

Reconfigure the committee system by eliminating the District of Columbia, Merchant Marine and Fisheries, and Post Office and Civil Service Committees and by shifting some committee jurisdictions, including a reduction in scope of Commerce Committee responsibilities.

Require that, with few exceptions, committee meetings be open to the public and subject to broadcast, if requested.

Although the limitations on subcommittees and the full-committee control of staff did enhance the power of chairs, most of the other changes have weakened committees. For example, no longer can chairpersons dominate committee decisions by controlling the proxy votes of their partisan colleagues, a tactic often employed in the past by Democrats. And term limits for chairs ensure that Republican committee leaders cannot gain undue advantage from extended tenure — either by building up debts or by shaping expectations about future rewards. In addition, the Republican leadership has often employed party task forces — whose business is conducted in private — to move important legislation. Committees and their chairs thus face the threat of an alternative venue for the development of legislation.[23] Without question, the party-committee balance of power has shifted in the House, as Republican leaders have accomplished much of what their Democratic counterparts would have liked to have done. That is, they now exercise greater control over the potentially autonomous committee units.

Ironically, as the first set of term-limited committee chairs approach their three-term limits in the 106th Congress, party leaders have diminished control over them. As Transportation chairman Bud Schuster (R-Pa.) put it, "We're all lame ducks now. So that means that we're in no position to vigorously support the party . . ."[24]

Even so, the essential structure of the committee system remains. Different panels offer differing patterns of benefits and opportunities to their members, who eagerly seek (Appropriations) or reluctantly accept (Standards of Official Conduct) their assignments.

DIFFERENT COMMITTEES AND THEIR VALUE TO MEMBERS

In that the bulk of legislative work takes place within committees, obtaining good committee assignments is crucial to most legislators.[25] But what constitutes a "good" assignment? This depends on members' motivations. To be sure,

---

[23]See Steven S. Smith and Eric D. Lawrence, "Party Control in The Republican Congress," in Lawrence C. Dodd and Bruce I. Oppenheimer, eds., *Congress Reconsidered,* 6th ed. (Washington: CQ Press, 1997), pp. 177–178.

[24]Chuck McCutcheon, "Young, Combest, Dreier Ascend to Committee Chairmanships; House Gift Rule May Be Erased," *CQ Weekly,* November 21, 1998, p. 3167. See also, Guy Gugliotta, "Playing Musical Chairs in the House," *Washington Post National Weekly Edition,* March 30, 1998, p. 13.

[25]Kenneth Shepsle, *The Giant Jigsaw Puzzle* (Chicago: University of Chicago Press, 1978).

virtually all want to be reelected, so the first thought of many newcomers is to gain a committee slot that will help them win reelection.[26] As we saw with its tobacco subcommittee, the Agriculture Committee has attracted disproportionate numbers of lawmakers with farm or rural interests, and members of the Resources Committee (formerly Natural Resources, and before that, Interior) reflect concerns of the Western states, with their large expanses of federal lands. Such simple geographic relationships are exceptional, however, in that many committees can benefit legislators from virtually any district. The more powerful the committee, the more this is true. The committees that write tax laws and control appropriations certainly contribute to their members' reelection successes, but much more important are their roles in fulfilling two other goals of legislators: to influence policy and obtain power within the House.[27]

Although many veteran legislators who enjoy seniority and key committee positions are able to exercise more internal power and affect a wider range of policies than their less senior colleagues, most Representatives and senators can use their committee service to pursue multiple goals. Comparing three cohorts of new House members, Smith and Deering found a mix of motivations for seeking committee seats, especially on panels offering power and prestige.

Committees in the Senate are not quite as central to the day-to-day behavior of their members as are House panels. Senators have more committee and subcommittee assignments than their House counterparts, and their memberships overlap more. For example, all members of the Senate Appropriations Committee sit on at least two other committees, whereas House members hold exclusive assignments to the Appropriations panel. In both chambers, however, committees generally serve the members' interests. The jurisdictional fragmentation of the committees allows lawmakers, especially Representatives, to find assignments that serve their particular mix of goals.[28]

Historically, junior members have waited a term or two before moving to the House's "power" committees of Rules, Appropriations, and Ways and Means. In the 104th Congress, however, given the large number of slots that opened up for Republicans, first-termers won six seats on Appropriations, three on Ways and Means, and most remarkably, one on Rules, where insiders and the leadership dominate.[29] In addition, three first-term Republicans won appointments as subcommittee chairs.

The Republican leadership continued to reward the 104th freshmen in the committee appointments for the 105th Congress, where sixteen of the remaining fifty-nine (27 percent) have received seats on one of the traditional power

---

[26]The classic statement here comes from David Mayhew, *Congress: The Electoral Connection* (Cambridge, MA: Harvard University Press, 1974).

[27]Richard F. Fenno, Jr., *Congressman in Committees* (Boston: Little, Brown, 1973), p. 1.

[28]See Smith and Deering, *Committees in Congress,* 2nd ed., p. 110.

[29]In the 103rd Congress, in comparison, two Democratic freshmen won Appropriations slots and one was grudgingly accepted by Representation Dan Rostenkowski (D-Ill.) for Ways and Means.

committees: Rules, Appropriations, and Ways and Means.[30] Such a pattern is important for two reasons. In historical context, no post–World War II class has even occupied more than fifteen power committee slots at one time. This augurs well for the long-term influence of these members. Second, many of these members do not come from safe constituencies. Indeed, of the four who won power committee seats in the 105th Congress, none won reelection in 1996 with more than 52 percent of the vote. Republican leaders anticipated that these marginal-seat legislators would benefit from these appointments, but that they would not abandon the party on tough votes to cut spending. In a ideologically homogeneous party, one GOP staffer noted that while "Democrats historically have rewarded their loyal members, Republicans are much more of a team."[31] In sum, Republicans have confidence that their electorally endangered colleagues will not fall prey to the temptation to vote for more spending (or for smaller cuts) than their leaders desire.

Beyond the motivations of their members, committees also reflect a range of environments such as the visibility of their actions or the partisanship of their decision-making. Holding high-profile hearings on health care reform, for example, differs substantially from writing regulations for purchasing military equipment. Various legislators and their committee roles illustrate these differences among committees. Representative John Murtha (D-Pa.), a veteran legislator with a talent for cutting deals and avoiding publicity, is perfectly placed on the low-profile, but very powerful, Appropriations Committee, where he served as a key subcommittee chair. On the other hand, Senator Jesse Helms (R-N.C.), with his continuing desire for the spotlight, has enjoyed his role first as ranking member and then as chairman of the highly visible Foreign Relations Committee. Combining a penchant for publicity and an extensive issue agenda, for sixteen years Representative Henry Waxman (D-Calif.) operated effectively as an Energy and Commerce subcommittee chair, where he successfully pursued a host of initiatives on health and environment issues.

Not only do committees differ but over time they can change, sometimes dramatically. The once-prestigious House Judiciary Committee had a difficult time finding willing members in the 1980s. The obscure, constituency-oriented Interior Committee became an increasingly important battleground for environmentalists and property rights advocates as the Resources Committee in the 1990s. More generally, members of the Congress wanted more subcommittees and greater decentralization in the reform era of the 1970s. Twenty years later, both Democratic and Republican members have opted for fewer subcommittees and less fragmentation, although the basic division-of-labor principle continues to structure most lawmakers' work on Capitol Hill.

---

[30]See Tim Barnett and Burdett Loomis, "The 104th Congress: Of Classes and Cannon Fodder," *Extension of Remarks/Legislative Studies Newsletter*, January 1997, p. 14.

[31]Richard E. Cohen, "Congressional Committee Custom Bites the Dust," *National Journal*, November 30, 1996, p. 2604.

THE CONTINGENT NATURE OF COMMITTEE POWER

Committees are advantaged by their positive capacity, within a large and diverse Congress, to write detailed legislation on hundreds of separate, often complex, topics. Committees possess the tactical advantages of great informational resources, the ability to block legislation desired by other lawmakers, and the capacity to shape conference committee agreements at the end of the legislative process.[32] In addition, bringing legislation to the floor, especially in the House, is exceedingly difficult without gaining the approval and cooperation of the relevant committee. Committees are thus powerful, but not all-powerful. They cannot legislate; they cannot require the executive to comply with their wishes; they cannot implement policies once they have been approved.

Even when legislators such as former Ways and Means chairs Wilbur Mills (D-Ark.) and Dan Rostenkowski (D-Ill.) gained a reputation for power, an important element of powers in itself, their authority and influence were limited.[33] In the postreform Congress the Democratic Caucus and the Republican Conference alike have chosen to limit the clout of even the strongest, most assertive committee chairs, who must respond to their own committee members, the party leadership, the party caucus, and the wishes of the House as a whole, as expressed through a majority of the 435 members.

What follows are sketches of how two contemporary committee chairs, Representatives John Dingell (D-Mich.) and Thomas Bliley (R-Va.), have worked to shape legislation within their domains. Dingell represents a throwback to an earlier age of strong chairmen, while Bliley owes his seat to former speaker Gingrich, who elevated him over a more senior committee colleague. In distinct ways, they are chairmen for a postreform era, but their experiences also illustrate the differences between the congressional parties' approaches to committees and their ability to centralize the direction of the legislative process.

John Dingell, the Energy and Commerce Committee, and Clean Air

After the sudden death of Representative John Dingell, Sr., in 1955, his son and namesake won the special election for his seat and has served ever since, building seniority on the Energy and Commerce Committee (the Energy label was dropped in 1995) and becoming chairman in 1981 after thirteen terms of

---

[32]For a more extensive discussion of positive and negative power, see Steven S. Smith, *The American Congress* (Boston: St. Martin's, 1999), 2nd ed., pp. 223ff.

[33]Mills gave up his Ways and Means chair in 1974 after an ill-fated presidential bid in 1972 and a series of public, alcohol-related embarrassments. He retired from the Congress in 1976. In mid-1994, under indictment on various charges, Representative Rostenkowski stepped down as Ways and Means chair, as prescribed by Democratic Caucus rules. He subsequently lost his reelection bid to a Republican challenger.

service. As chair, Dingell expanded the committee's already extensive jurisdiction, which touched on most important domestic issues.[34] Supported by a large, talented staff that reflected the chair's instinct for the jugular, Dingell influenced governmental approaches to dozens, even hundreds, of issues ranging from health care to university research procedures. At the same time, he protected his basic constituencies in his Detroit district and within the entire auto industry.[35] This has meant that he has fought relentlessly on its behalf against clean air legislation, remarking unapologetically. "That's what I'm sent here to do."[36]

During the 1980s, Representative Dingell and his committee labored fruitlessly to modify clean air legislation, failing in part because the Energy and Commerce Committee was split over various provisions of an extremely complex bill.[37] In particular, as head of the full committee, Dingell had to contend with Representative Henry Waxman (D-Calif.), who chaired the subcommittee on health and the environment and who represented a Los Angeles district that suffered greatly from auto emissions. The smart and politically savvy Waxman, who challenged a more senior member to win his chairmanship (see Chapter 6), has been both a worthy adversary and an often valuable ally for Dingell throughout his twenty years on the committee.

Even more important than the intracommittee politics of the 1980s was the unqualified opposition of President Ronald Reagan to any new law regulating air quality. Richard Cohen bluntly recounts.

> The end of the Reagan era meant that lawmakers could no longer posture on clean-air legislation. . . . The key change . . . happened at the White House: Nixon and Carter supported clean-air laws and legislation went through. Reagan opposed it so nothing happened. With the [1988] election . . . of George Bush, the self-proclaimed "environmental president," the gridlock of divided government would no longer be an excuse for inaction.[38]

For John Dingell and Henry Waxman, Bush's potential cooperation meant that they could finally legislate, if they could first find common ground between their own positions and then with the president's approach.

Understanding that indefinite delay was no longer possible, and unsure of his ability to control results either within his committee or on the House floor,

---

[34]Republicans substantially cut back the jurisdiction of the Commerce Committee, in part as a rebuke to Dingell's success in expanding it during his fourteen years as chair.

[35]Dingell's wife is employed by General Motors in a government relations position. She does not directly lobby the Congress.

[36]Quoted in Phil Duncan, ed., *Politics in America 1994* (Washington, DC: CQ Press, 1993), p. 802.

[37]This account relies on Richard E. Cohen, *Washington at Work* (New York: Macmillan, 1992), and Gary C. Bryner, *Blue Skies, Green Politics* (Washington, DC: CQ Press, 1993).

[38]Cohen, *Washington at Work,* pp. 43–44.

Dingell sought to forge an alliance with his subcommittee adversary (on clean air legislation, at least). Waxman had begun to rework the Bush administration's proposed bill in his subcommittee and had made some progress by late 1989, when Dingell joined the discussions. Within a few days, the unlikely duo announced an agreement on the difficult issue of tailpipe emissions, as well as several related items. Dingell had placed his trust in Waxman, and vice versa; these two skilled legislators could then join together to work on behalf of the bill, even as their own constituents expressed reservations about the unexpected alliance.

Although it would take several months for the full committee to agree on a bill and more than year for clean air legislation to win final congressional approval, the Dingell-Waxman deal held firm; committee member Representative Phil Sharp (D-Ind.) observed that the agreement "allowed the process to go forward dramatically and . . . made it clear that we were going to move forward on a bill."[39] In sum, neither the full-committee chair nor the subcommittee chair felt assured of victory, so they reached a compromise agreement, forged in private, that they hoped would serve as a basis for building an entire bill that could survive intact on the House floor and through the remainder of the legislative process. They more or less succeeded. At least as important for the principals, Waxman won a substantial number of policy points, and Dingell, in the words of one legislator, "prevailed on issues important to him *and he kept control of the committee.*"[40] Even for a strong committee chair like John Dingell, power remained contingent on the support of this committee members and the ability to win majorities on the House floor.

Thomas Bliley and the Commerce Committee

The Republican era in the House brought with it no old-line committee chairmen, like John Dingell, who had accumulated knowledge, turf, staff, and power over an extended congressional career. In fact, no House Republican in the 104th Congress had ever served in the majority. Dingell's successor as Commerce Committee chair, Thomas Bliley (R-Va.), illustrates both the similarities and differences between the ways Democrats and Republicans have operated in the postreform House. First elected in 1980 (at age 48) and a natty dresser, complete with bow tie, Bliley has consistently reflected his Virginia roots as an aggressive defender of the tobacco industry. Still, fourteen years of service on Commerce, with its wide jurisdictional range, did expose him to many pressing national issues. In particular, his work on the Health/Environment and Telecommunications subcommittees gave him important experience in crucial policy areas.

---

[39]Quoted in Cohen, *Washington at Work*, p. 77.

[40]Representative Tom Tauke (R-Iowa), quoted in Cohen, *Washington at Work*, p. 171. Emphasis in original.

Standing second in seniority on the Commerce Committee, Representative Bliley would have played an important role in health and telecommunications legislation in the 104th Congress, but Speaker Gingrich elevated him to the panel's chairmanship with firm expectations that he would mesh the committee's work with the Republican agenda. Bliley observed: "The Speaker made it very clear from the outset that he looks to the chairmen of the committees, and that the chairman runs his or her committee."[41] In other words, committees were to serve as the agents of the party leadership, and indirectly the Republican members at large.

Bliley discovered that — no matter how well he ran his committee — there were unspoken, but real, limits to the freedom granted by the Speaker. On telecommunications deregulation, the central issue for Commerce in the 104th Congress, the chairman initially succeeded in leading the committee to adopt a bill that generally favored the long distance side of the industry at the expense of the regional Bell companies. As one participant noted, "He was in clear command without being dictatorial," and the committee voted in favor of the Bliley package by an overwhelming 38-5 margin in May 1995.[42] Given the huge stakes involved in deregulation, the regional Bells, with their strong local presence across the country, appealed to the House leadership to revise the legislation. Less than two months after the lopsided Commerce vote, Bliley capitulated to Speaker Gingrich and other leaders in adding "refinements" to the committee's bill. In fact, the Republican leadership dictated major new provisions in the telecommunications package that benefited the regional Bells. In a meeting with long-distance executives, Bliley "appeared to be reading from a script," stating "he did so because he was under instructions by the leadership. . . ."[43] The apparently powerful chairman had become a messenger for the party leadership.

In the end, this was but a single chapter in the long, complex story of telecommunications reform, but it dramatically illustrates the essential relationship between party leadership and committees in the early days of the Republican era. Representative Bliley owed his chairmanship to Speaker Gingrich, both in general (the creation of a Republican majority) and in particular (the bypassing of a more senior committee member). The chairman was in no position to protest the leadership's desire for substantial policy changes on telecommunications policy. Still, the passage of the complex piece of legislation, which included far more than telephone deregulation issues, stood as a victory for Chairman Bliley, who helped win the support of Representative Dingell by not pressing too much deregulation, too soon, on consumers (e.g., a three-year delay in freeing large cable systems from some regulatory rules). In the 105th

---

[41]Quoted in Kirk Victor, "Mr. Smooth," *National Journal,* July 8, 1995, 1758.

[42]Victor, "Mr. Smooth," p. 1759.

[43]Kirk Victor, "How Bliley's Bell Was Rung," *National Journal,* July 22, 1995, p. 1892.

and 106th Congresses, Bliley gained more leeway in setting the Commerce Committee's agenda, in part due to the narrowing Republican majority in the House. Given the broad reach of Commerce's jurisdiction, Bliley could push more of his own priority items through the legislative process.

One Last Chance: The Politics of Conference Committees

Whereas Dingell's deal with Waxman probably meant that a clean air bill would eventually pass, Bliley's early victory was merely one step in a long and winding journey: Bliley and Dingell did each have one more important chance to affect the outcomes of the legislative process — in the conference committees composed of representatives from both House and Senate that would meet to iron out the differences in the versions of the bills passed by the two chambers. Most, though not all, major legislation requires an ad hoc conference committee, whose composition is determined by party and standing committee leaders. Traditionally, the key committees are well represented in conferences, where the participants must choose how vigorously to defend their chamber's version of the legislation at hand. Indeed, on telecommunications, most House members, even Republicans, complained that they were being shut out of the negotiations.[44]

The ability of standing committees to influence the outcomes of conference committees has been labeled "ex post veto" power.[45] By virtue of their members' potentially influential participation in conference committee decisions near the end of the legislative process, committees can exercise substantial power, especially when their original proposals are modified on the floor of the House or Senate. The conferees may choose not to lobby hard against such changes; rather, they might support a version of the legislation closer to the committee's original proposition. The full House or Senate can only vote a conference report up or down; thus, committee members can often have the last word in terms of the shape of a given piece of legislation. Of course, this power is hardly absolute. One of the chambers may reject the conference version, or, on major legislation, there may be conferees from several committees, which negates any advantage a single panel might enjoy.[46] Indeed, on telecommunications the requirement that a package be constructed to pass both House and Senate led, in the end, to considerable accommodation to most interests and a wide range of individual legislators.

---

[44]Dan Carey, "Overhaul Comes Down to Issue of Broadcast Ownership," *Congressional Quarterly Weekly Report,* December 16, 1995, p. 3796.

[45]See Kenneth Shepsle and Barry Weingast, "The Institutional Foundations of Committee Power," *American Political Science Review* 81 (March 1987): pp. 85–104.

[46]On conferences generally, see Lawrence Longley and Walter Olezsek, *Bicameral Politics* (New Haven, CT: Yale University Press, 1989).

HOUSE COMMITTEES IN A PARTISAN ERA

What can we learn about the power of committees and their chairs from the Dingell and Bliley experiences on clean air and telecommunications? First, chairing a key prestige or policy committee remains one avenue to power within the Congress, especially in the House. Any major legislation within their broad jurisdictions must accommodate the preferences of these chairmen. Second, subcommittees, although important, remain limited in their impact, even with veteran legislators such as Henry Waxman at their helm. Third, on important, divisive issues, a committee's partisan majority is the crucial locus of power, at least in the House. For example, in September 1995, then-Representative Pat Roberts (R-Kans.), chairman of the House Agriculture Committee, found himself unable to hold together a Republican majority of his panel as he sought to reform crop subsidy programs. Only after the leadership intervened was he able to construct a majority that would remain cohesive on the floor.

Finally, and perhaps most important in terms of assessing their roles in the contemporary House, committee chairs act increasingly either as or with party leaders. The capacity to act effectively in league with the party leadership has grown in significance for prestige committee appointments. In the 1970s and 1980s, both the Rules and Budget committees fell under the domination of the party leadership, and in 1994 the Democratic Caucus chose Representative David Obey (D-Wis.) to chair the Appropriations Committee over the more-senior Neal Smith (D-Iowa). Although Smith was well respected and generally supported most Democratic programs, the caucus chair noted that the majority Democrats "want[ed] a more activist chairman, someone who is a player, who is aggressive with party initiatives and who takes a larger role in interpreting the work of the committee."[47] With close ties to the Democratic party leadership, a twenty-five-year record of tough-minded liberalism, and strong support from the first-term members in the large class of 1992, Representative Obey was a good chairman for a highly partisan House, where the most significant budget and spending decisions often must win approval with little or no minority support.

If Democrats moved incrementally toward greater party control over committees, the Republican majority under Speaker Gingrich embraced the idea with few reservations. In fact, the early days of the so-called Republican revolution witnessed legislators questioning the very need for committees that might hinder the leadership's control of the agenda. In the wake of restiveness on the Agriculture Committees, conference chair John Boehner (R-Ohio), the fourth-ranking House Republican, argued — at least for public consumption — that "the future of the committee is in doubt."[48] Potential dissidents and defectors

---

[47]Representative Vic Fazio (D-Calif.), quoted in Richard E. Cohen, "A New Dean in the College of Cardinals," *National Journal,* March 26, 1994, p. 735.

[48]Quoted in John H. Aldrich and David W. Rohde, "Conditional Party Government Revisited: Majority Party Leadership and the Committee System in the 104th Congress," *Extension of Remarks/Legislative Studies Newsletter,* December 1995, p. 6.

were threatened with the loss of subcommittee chairmanships; party-based task forces, their members appointed by the Speaker and other party leaders, often developed legislative proposals in private, rather than having committees do the work in public.

Political scientists Lawrence Evans and Walter Oleszek, close students of congressional reform, argue that the post-1994 shifts in committee structure and practice have reflected partisan rationales. They conclude: "The personal power agendas of Republican committee leaders were dominated by rank-and-file Republicans who wanted to center power in the leadership and the Republican Conference as a whole. . . . [Thus,] throughout the mid-1990s, key decisions on major bills were made in private by Republican leaders rather than openly, with minority party participation, in the primary committees of jurisdiction."[49]

In the 105th and 106th Congresses, Republican chairs recovered some of their autonomy, as their party's control of the House became more tenuous. Although some Republicans sought to ensure that chairs would support the leadership on virtually all votes, Speaker Hastert argued that some real cross-party alliances would be necessary between chairs and ranking members.[50] More importantly, sitting Republican chairs had to worry about their own futures, in that the 1995 reforms limited their committee leadership terms to six years — the end of the 106th Congress. This limitation precluded any Republican from developing the kind of tenure that Representative Dingell used to his advantage.

Committee and party leaders, however, continue to view the legislative process from different perspectives. Committee chairs desire a degree of autonomy; party leaders want greater control and coordination. It is unlikely that such a fundamental division will be easily bridged, especially in an era of declining resources and difficult, often painful, decisions directed at programs and constituencies (such as ranchers, defense contractors, and the oil industry) that the standing committees have historically protected. As congressional scholar Steven Smith concludes, "The *direction* of change over the last two decades or so — toward less autonomous committees and a less committee-oriented process — must not be confused with the *degree* of change."[51] Although committee power has been diminished by the assignment process, bill referrals, and the growing importance of omnibus legislative packages, committees continue to represent the source of most legilsation. Moreover, the very size of the House virtually requires that these units will retain substantial

---

[49]Evans and Oleszek, *Congress under Fire*, p. 157.

[50]Karen Foerstal, "From Panel Ratios to Paychecks: Parties Tackle the Nuts and Bolts of Working Together on the Hill," *CQ Weekly*, November 28, 1998, p. 3218; Jim VandeHei, "Back to the Future: Hastert Tries to Return House to Michel Era," *Roll Call*, February 22, 1999.

[51]Steven B. Smith, *The American Congress*, 2nd ed. (Boston: Houghton Mifflin, 1999), p. 235. Emphasis in original.

power, as they find ways to use the legislative process (special rules, designated spending in omnibus bills) to influence policy outcomes.

COMMITTEES AND THE SENATE: STRUCTURED INDIVIDUALISM

Most extensive analyses of congressional committees focus the bulk of their attention on the House, where the committee system dominates the members' daily activities. Although Senate committees roughly parallel those in the House, they are less significant — to both the senators and the chamber as a whole — than their counterparts on the other side of the Capitol. As a former House member, Senator Phil Gramm (R-Tex.) expressed surprise at committees' modest significance in the Senate: "Subcommittees are almost meaningless over here. The committees are small enough that all the work is done in full committee. . . . And quite frankly, Senate committees don't do a whole lot. . . . Much of the work is done on the floor."[52] That might come as a surprise to former Armed Services chair Senator Sam Nunn (D-Ga.) or Senate Appropriations chair Ted Stevens (R-Alaska), but for most senators, committee assignments are important in affecting their overall ability to act, rather than in shaping most of their day-to-day actions. Take, for example, the committee-related shifts of Senator Jesse Helms (R-N.C.) in the past fifteen years.

Helms has concurrently held seats on the Agriculture and Foreign Relations committees, rising by seniority to chair the Agriculture panel when the Republicans controlled the Senate from 1981 to 1987. Helms could serve North Carolina tobacco interests from this position, and his promise to retain it despite a chance to become chair of Foreign Relations helped him win a tight reelection campaign in 1984. Still, the highly visible Foreign Relations committee offered great possibilities for the conservative Helms, who chose to serve as that panel's ranking minority member in 1987, after the Republicans lost their Senate majority. Senator Richard Lugar (R-Ind.) had served as Foreign Relations chair in 1985–1986, and he challenged the more-senior Helms' right to the ranking position. Despite general agreement over Lugar's effectiveness as chairman, Helms won the ranking position on a 24-17 vote. Many moderate Republican senators supported Helms, not because they favored either his conservative or, often, obstructionist brand of politics but because they endorsed the seniority principle.

Helms could thus use his Agriculture chairmanship for reelection purposes and then move to the leadership of Foreign Relations, where he became chairman in 1995, to increase his policy reach on important international policies and appointments during the breakup of the Soviet Union and the search for post–Cold War foreign policies. Even as he practiced the disagreeable politics

---

[52]Quoted in Ross K. Baker, *House and Senate* (New York: Norton, 1989), pp. 59–60.

of delay, to the extent that his own party colleagues reacted strongly against his tactics Helms could employ his committee positions to bolster his individual career goals. In the first few years of his Agriculture Committee chairmanship, for example, Helms "virtually abdicated control of the committee . . . , allowing a coalition of Republicans, led by [Finance Committee chair] Bob Dole of Kansas, to take the lead on farm legislation." Subsequently, Helms's "invariable opposition to provisions in [Foreign Relations] legislation contributed to the committee's failure to pass foreign aid authorizations in [the early 1990s]."[53]

Helms's choices reflect the Senate's individualism, which shapes its committee system. In general, Senate committees are less important than their House counterparts, and Senate subcommittees are considerably less significant. Most House markups (the actual line-by-line writing of legislation) occur in subcommittee, and House subcommittee chairs ordinarily manage the bills when they move to the chamber's floor. The full committee is the venue for Senate markup activity, and individual senators, serving as sponsors, generally manage individual pieces of legislation on the floor. With talented, veteran staff members, Senate committees are important units, both for the Congress as a whole and as they shape their members' actions. However, committees often bolster the individualism of the Senate, as opposed to the House, where the structure of committees and subcommittees produce fragmentation in that chamber.[54] Once the GOP obtained the majority, some junior Republican Senators pressed for more party control over committees, but Senate party leaders nonetheless remain much less capable of shaping committee actions, in marked contrast to the centralization fashioned by House Republicans in the 104th Congress.

Still, the Senate's Republican era has not proceeded without some modest, but potentially important, committee changes. In muted form, the partisan overlay that has dramatically affected the role of House committees has also had its impact in the Senate. As Senate membership has changed from a Democratic to a Republican majority, from older to younger legislators, from moderate partisans to more intense ones, the role of committee chairs has come under increased scrutiny. The mini-drama that illustrated the new parity of forces in the Senate developed around the chamber's vote on a balanced budget amendment in 1995. As the vote approached, virtually all Republicans and a substantial number of Democrats combined to produce sixty-six votes, one shy of the two-thirds majority necessary to approve submitting a constitutional amendment to the states. Only one Republican, veteran Appropriations Chairman Mark Hatfield (R-Ore.), opposed the amendment, but he would not alter his position. After the Senate vote fell a single tally short,[55] several Repub-

---

[53]Duncan, *Politics in America,* p. 1115.

[54]See King, *Turf Wars,* ch. 7.

[55]The final vote was 65-35, with Majority Leader Bob Dole voting with the minority so that he would have the standing, as a member of the losing side, to move for reconsideration of the amendment if he could later find another supporter. This did not happen.

lican senators called for a party caucus that would entertain the possibility of disciplining Senator Hatfield and perhaps even stripping him of his chairmanship. Although no caucus vote was taken, such an initiative was important for two reasons. First, the leading proponents of retribution, such as Senators Rick Santorum (R-Pa.) and Connie Mack (R-Fla.), had earlier served in the House and felt few qualms about enforcing partisan discipline. Second, although Hatfield escaped sanctions, Majority Leader Dole did appoint a Leadership Working Group, well populated by former House members with ties to Speaker Gingrich, to explore the relationships between the body of Senate Republicans, their party leaders, and the committees and chairs.[56] In the end, Senate Republicans adopted a set of modified working-group proposals that included six-year term limits for committee chairmen and minor party leaders, the adoption of a party agenda at the start of a new congress (by a three-fourths vote), secret ballot selection of committee chairmen by committee members and subsequent ratification of the choice by the Republican Conference, and a limitation on members to a single full or subcommittee chairmanship, except on Appropriations. All of these provisions went into effect as of the 105th Congress, in January 1997.

Although Senate Republicans did feel many of the same pressures for partisan control as did their House colleagues, their responses were in keeping with the normal, evolutionary nature of change in the upper house. Senate party leaders neither sought nor won any significant new weapons in their efforts to limit the individualism that continues to characterize their chamber. Partisanship has certainly increased in the Senate, but not to the point at which it can overcome the individualism, only partly based in committees, that remains the core characteristic of that body.

---

[56]Evans and Oleszek, *Congress under Fire,* p. 155.

Six

THE INDIVIDUAL ENTERPRISE

I n September 1997, Dennis Moore was a defense attorney in the affluent Kansas City suburb of Lenexa. A month later he had decided to
run in Kansas's Third Congressional District and had hired his first
campaign staffer, a young fund-raiser. By early 1998, a campaign manager
came on board. The Moore enterprise grew steadily through the first half of the
year, with a scheduler and a field director in place by June. A professional
press secretary followed in September, along with dozens of volunteers. During the year, Moore also hired a polling firm, a DC fund-raiser, media consultants, a direct mail specialist, and an opposition research analyst. With a
million dollars in funding, plus significant Democratic party and labor union
assistance, Moore created a substantial campaign organization that helped him
defeat incumbent Republican Vince Snowbarger in the November 1998 general election.[1]

Moore's organizational tasks had just begun, however. In the basement of
his suburban home, his campaign metamorphosed into the beginnings of a
full-blown congressional enterprise. He immediately hired a veteran administrative assistant, a loyal district director, and a young woman from the campaign who would become his scheduler. By early January, when Moore
moved into his cramped, hidden three-room office suite in the fifth floor "attic"
of the Cannon House Office Building, he had almost an entire staff in place,
including his former campaign manager, who had become his press secretary.

Back in the district, Moore opened three offices, with staffers for casework
and interns. Nor was the new congressman ignoring the political side of his
operation; his campaign continued to operate, raising funds for what would
surely be an expensive reelection campaign in 2000. The Moore enterprise —
reduced to a couple of aides in the days after his election victory — numbered
more than 20 individuals by January 15, 1999.

---

[1]For a full description of the Moore campaign, see Burdett A. Loomis, "Kansas 3: The 'Pros from
Dover' Set Up Shop" (paper presented at "Money, Media, and Madness" conference, Center for
Congressional and Presidential Affairs, American University, Washington, DC, December 4, 1998.

Two major elements made up the Moore enterprise. First were the personal office resources available to every member of the House, which include more than $800,000 in salaries and benefits for Moore and his staff, along with the ability to send franked mail and an allowance of more than $150,000 for travel, telephones, computers, rent on district offices, and other, miscellaneous expenses.[2] The campaign organization represented a second distinct part of the enterprise; it would provide Moore with political expenses throughout his term of office, as well as raising funds for the 2000 campaign. More senior members often enjoy an additional source of resources for their enterprise — committee or leadership staffers. As a first-term member, Moore would benefit from none of these, but many veteran legislators can take advantage of these assets.

Making Moore's — or any legislator's — enterprise all the more formidable was its overall flexibility. Even with strict adherence to the formal rules prohibiting campaign work on government time, staffers could fulfill their job obligations and perform political work. Campaign funds could cover a wide variety of political expenditures during the 1999–2000 period. Office staff could go off the payroll to work on the campaign. Two elements of the enterprise remained clear: Representative Moore was in charge, a chief executive officer, so to speak; and the organization had one major "product" to push — Dennis Moore as U.S. representative, policymaker, service provider, and candidate for reelection, all in a district where he had won his initial election by a mere four percentage points.

THE LEGISLATOR AS ENTERPRISE

Nothing captures the fragmentation of congressional politics better or contributes to it more than the husbanding of resources in 535 separate congressional enterprises.[3] The enterprise notion is extremely useful in understanding the actions of individual legislators within the context of the Congress as a whole. To put it simply, House members and, even more so, senators must allow others to act for them; there is so much to do and so little time. Thus, staffers negotiate agreements, answer letters, feel out allies, return constituents'

---

[2]For details on congressional offices, see various useful publications from the Congressional Management Foundation, including *Setting Course: A Congressional Management Guide,* various editions. (Washington, DC: Congressional Management Foundation).

[3]See Robert Salisbury and Kenneth Shepsle, "U.S. Congressman as Enterprise," *Legislative Studies Quarterly* 6 (November 1981): pp. 559–576; and Burdett A. Loomis, "The Congressional Office as a 'Small (?) Business,'" *Publius* 9 (Summer 1979); and Loomis, *The New American Politician* (New York: Basic Books, 1988).

calls, and perform a thousand other tasks. On occasion, staffers may act on their own, but ordinarily their actions follow the dictates — however general — of their bosses, who historically have had the absolute power to hire and fire their congressional employees.[4]

The idea of an enterprise purposefully blurs the distinction between members of Congress and those who work on their behalf. In the end, the legislators will gain the accolades for the actions of the staffers, whose careers will rise or fall with their bosses' fortunes. Using this idea, we can examine a legislature filled with enterprise — a hallmark of the post-1960 Congress. As Salisbury and Shepsle conclude, "The result of the actions and interactions of one hundred senatorial enterprises . . . generates a quite different institution than the one of a century ago, or even a few decades ago, consisting of individual senators acting more or less alone."[5] If enterprises provide more structure to Senate individualism, they exert even more influence on the larger House, where 435 separate legislators have come to possess enough resources to insert themselves into policy making and constituency affairs in dozens of ways.

Since World War II, congressional resources have grown steadily and profoundly (Figure 6–1). Personal office and committee staff numbers have risen sharply, as have the number of special interest caucuses, the budgets of legislative support agencies,[6] and campaign expenditures. In short, senators and Representatives command adequate resources to pursue multiple, individually defined goals, which range from winning reelection to influencing policy decisions to running for higher office.

Congressional enterprises for veteran legislators often become multimillion-dollar small businesses that must maintain themselves as they seek to promote their members' interests. Despite some variation, most enterprises look roughly like the one depicted in Figure 6–2. At the heart of the miniconglomerate is the legislator, often in tandem with his or her top aide — usually the chief of staff. Around this essential nucleus each legislator builds a unique combination of contributing components. Although some senior members may construct their organizations from all the building blocks, most emphasize a few key elements, always including the personal office.

---

[4]An excellent example here is Eric Redman's description of his work on behalf of former Washington Senator Warren Magnuson, who gave Redman and other staff members broad latitude to formulate legislation encouraging doctors to serve in needy areas. See Redman, *The Dance of Legislation* (New York: Touchstone, 1974). In 1995, the Congress adopted the Congressional Accountability Act, which requires it to adhere to almost all federal laws, including those on conditions of employment. This may have some modest effect on the relations between legislators and their staffers, but the essentially personal and political nature of these ties remains.

[5]Salisbury and Shepsle, "U.S. Congressman as Enterprise," p. 563.

[6]These include the General Accounting Office, the Congressional Research Service, and the Congressional Budget Office.

FIGURE 6-1
Growth in Congressional Staff, 1891-1997

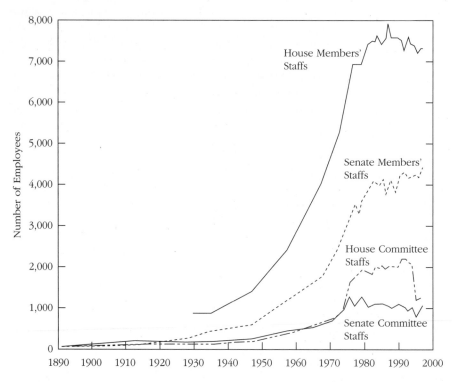

Source: Norman J. Ornstein, Thomas Mann, and Michael Malbin, eds., *Vital Statistics on Congress, 1997–1998* (Washington, DC: CQ Press, 1997).

FIGURE 6-2
The Congressional Enterprise

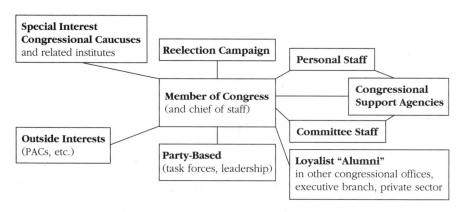

The Personal Office

Except for a handful of lawmakers such as top party leaders or committee chairs, the personal office lies at the heart of each legislator's congressional enterprise. In the House, even the most junior minority-party Representative is entitled to exactly the same personal office allowances as the most senior majority-party member: up to eighteen staffers and an overall budget of approximately $1 million.[7] Thus, Representative Charlie Gonzolez (D-Tex.), elected to his first term in 1998, can purchase the same basic personal office resources (staff, travel, communications, computers, etc.) as does his fellow Texan, Majority Leader Dick Armey, who has served in the House since 1985.

Although there is some variation in structure and work assignments, the cast of characters in most congressional offices is roughly the same. It includes an administrative assistant responsible for overseeing the entire operation; several legislative aides, with one often designated as a legislative director; a personal secretary; an office manager; a press secretary; caseworkers (in Washington and in the home district); a top district aide; and other district staff.[8] Senate offices are larger and more likely to encourage specialization, but the basic configuration is similar.

Variation also occurs in *what* legislators do with their office staff and other resources — and *where* they do it. Two major generalizations hold true here. First, there are some tasks that virtually all legislators must attend to: answering constituent mail, pursuing "cases" (often regarding bureaucratic snafus) that constituents bring to their attention, seeking new benefits and protecting existing ones for local interests, and maintaining at least minimal knowledge about major legislation under consideration. Much of this work reflects the service and allocation responsiveness that make up a good part of representation.

Beyond these essential tasks and routine office maintenance such as personnel and scheduling, the personal office can be constructed to serve the specific interests of a particular legislator. Thus, the second generalization: Members of Congress have tremendous discretion over how they use their basic resources. A marginal-seat congressman may establish several district offices to deliver the best possible constituency service; he may use substantial amounts of franked mail and send out the maximum number of newsletters each year, all the while making do with a couple of legislative assistants. Conversely, a member who considers herself relatively safe, having consistently won 65 percent of the vote in reelection contests, might hire six or seven legislative aides to assist in achieving her own policy goals.

---

[7]This is the 1999 figure, which varies somewhat among offices because of disparities in travel costs from the district to Washington.

[8]Not all offices have all these positions; the best data here come from the private Congressional Management Foundation, which annually surveys congressional offices and reports on the changing nature of office organization and salary levels. In particular, see Bradley S. Keare, *1998 House Staff Employment Study* (Washington, DC: Congressional Management Foundation, 1998).

An ambitious House member might well want to hire a top-notch press secretary in anticipation of running for a Senate seat, whereas a junior senator might hope to use a couple of legislative aides to research and write a bill to correct a modest, but real, policy snarl. All House offices receive almost identical resources,[9] but Senate operations vary considerably, given the great differences among state populations. (See Table 6–1.)

In 1995 the Congress placed itself under the Fair Labor Standards Act and adopted the Congressional Accountability Act, both of which imposed some modest limitations on staff hiring and working conditions. Overall, however, staff serve at the pleasure of the legislator and remain part of the overall enterprise.[10]

In sum, the annual personal office resources can be used, within broad limits, to pursue legislators' individual goals. Offices tend to look roughly the same, but this is largely because of a general similarity in members' goals — to win reelection (and perhaps advance to higher office), produce good public policy, and exercise power within the Congress. Their considerable resources allow members a base from which to act effectively as individuals; in particular, they can establish strong constituency ties that make it very difficult for them to be effectively challenged for reelection. Given the resources that allow 535 legislators to play to their constituencies and to operate with such flexibility, the personal office contributes greatly to the centrifugal tendencies of the Congress. Along with the control of their individual votes in committee and on the floor, personal office resources represent a key source of individual power for any legislator. These resources can also be used to build coalitions and seek consensus; even the most isolated and iconoclastic members need cooperation from their legislative peers if they are to act effectively in passing legislation.

Committees and Subcommittees

There are strict limits on personal office resources, particularly on the numbers and salaries of staff. Whatever the member's goals might be, if a congressional enterprise is to grow it must lay claim to other assets. Since the 1970s, the Congress has been generous in complementing the resources available to all its members, especially for those in the majority party, who, by dint of their status, chair all committees and subcommittees.

As Figure 6–1 illustrates, committee-based staff in the House tripled in the 1970s, and committee budgets grew even faster. If the committee system of the 1950s and early 1960s had remained intact, this change would simply have meant more resources under the control of a handful of powerful full-committee chairs. As noted in Chapter 5, however, subcommittees proliferated in the 1970s, and their chairs came to control substantial resources and power. Not

---

[9]House travel funds differ, but only because the costs of returning to 435 districts vary greatly. In 1996, they ranged from $6,200 to $67,200.

[10]See *Setting Course: A Congressional Management Guide*, 105th Congress ed., chap. 9.

TABLE 6-1

Average 1998 Salaries for Staff Positions, House and Senate

Washington Positions	House	Senate*
Administrative Assistant/Chief of Staff	$88,936	$109,638
Legislative Director	$55,453	$83,156
Press Secretary	$42,578	$59,881
Office Manager	$39,691	$49,367
Executive Assistant/Scheduler	$36,737	$41,230
Legislative Assistant	$34,275	$46,717
Systems Administrator	$28,901	$35,822
Legislative Correspondent	$24,048	$24,209
Staff Assistant	$21,762	$22,371
State/District Positions		
State/District Director	$58,265	$69,070
State/District Scheduler	$31,775	$34,779
Caseworker/Constituent Services Rep.	$29,269	$30,150
State/District Staff Assistant	$22,984	$23,732

*Senate figures are for 1997, most recent year with comparable data.

Source: 1997 Senate Staff Employment and 1998 House Staff Employment (Washington, DC: Congressional Management Foundation).

only did total committee staff in the House grow from 461 to 1,600 between 1970 and 1990, but the subcommittee allocation of staff grew from 23.2 percent (107) of total committee staff in 1970 to 45.2 percent (723) twenty years later.[11] In 1970, only one in four subcommittee chairs controlled their own staff, an average of four aides. By 1989, almost half the subcommittee chairs had such control, and their average staff size stood at ten. These figures understate the actual control of staff by subcommittee chairs in the pre-1995 era, however. Although various full-committee chairs may have formally controlled hiring, their subcommittee chairs often chose their own aides.

In short, many members of the majority party in the House greatly expanded their enterprises in the wake of subcommittee changes of the 1970s. Minority staffing on committees and subcommittees has not increased nearly as much as for the majority — a constant irritant for Republicans during the long period of Democratic control. Republicans long requested a third of all committee staff, only to be continually rebuffed.

In the 104th Congress, the majority Republicans moved immediately to bolster the power of full committees by placing the responsibility for hiring staff with committee chairs and by limiting to five the number of subcommittees permitted for most committees. In addition, committee staff numbers were cut by one-third, as Republicans made good on their promise to trim committee staffing levels (see Figure 6–1). Overall, the individual enterprises of many

---

[11]Data from Steven S. Smith and Christopher J. Deering, *Committees in Congress,* 2nd ed. (Washington, DC: CQ Press, 1990), p. 152.

members — most notably Democrats and subcommittee chairs — were substantially reduced, while Republican committee chairs have come to control a much greater proportion of available resources. In an admittedly extreme example, former Energy and Commerce Committee Chair Representative John Dingell (D-Mich.) was not able to keep Republicans from slashing his committee staff from almost 100 aides to about 20.[12]

On the Senate side, subcommittee staff have not grown nearly as fast as in the House; nor are subcommittee aides as important to individual enterprises, given the much larger personal staffs that most senators command. In addition, more than a fourth of majority-party senators chair full committees and thus control their considerable resources. Even so, with the relatively small number of senators, committee staff play major roles in developing policies, and Senate staff are ordinarily much more aggressive in their efforts on behalf of their bosses.[13] Given senators' larger numbers of committee assignments and attendant responsibilities, it makes sense that staff members take on great responsibilities in the Senate. Indeed, many top Senate aides function as entrepreneurs who operate to further the influence of their own bosses.[14] Such reliance serves to extend the reach of individual senators, as they designate knowledgeable, skilled, and unelected staffers to act in their stead.

Special Interest Caucuses

Much as House members have taken advantage of expanding subcommittee resources, so too have they expanded their enterprises by advancing to leadership positions in a host of special interest caucuses. By the mid-1980s, almost 150 such groups had formed, with House organizations outnumbering those in the Senate by a three-to-one margin (ninety-one in the House to thirty-one in the Senate; twenty-five more were bicameral groups).[15] For members, especially junior ones, caucuses have provided opportunities to participate in the policymaking process in various ways, from constituency service, as with the Auto Task Force, to building a policy-based coalition such as the Military Reform Caucus. Resources vary greatly across caucuses, but the strongest groups often command budgets into the hundreds of thousands of dollars and substantial numbers of staff. Some of these groups won House designation as officially sanctioned legislative service organizations (LSOs), which were granted office space and were allowed to receive financial support from

---

[12]Allen Freedman, "A Survivor Steps into Minority Role," *Congressional Quarterly Weekly Report,* April 8, 1995, p. 989.

[13]See Michael J. Malbin, *Unelected Representatives* (New York: Basic Books, 1980).

[14]See David Price, "Professionals and 'Enterpreneurs': Staff Orientations and Policy Making on Three Senate Committees," *Journal of Politics* 33 (May 1971): pp. 316–336.

[15]Susan Webb Hammond, "Congressional Caucuses in the Policy Process," in Lawrence C. Dodd and Bruce L. Oppenheimer, eds., *Congress Reconsidered,* 4th ed. (Washington, DC: CQ Press, 1989), p. 355. See also, Susan W. Hammond, *Congressional Caucuses in National Policy Making* (Baltimore: John Hopkins University Press, 1998).

members' accounts. In 1995, the Republican-controlled House denied funding and office space to the twenty-eight groups that qualified as LSOs. This affected most of the major caucuses, but many of these groups obtain much of their funding from outside sources, so the ultimate impact was muted.

Although House Republicans made caucuses one of their first targets as they sought to trim back congressional bureaucracy, as of 1996, 129 caucuses were active; most were House-based or bicameral, although 24 existed in the Senate alone. Even as they were being denied financial backing from the House, caucuses continued to prosper. Susan Webb Hammond, the foremost student of these groups, argues that caucuses are significant precisely because the Congress requires "centralization to build majorities from disparate points of view" as well as to reflect the decentralizing pressures of representation.[16] Caucuses play significant roles in both overcoming congressional fragmentation (as in building bridges between committees) and sometimes furthering decentralization, as they represent particular interests (the Mushroom Caucus? the High Altitude Caucus? the Auto Task Force?) within the Congress.

In the 104th Congress, not only did 129 caucuses retain their identities, but the House also invented a new status for these groups, labeling them "congressional member organizations," a designation that allows their members to share staff resources (e.g., two offices may each pay half the salary of a staffer who manages caucus activities).[17] Although caucus leaders have some power to hire and fire, the chief benefit for legislators in being a member of a caucus comes with the ability to employ resources to push favored ideas and to have adequate staff to react to opportunities or challenges as they arise. The variation is great in staff resources among the 150 or so caucuses; some — the Congressional Black Caucus, the Hispanic Caucus, the Northeast-Midwest group, and the Environmental and Energy Study Conference — have established separate institutes outside the Congress, which have served them in good stead in the wake of the 1995 cutbacks. Others have no staff at all and operate out of their chairs' offices, which can amount to a net drain on that legislator's resources.

The benefits for less senior members, especially in the House, have been clear. Party leaders and committee chairs check with them on policies relevant to their groups, and many command substantial resources early in their careers. For example, Representatives Bob Edgar, a liberal Democrat, and Curt Weldon, a moderate conservative Republican, who have represented Pennsylvania's Seventh District since 1974 and 1986, respectively, have demonstrated how junior legislators can profit from caucus leadership. In the late 1970s,

---

[16]Susan Webb Hammond, "Congressional Caucuses in the 104th Congress," in Lawrence J. Dodd and Bruce I. Oppenheimer, eds., *Congress Reconsidered*, 6th ed., (Washington, DC: CQ Press, 1997), p. 276. See also, Hammond, *Congressional Caucuses in National Policy Making*.

[17]Hammond, "Congressional Caucuses in the 104th Congress," p. 284. The exact number of caucuses that operate at a given time is difficult to ascertain, precisely because they are informal organizations. As of the 106th Congress, 150 caucuses represent a fair estimate.

Edgar used his positions as head of the Northeast-Midwest Economic Advancement Coalition and the Congressional Clearinghouse on the Future to push for strong environmental policies, especially in the realm of modernizing water infrastructure in older cities — such as his Philadelphia-area district. Although much more liberal than many of his constituents, Edgar used his caucus roles and resources to frame issues that attracted support from his suburban Republican seat.[18]

When Edgar left the House after unsuccessfully running for the Senate in 1986, Weldon won his seat in the House and set new entrepreneurial standards for caucus activity. Weldon's unlikely vehicle has been the Fire Services Caucus, the largest single caucus in the Congress. Not only has this group won some legislative victories, but Weldon, as its founding entrepreneur, incorporated many of its resources into his congressional enterprise (and vice versa, using campaign funds to buy an old fire truck). Given his status as a junior Republican, the caucus leadership role allowed him a wider range of possible actions than those available to his GOP peers. In addition, Weldon's strong ties to the caucus and its resources may well prove a boon to him if he chooses to run for statewide office. In such an effort, he would again follow Edgar's lead; the Democrat actually incorporated a statewide environmental organization into his campaign operation during his bid for the Senate.

As of the 1990s, representatives belonged to an average of sixteen caucuses, and senators averaged fourteen such memberships, all in addition to their positions on committees, subcommittees, and within their parties. Why would busy legislators want to take on so many obligations?

First, joining most caucuses is a painless task, often requiring little more than agreeing to place one's name on the membership roster; subsequently, a lawmaker can be as active as he or she wants to be. Mere membership in a caucus does have its benefits. Former Representative Bill Richardson (D-N.M.) observed, "If someone writes me on an arts issue, I can write back and say, 'I'm a member of the Congressional Arts Caucus.'"[19]

Second, depending on the caucus, members can obtain different kinds of useful information. For example, *party-based* caucuses, such as the moderate-to-conservative Democratic "Blue Dogs," frame issues from their own perspective. *Personal interest* caucuses offer information on subjects that unite members with similar interests (e.g., the arts, environment). And various *constituency-based* caucuses provide members who represent given national (the Congressional Black Caucus), regional (the Sunbelt Council), state/district (the Suburban Caucus), and industry (the Textile Caucus) interests with organized means to share information and help set the legislative agenda.[20] (See Table 6–2.)

---

[18]For an extended discussion, see Loomis, *The New American Politician,* pp. 152ff.

[19]Loomis, *The New American Politician,* p. 150.

[20]Hammond, "Congressional Caucuses in the 104th Congress," pp. 278ff.

TABLE 6–2
Caucus Establishment, 1959–1996 (by type)

	Caucus Type						
Time Period	*Party*	*Personal Interest*	*National Constituency*	*Regional*	*State/District*	*Industry*	*Total*
1959–1970	2	1	0	1	0	0	4
1971–1976	5	6	2	5	1	1	20
1977–1980	1	5	3	5	9	15	38
1981–1986	6	25	0	7	10	16	64
1987–1990	2	17	0	7	8	16	50
1991–1996	7	21	1	9	21	17	76
Total	23	75	6	34	49	65	252

Source: Susan W. Hammond, *Congressional Caucuses in National Policy Making* (Baltimore: Johns Hopkins University Press, 1998), Table 3–2, p. 42.

Third, junior members such as Edgar (in the 1970s) and Weldon (in the late 1980s) have often found opportunities for action within caucuses that committees or party structures would not have provided them for years. Although many caucuses provide no resources to their leaders, some well-established groups have staffs that complement their leader's regular enterprises. Groups such as the Congressional Black Caucus and its Hispanic counterpart host expensive fund-raising galas ($500 per seat) to support outside institutes that complement the inside groupings of members. The access to such resources makes these caucus leaders important forces within the House, all the more so as the numbers of African American and Hispanic members have grown sharply in the 1990s.

Finally, there can be some tangible benefits for holding a caucus leadership position, as individual donors and PACs seek out those with apparent influence on their specific issue. For example, in 1990 Representative Bud Schuster (R-Pa.), the cochair of the Congressional Truck Caucus, received more than $32,000 in PAC contributions from Ryder, the Teamsters Union, North American Van Lines, and other related groups.[21]

The policy, campaign, and power incentives to join and become active in caucuses are substantial for most legislators, even senators and senior House members like Schuster. The costs of affiliation are often minimal, usually outweighed by the symbolic benefits of membership. For those who invest time and energy in caucus activity, the returns can be great in terms of campaign funds, access to the executive branch, and attention from party leaders. It's no

---

[21]David Segal, "Caucus Crazy," *Washington Monthly* (May 1994): p. 23. Representative Schuster was the ranking Republican on the Public Works and Transportation Committee, which also made him a target for such contributions. Caucus positions can and do pull together various parts of a member's enterprise—in this instance his committee position and campaign. Schuster's leverage grew further when he became committee chair in the 1995–2000 period.

wonder that Curt Weldon founded the Fire Services Caucus in 1987; by providing an attractive, cheap benefit to many of his peers, he could become a force
on a narrow, but not insignificant, set of policies. Such an achievement is one
basis for influence within the Congress.

Congressional Offices and the Continuing Campaign

In the 1960s and early 1970s, legislators' enterprises grew mainly within
the Congress. In 1957, the average House office employed 5.6 staffers; twenty
years later, that number had almost tripled, to 15.9. Through the mid-1970s,
however, congressional election campaigns remained relatively inexpensive.
In 1974, for example, the cost of a typical House campaign stood at $54,000,
and incumbents spent less than $57,000 on average (while challengers spent
not much less, around $40,000). By 1990 expenditure patterns had changed
greatly: Average expenditures had risen to $266,000 (incumbents had increased
their spending to $390,000, but challengers could muster only an average of
$133,000). (See Chapter 4 for more details.)

Members of Congress obviously had learned to raise and spend vast
amounts of funds, to the point that *unopposed* incumbents spent $250,000 on
average in the 1989–1990 election cycle. This combination of no opposition
and a quarter-million dollars in expenditures means that all funds went to support the political side of the individual enterprise, rather than being siphoned
off for advertising, direct mail, or consultants' expenses.[22]

Perhaps the most interesting trend in the growth of election-oriented
enterprises is the number of House campaigns that spend more than a million
dollars in a two-year election cycle (Table 6–3). Although some challengers
and open-seat aspirants reach this mark, the vast majority of big spenders
come from the ranks of incumbents, who use their ability to raise funds to
scare off prospective opponents or to meet the demands of a tight race with an
effective challenger. Of course, the fund-raising requirements of million-dollar
campaigns are staggering; a candidate would have to raise approximately
$10,000 per week throughout a two-year cycle to accumulate such a total. Few
challengers can raise this kind of money, although increasing numbers do self-
finance their campaigns with large sums.

Despite the escalation in campaign expenditures, the most important
building block of any sitting member's campaign enterprise remains the personal office, with its extensive resources and staff. As one close observer of the
local arms of congressional enterprises has noted,

> No matter how dazzling a campaign organization a challenger puts
> together, it will always be an ad hoc group, unfamiliar with the territory
> and with each other, while the incumbent fields a publicly paid team of

---

[22]For the breakdown of expenditures in a typical House campaign, see Paul Herrnson, *Congressional Elections: Campaigning at Home and in Washington* (Washington, DC: CQ Press, 1995),
p. 74.

TABLE 6-3
House Campaigns Spending More Than $1 Million, 1979-1998

	Incumbents	Challengers	Open Seats	All
1979–1984	6	3	2	11
1985–1986	10	2	6	18
1987–1988	13	4	5	22
1989–1990	9	1	4	14
1991–1992	44	3	7	54
1993–1994	34	10	4	48
1995–1996	55	14	7	76
1997–1998	69	19	22	110

Source: Modified from *Congressional Quarterly Weekly Report,* December 21, 1996; and "U.S. Candidate Money Leaders," <www.tray.com>. Figures for 1997–1998 are through December 31, 1998.

experienced veterans to do a task they have succeeded in before . . . and which differs very little from their everyday jobs [such as seeking benefits for constituents as opposed to promising them to voters].[23]

With the congressional staff taking care of routine tasks, the congressional enterprise can exercise great flexibility in expanding its political and electoral dimensions.

Political Expenditures

On top of staff and office resources are piled hundreds of thousands of dollars of political expenditures, which the Congress has defined exceptionally broadly. For example, former Representative (and, as of 1994, convicted felon) Carroll Hubbard (D-Ky.) paid $3,000 in campaign funds for a portrait of his father. Although the exact political purpose of the painting remains unclear, the congressman enjoyed great freedom in defining political expenditures as he saw fit.[24] One intensive study of campaign financing identifies a wide range of so-called political expenditures that systematically contribute to the overall congressional enterprise of many, though not all, incumbents. These include:[25]

- ▶ A professional campaign staff
- ▶ Substantial entertainment budgets
- ▶ Travel expenses (such as auto leases)
- ▶ Political consultants
- ▶ Lawyers and accountants

---

[23]John McCartney, "Congressional District Offices: Their Staff and Functions" (paper presented at the 1979 meeting of the American Political Science Association, Washington, DC), p. 48.

[24]Fritz and Morris, *Gold-Plated Politics,* p. 66.

[25]Fritz and Morris, *Gold-Plated Politics,* pp. 29–30.

► Civic and political donations

► A fund-raising apparatus (parties and direct mail)

► Investments such as certificates of deposit[26] and a building that housed former Representative Steve Neal's (N.C.) campaign organization

► Contributions to civic groups and establishment of college scholarships

Although congressional rules formally require expenditures to have a direct political purpose, almost no enforcement has taken place. Indeed, when contemplating a run against an entrenched incumbent, a challenger not only faces the Herculean task of raising funds to match those of the sitting legislator, but also confronts an established enterprise that has often been constructed over years by substantial spending of both federal funds and privately raised political monies.

To be capable of making political expenditures, one must amass substantial campaign resources, and contemporary legislators have proven most adept at raising these funds. Although academics have debated the ultimate impact of incumbents' spending patterns, there is little debate over the rise in costs since the mid-1970s, when the Federal Election Commission was established and began to publish, and make widely available, accurate figures on receipts and expenditures. As we saw in Chapter 4, the average Representative's political expenditures have risen from $54,000 in 1974 to $544,000 in 1996, a hefty increase even when taking inflation into account. During the same period, average Senate expenditures have grown from $437,000 to $3,900,000. Crucial here is that many of these funds were expended to perpetuate strong, continuing enterprises — organizations that allow incumbents maximum flexibility in pursuing their individual goals. In 1996, the average House incumbent raised more than $700,000, and the average sitting senator who sought reelection received $3.9 million. The cost of campaigning continues to increase, especially in the House.

In many ways, the enterprises of incumbents in uncontested races and those in the most competitive ones are remarkably similar. Both are very different from those of challengers, even in relatively close electoral contests. Only those candidates who are seeking an open seat regularly put together a campaign that looks much like that of an entrenched incumbent — without, of course, the personal office resources that sitting members traditionally employ. Challengers who can fund a major campaign effort remain few and far between. In 1998, just nineteen challengers raised more than $1 million. (See Tables 6–3 and 6–4.)

---

[26]Investment income in the 1980s was often truly substantial, in that bank CDs paid handsomely. With lower rates of return in the 1990s, some members have invested their excess cash in the stock market.

TABLE 6-4
Dennis Moore (D-Kans.) for Congress Budget (as of election day)

Receipts:	$982,000	
Individuals:	$646,000	(66.0%)
PACs and Party:	$336,000	(34.0%)
Labor	$230,000	(23.0%)
Other	$106,000	(11.0%)
Democrats	$ 50,000	(5.0%)
Member/Leader	$ 30,000	(3.0%)
State/Local	$ 10,000	(1.0%)
Nontraditional/Business	$ 10,000	(1.0%)
Expenditures:	$950,000	
Approximate Allocations:		
Radio/TV time purchase	$625,000	(66.0%)
Staff salaries, expenses	10,000	(12.0%)
TV/Radio production	70,000	(7.0%)
Polling	50,000	(5.0%)
Research	25,000	(3.0%)
Field (printing, etc.)	20,000	(2.0%)
Paid phone banks	15,000	(1.5%)
Fund-raiding costs	15,000	(1.5%)
Administration (phones, rent, etc.)	15,000	(1.5%)
Miscellaneous	5,000	(.5%)

Source: Moore campaign, November 6, 1999. Moore's total receipts as of December 31, 1999, exceeded $1 million.

Most notably, incumbents in tight races spent only modestly more on overhead and fund-raising than did those who were unopposed; the latter spent more on constituents and donations to other races. But candidates who felt their opponents breathing down their necks could ratchet up their spending on polling, advertising, and other campaign activities (such as direct mail). Even when they were engaged in a potentially close race against an incumbent, challengers could not begin to muster adequate resources to guarantee a strong challenge. They could not match the incumbents' overhead expenditures, which is not surprising. Nor could they come close, even in tight contests, to the figures incumbents could spend on polling, advertising, and other electoral activities — the heart of any campaign. Only open-seat candidates build organizations that resemble an incumbent's enterprise (with no accounting for congressional staff, district offices, communications capacities, and travel expenses). In the end, that is what much of the struggle for open seats is all about — to obtain the resources of incumbency for the future. One measure of the Republicans' 1994 success is that they won twenty-one open seats previously held by House Democrats and six such seats in the Senate.[27]

---

[27]Republicans lost four previously held House seats that were open, for a net gain of seventeen. They lost no open Senate seats.

Additional Enterprise Resources

Legislators' enterprises extend far beyond the structures of personal offices, committees, caucuses, and reelection operations. Many additional resources are available to all, and access to others resides formally or informally with key committee and party leaders.

CONGRESSIONAL SUPPORT AGENCIES   The most democratic resource on Capitol Hill is the Congressional Research Service (CRS), which responds to requests from all members in a reasonably equitable manner. In terms of providing basic information on a wide range of questions (from setting up an office to an economic analysis of the North American Free Trade Agreement), CRS is an invaluable source of timely insights. On more complex questions, which might require extensive staff time (from approximately 800 researchers), CRS is more likely to act quickly and comprehensively on requests from formal leaders within the committee or party hierarchy.

Likewise, the General Accounting Office (GAO) and the Congressional Budget Office (CBO) provide only modest assistance to legislative backbenchers, even though any member can request studies or information.[28] On the other hand, all members of Congress benefit from the independent information generated by these support agencies through reports and testimony. More than any other legislative body in the world, the Congress has sources of information and analysis that are intentionally separate from the executive branch and the federal bureaucracy. All members can use the volumes of information to help form their own policy positions, explain these positions and related votes to their constituents, and resist the entreaties of party leaders and presidents alike.[29]

LEADERSHIP RESOURCES   During the Democratic postreform era in the House (1981–1994) the joke went that any time one wanted to get the attention of a House Democrat and couldn't remember his name, all one had to do was call out "Mr. Chairman," and the legislator would respond; approximately half the 258 Democrats in the 103rd Congress chaired a committee or subcommittee, and almost all Democratic senators were chairs of some committee or subcommittee. Much the same could be said of the House Democratic leadership in recent Congresses. For example, in the 103rd Congress almost half the 256 House Democrats held some kind of formal party leadership position, including 92 who were considered part of the party's whip system. This inclusive leadership structure helped to define the postreform House, but relatively few

---

[28]Another support agency, the Office of Technology Assessment, was defunded and dismantled by the Republican-controlled 104th Congress.

[29]At the same time, party and committee leaders can commission studies that will serve to support their own positions. Information can serve both centrifugal and centripetal purposes.

resources accompany the vast majority of these positions. Only at the top of the ladder do leadership roles confer many resources, for either political party in either chamber.

For these few Representatives and senators, though, the benefits are substantial. For example, in the 106th Congress, House Whip Tom Delay (R-Tex.), the third-ranking Republican leader, controls an office staff of seventeen, and Senate Majority Leader Trent Lott (R-Miss.) has a party leadership staff of twenty. Other top leaders command similar resources. In addition, the four chairs of the respective parties' House and Senate campaign committees enjoy large staffs and travel budgets as they seek and allocate campaign funds and attempt to recruit candidates for upcoming elections. For those legislators who succeed at helping elect (and reelect) their colleagues, the rewards can be great, as former Senate Majority Leader George Mitchell (D-Maine) and presidential aspirant Senator Phil Gramm (R-Tex.) have demonstrated. As a relatively junior senator, Mitchell chaired the Democratic Senate Campaign Committee and took credit for returning the Democrats to majority status with their 1986 election results. When Senator Robert Byrd stepped down from his majority leader position in 1988, Mitchell won the right to succeed him, in part because of his general performance as campaign committee chair and the contributions he had directed to many of his colleagues. Senator Gramm's ambition has taken a different direction, but many senators were beholden to him for raising and funneling funds to their campaigns as head of the Republican Senate Campaign Committee.

For the most part, party-based resources assist in centralizing the power of leaders, but this is not always the case. In 1993, House Democratic Whip David Bonoir (D-Mich.) emerged as the leading critic of the North American Free Trade Agreement, a pact that Speaker Tom Foley and President Clinton strongly supported. Bonoir pledged not to use the resources of his office to oppose the treaty, but given the integrated nature of the congressional enterprise, it was difficult for him not to use — directly or indirectly — his party resources, as he fought the policy position of his legislative party and his president.[30]

PERSONAL PACS, INTERCAMPAIGN DONATIONS, AND OTHER ORGANIZATIONS
In 1978, Representative Paul Rogers (D-Fla.), chairman of the important Energy and Commerce Subcommittee on Health and the Environment, retired from the House. The next most senior subcommittee member was the well-respected Representative Richardson Preyer (D-N.C.), and it was widely assumed that the full committee's Democratic caucus would select him to replace Rogers. Representative Henry Waxman (D-Calif.), a talented and

---

[30]Majority Leader Richard Gephardt (D-Mo.) also opposed the pact, but took a less publicly aggressive stance. He announced that any actions against NAFTA taken by him would emanate from his personal office, but, again, the relationships among various parts of the enterprise make such a commitment difficult to monitor.

aggressive member first elected in 1974, had different ideas, however. Wax-man sought the chairmanship, arguing that Preyer's family ties to the pharma-ceutical industry and his district's tobacco interests would compromise his leadership of the subcommittee. Ordinarily, a vote among the full committee's Democrats would probably have resulted in a Preyer victory. But Waxman waged an exceptional campaign. Drawing on his fund-raising experience in California, he actively sought the subcommittee position by contributing $24,000 of his own campaign funds to members of the Energy and Commerce Committee.[31] The resulting 15-12 Waxman victory derived at least in part from the contributions, and this action set a precedent for subsequent contests for open committee and leadership positions. Much of Waxman's funding came from health interests, which had specific goals within the legislative process.[32] As a reformer and legislative activist, Waxman was an important target for health interests that desired access to him, regardless of their frequent dis-agreements with him on the issues.

By the late 1980s, many races for party leadership slots and key committee chairs employed funds from so-called leadership PACs. Organized interests often see great advantages in supporting potential leaders, who have little trouble in soliciting contributions for their own PACs. The resulting monies provided a great edge to Representative Tony Coelho (D-Calif.), who con-tributed $570,000 to House candidates prior to his election by the Caucus as Democratic Whip, and to Representative William Gray (D-Pa.), who spread around more than $60,000 in his successful 1988 bid to chair the Democratic Caucus.[33]

In the Senate, leadership PACs have proliferated, in large part owing to the presidential aspirations of so many senators. For example, former Senator Bob Dole used his Campaign America PAC to support his activities as a presidential candidate, his work as legislative leader, and his general political expenses for frequent trips to support incumbent legislators, governors, and dozens upon dozens of Republican challengers. Well-heeled interests such as agriculture's Archer Daniels Midland corporation received credit from Dole for their contri-butions to Campaign America, which then distributed some of these funds to other candidates, who, in turn, subsequently credit Dole for their good for-tune.[34] Taking in and disbursing millions of dollars since 1978, Campaign America became an integral part of the total Dole enterprise, which employed,

---

[31]This account is drawn in part from Ross K. Baker, *The New Fat Cats* (New York: Priority Press, 1989).

[32]Baker, *The New Fat Cats,* p. 50.

[33]Baker, *The New Fat Cats,* pp. 35–40.

[34]See Jake Thompson, *Bob Dole* (New York: Donald Fine, 1994). Thompson lists one other large-scale fund-raising component of the Dole enterprise: the Dole Foundation, a nonprofit entity established in 1984 to provide training and education grants to the disabled. Thompson notes the "critics have contended the foundation has been a means for big corporations to earn Dole's favor with large contributions" (p. 229).

directly or indirectly, well over one hundred individuals at any given time, all of whom owed their positions to the senator.

In the 1996 and 1998 election cycles, Senate GOP leadership PACs — most notably that of Majority Leader Trent Lott — raised large sums that were directed toward tight races. Lott's New Republican Majority Fund amassed contributions of $6 million in 1998 and disbursed $5.4 million to support candidates, the third highest total of all PACs.[35]

Leadership PACs like Lott's do hold some potential for integrating the legislative process. After all, a Waxman or a Dole desires to do more than simply win an important legislative office; such individuals want to have an impact on policy results. However, with more than fifty legislators establishing such organizations, the tendency toward fragmentation dominates.[36] As congressional scholar Ross Baker concludes after his careful study of this trend, the PACs will "magnify the influence of individual members, . . . [who], armed with their own checkbooks, [will make] harder the job of party leaders as they try to manage the delicate balance and often frustrating task of building party majorities."[37] In the House and, especially, the Senate, where every legislator can hope to exercise some policy leadership, the additional resource of personal PACs has often served to further fragment an already decentralized institution.

The most noteworthy counterexample of a centralizing set of forces lies in the overlapping organization that Speaker Newt Gingrich created in his rise to power. Providing fund-raising clout, technical expertise, and issue-based themes, Rep. Gingrich and his staff directed a political action committee (GOPAC), established a think tank (the Progress and Freedom Foundation), and cajoled fellow Republican incumbents to contribute funds to GOP challengers' campaigns. In the end, as Speaker, Gingrich could take advantage of the favors, services, and funds that he had provided through his extensive enterprise.

In 1996 and 1998, Gingrich and the House Republicans once again acted to centralize funding by soliciting substantial funds from safe Republican House members to redistribute to open seats and threatened incumbents. Although Republicans lost seats in both 1996 and 1998, the fund transfers may have reduced the losses.

THE CONGRESSIONAL ENTERPRISE: BLESSING AND CURSE

Of all the changes that have affected the U.S. Congress in the post–World War II era, none has been more striking than the expansion of the individual lawmaker's enterprise. From the moment new members take the oath of office,

[35]Federal Election Commission figures, <www.tray.com>, February 11, 1999.

[36]Baker, *The New Fat Cats,* Table 2, pp. 78–80.

[37]Baker, *The New Fat Cats,* p. 71.

they all control million-dollar-per-year operations of staff, communications, travel, and research capacities that allow them to commit substantial resources to reelection efforts, drafting legislation, overseeing the bureaucracy, or seeking higher office. Moreover, if clever at all, they will raise campaign funds that can be spent for broadly defined political purposes. The congressional enterprise helps all lawmakers claim credit for governmental programs, take positions on the issues of the day, and relentlessly advertise their accomplishments. But this is just the minimum enterprise, the stripped-down model that every first-term member gets upon arriving on Capitol Hill (and obtaining the smallest, most distant office from the floor of the House or Senate).

Virtually all senators and many House members enjoy the services of committee staffers, many benefit from caucus positions, and some even create their own PACs to reward their fellow legislators. At the heart of every congressional enterprise stands the individual senator or representative, to whom each of their respective staff members, campaign consultants, and fund-raisers owes his or her job. And their collective task is to promote the career and interests of their principal — the House member or senator. Party leaders and committee chairs regularly seek their support, but legislators know that, save in extraordinary circumstances, they remain largely unaffected by others' actions. Especially when it comes to reelection, party leaders and committee chairs enjoy no control over the average legislator's enterprise. All House members understand that, if reelected, they will retain the core personal staff of their enterprise, to say nothing of the other campaign, committee, and caucus resources they may have accumulated. In short, party leaders must negotiate with 435 representatives and 100 senators, who control their own electoral destinies and have enough resources to affect the policy process when they so desire. For all the decentralizing forces of subcommittees, committees, and incumbency, the heart of congressional fragmentation and individualism lies in the strength and flexibility of the legislator as enterprise.

Seven

PARTIES AND LEADERSHIP: CAPTURING THE CONGRESS

The Contract [with America] can be understood as an effort to introduce responsible party government into a legislature that has heretofore been described as an inchoate collection of atomized interests.

James Gimpel, *Fulfilling the Contract*

A pril 7, 1995. Speaker of the House Newt Gingrich and many, though not all, of his fellow Republican representatives marched out to the Capitol steps to proclaim the success of their hundred (actually ninety-three days) forced-march passage through the House of all but one (term limits) of their Contract with America agenda. Speaker Gingrich, supported strongly by old and (especially) new House Republicans, had captured the congressional agenda, even if only two Contract items had become law by the April rally.

April 1996. With Majority Leader Bob Dole well on his way to the Republican presidential nomination, Speaker Gingrich was no longer the focal point of Washington politics. In the wake of his budget confrontations with President Clinton that resulted in shutting down many federal programs and facilities, Gingrich — who prided himself on a capacity to think strategically — had long recognized that he had failed to make a correct assessment of the budget impasse between the Congress and the Chief Executive.[1] Equally seriously, he was faced with the real possibility that Republicans might lose control of the House after a single term in the majority, as they had in 1948 and 1954. The so-called Republican Revolution might well be stopped in its tracks.

January 6, 1999. The Gingrich era has ended, as the mostly unknown, distinctly conservative, and generally well-liked Representative Dennis Hastert (R-Ill.) is elected Speaker of the House. That Hastert has risen to the Speakership is nothing short of astounding. In November, Representative Bob Livingston (R-La.), the Appropriations Committee chairman, announced his candidacy for the speakership, and the sitting Speaker responded to his almost-certain ouster by declaring his intent to resign from the House as of the start of the 106th Congress.

---

[1]Among many sources, see David Maraniss and Michael Weisskopf, *Tell Newt to Shut Up* (New York: Touchstone, 1996), pp. 188ff.

Then, almost unbelieveably, he hustled out of Washington for an extended Florida vacation. Just as the House turned its attention to the impeachment of Bill Clinton, the man who challenged the president for national leadership in 1994–1995 handed the reins of power to Livingston, the presumptive but unelected Speaker, and the remaining, weakened House leadership.

Livingston owed his position and prominence to Gingrich, who elevated him to head the Appropriations panel over three more senior colleagues (see Chapter 5). Although he compiled a strong conservative record, Livingston was much more of a House insider and deal-maker than Gingrich; with a mere twelve-vote majority in the 106th Congress, Republican House members sought an astute legislative leader, rather than a fading partisan revolutionary, however successful he had been in building the GOP majority in 1994. But politics in the late 1990s, both inside the House and out, was scarcely so settled as to allow an easy transition for the Republican leadership.

Just as the impeachment process was to begin on the House floor, Representative Livingston announced that he would not seek the speakership in the 106th Congress and that he would resign from the body in the upcoming months. Larry Flynt, publisher of the salacious *Hustler* magazine, was ready to publish details of several of Livingston's extramarital affairs. Despite calls for him to remain, from both sides of the aisle, Livingston resigned and thus left the Republican House majority with no functioning Speaker, and a slate of leaders who, with the exception of Whip Tom DeLay (R-Tex.), had either been successfully challenged in December Republican conference elections or who had withstood a tough challenge (Majority Leader Richard Armey, R-Tex.).

Representative Hastert emerged as a consensus candidate for the Speakership in the wake of Livingston's resignation, in part because of his own qualifications and experience (as chief deputy whip), and in part because of the almost-desperate need for House Republicans to coalesce around a single figure. With his 223-211 majority and weakened Republican party, both in the legislature and in national polls, Speaker Hastert had his work cut out for him in the 106th Congress.

This chapter focuses on the extent to which party leaders, especially in the House, can gain the confidence of their colleagues to the point they are granted substantial powers, such as appointing committee chairs and committee members. The House, under Democrats and Republicans alike, has encouraged strong party leadership, while the Senate, despite some increased partisanship, remains the bastion of individualism within the legislative process.

THE CONGRESSIONAL PARTY: CENTRALIZATION IN CONTEXT

Legislatures, like all institutions, must function with some overall coherence. Political parties provide much of the glue that holds together the disparate ambitions of 535 legislators, buttressed by their enterprises, as well as the fragmented collection of committees, subcommittees, and special interest caucuses. Yet in the United States, political parties have proven much weaker and less capable of producing strong centripetal effects within the legislature than have parties in most other Western-style democracies, and especially those with parliamentary systems.[2]

Assessing the role of parties in the early 1960s, a strong committee era, Richard F. Fenno, Jr., concluded that parties "organize decision-making across committees and across stages [of the legislative process], thereby functioning as a centralizing force in the making of House decisions."[3] Although most members shared emotional attachments to their party and regarded it as one means to exercise power, Fenno, noted, "the . . . party label masks a pluralism of geographic, social, ideological, and organizational sources of identification, support, and loyalty. The roots of this pluralism lie outside the chamber, in the disparity of conditions under which the members are elected and in the decentralized organization of the parties nationally."[4] Congressional parties thus grow stronger when partisan divisions within the electorate have increased. In 1994, for example, congressional election results reflected strong partisan forces that helped form the basis for strong party leadership under new Republican Speaker Gingrich. In short, the best opportunities to exercise effective party leadership in the Congress, most notably within the House, have depended on forces largely beyond the control of the leaders, forces that emanate from the society and the electorate.

Not only does the diversity of constituencies constrain the impact of congressional parties, so too does the very resolution of issues that occasionally, but temporarily, divide the country into two broad, party-based factions. Periods of strong, centralized leadership and high levels of partisan voting on Capitol Hill reflect polarization between the parties in the electorate.[5] Circa 1900, Republican Speakers Thomas Reed and Joseph Cannon benefited from electoral results built on clear philosophical differences between two legislative parties that shouldered responsibility for ruling and accountability for their actions. In that era, individual representatives, having won their seats "on the basis of a party's platform," were expected to "support party positions, even against personal convictions or desires."[6] Internal allegiances to a party leader fit neatly into a world in which party machines controlled the candidate

---

[2]Parties in most parliamentary systems possess the power to select candidates rather than relying on primary elections to bestow the party label on a candidate.

[3]Richard F. Fenno, Jr., "The Internal Distribution of Influence: The House," in David B. Truman, ed., *Congress and America's Future* (Englewood Cliffs, NJ: Prentice-Hall, 1965), p. 61.

[4]Fenno, "The Internal Distribution of Influence," pp. 61–62.

[5]Joseph Cooper and David W. Brady, "Institutional Context and Leadership Style: The House from Cannon to Rayburn," *American Political Science Review* 75 (June 1981): pp. 411–425.

[6]Cooper and Brady, "Institutional Context and Leadership Style," p. 413.

selection process.[7] Opposing the party might well mean that a legislator would be denied renomination, and thus reelection, especially in an era before the widespread adoption of primary elections as the means of choosing nominees.

If party machines and a polarized electorate provided the external context for strong direction, the Speaker could act forcefully on party issues within the House.[8] Reed (1889–1891, 1895–1899) and Cannon (1903–1911) each combined their extensive formal prerogatives under the rules with their status as Speaker to carry out their legislative agendas. Moreover, the Speaker was also a party leader who could define those issues appropriate for partisan position-taking. As Speaker, Reed or Cannon could bring an issue to the majority Republican caucus, whose collective vote could require its legislators to line up behind the overall party position. Straying from the party might well mean that a dissident would be disciplined by the Speaker through removal from a powerful committee or the rejection of his preferences in fashioning a key piece of legislation, to say nothing of encouraging his local party organization to reject him as a candidate in the next election.

Why should we care much about century-old congressional voting alignments? (See Table 7–1.) Whatever the importance of the policies made at the time, this period's practices allow us to assess the actual possibilities for centralization with Congress. Given an external context that produces opposing voting blocs, legislators may opt to strengthen the hand of party leaders by providing them with the tools to lead forcefully, as the Democrats did in the 1980s, with Republicans following suit after winning control of Congress in 1995. Indeed, the Gingrich Speakership has left congressional scholars grasping for parallels in the modern Congress. For example, political scientist Charles Jones observed that the House Republicans' domination of the agenda, at least in the first year of 104th Congress, had no precedent in this century, including during the Cannon speakership.[9]

If the context of congressional politics can produce strong leadership and intense partisanship, it can also set conditions for relatively weak parties. In fact, from the 1920s through the early 1960s, parties within the Congress often reflected a social stalemate over the scope of governmental actions and, particularly, the role of federal involvement in matters of race and other domestic matters such as education and health care. To the extent that Americans were split by both ideology and region on these issues, so too were their representatives in Congress, where three party blocs developed in the wake of the pol-

---

[7]Peter Swenson, "The Influence of Recruitment on the Structure of Power in the U.S. House, 1870–1940," *Legislative Studies Quarterly* 7 (February 1982), pp. 7–36.

[8]The following discussion relies in part on Cooper and Brady, "Institutional Context and Leadership Style," pp. 412ff. See also, relevant chapters in *Masters of the House*, Roger H. Davidson, Susan Webb Hammond, and Raymond W. Smoek, eds. (Boulder, CO: Westview Press, 1998.)

[9]Comment made at American University forum on Congress and the president, April 17, 1995, televised on C-SPAN.

TABLE 7-1
The First and Last Congresses of the Twentieth Century

	57th Congress	106th Congress
Party Identification		
House	199 R	222 R
	151 D	211 D
	8 Other	1 Other
Senate	55 R	55 R
	31 D	45 D
	4 Other	0 Other
Average Age		
House	49	53
Senate	58	58
Average Number of Previous Terms		
House	2	4
Senate	1	1
African Americans	0	38
Women	0	65
Most Common First Name	William (45)	John (40)
Most Common Last Name	Smith (7)	Smith (6)
Members Named Elijah	1	1
Members Named Nehemiah	1	0
Members with Military Experience	28%	33%
Most common Former Profession	Lawyer (90%)	Lawyer (40%)
Former Blacksmiths	1	0
Former Plastic Surgeons	0	1
Members from Alaska, Ariz., Hawaii, N.M. or Okla.	0	28

Sources: Roll Call, January 18, 1999.

icy initiatives of Franklin Roosevelt's first term (1933–1937) as president: Republicans, Northern Democrats, and Southern Democrats.

Democrats organized both House and Senate for all but two Congresses between 1933 and the 1960s.[10] This means they named the Speaker, the majority leader, various other majority-party offices, and all the committee chairs, as well as holding a majority of seats on all legislative committees. But this "procedural majority," which ensured Democratic control in formal terms, often vanished when important, substantive issues came to a vote.[11] Not only was the Congress fragmented among constituencies in ordinary pluralistic ways, but it frequently split sharply along the related lines of region and ideology, as Southern Democrats joined with Republicans to form a "Conservative Coalition" that

[10]The exceptions were narrow Republican majorities in both houses for the eightieth and eighty-third Congresses (1947–1949 and 1953–1955, respectively).

[11]David S. Cloud, "Speaker Wants His Platform to Rival the Presidency," *Congressional Quarterly Weekly Report,* February 4, 1995, p. 331.

opposed the liberal initiatives of Democratic presidents and their Northern Democratic allies in the Congress, especially on civil rights and social welfare policies.[12]

As Brady and Bullock point out, "Understanding how the Conservative Coalition works furthers our understanding of the [Congress] as a whole. The voting alliance begun in 1937 between Southern Democrats and Republicans . . . greatly reduced the ability of the majority Democratic party to function as a governing party."[13] Although Republicans and Southern Democrats did consult with each other, the alliance remained informal; for example, there has never been a Conservative Coalition caucus. Rather, key Republicans such as House Minority Leader Joseph Martin (R-Mass.) or Southern Democrats such as Senator Richard Russell (D-Ga.) would communicate casually, if purposefully, with their allies and encourage the formation of a voting coalition.[14] With Texan Sam Rayburn (a moderate-to-conservative Southerner) at the helm of the House Democratic party for much of the 1940s and 1950s, the Conservative Coalition's ability to defeat liberal legislation was scarcely a great problem. The party and committee leadership, which was heavily weighted with Southerners, ordinarily deferred to the coalition, whose preferences roughly reflected those of the House as a whole.

Rayburn's greatest strengths as Speaker did not derive from his formal powers, which were modest at best. A brief comparison to Reed or Cannon — or Gingrich — demonstrates the personal and policy bases of Rayburn's influence. Speaker Cannon, for example, chaired the Rules Committee and his majority leader headed the Ways and Means panel — at the time, the two most powerful committees in the chamber. He appointed all committee members and all chairs and could delay making these appointments until well after the Congress had convened. He controlled the legislative schedule with an iron hand and used his power of recognition to reduce opponents' capacity to participate meaningfully in floor debate. Rayburn, in contrast, held relatively few formal powers. He could not control the Rules Committee; it had been captured by the Conservative Coalition during the 1950s under the strong-willed chairmanship of conservative Democrat Howard Smith (D-Va.), who owed his position to his seniority on the committee. More generally, the seniority principle had become so firmly entrenched within the Congress that advancement on committees was virtually automatic, regardless of one's loyalty to the party. Nor did

---

[12]See John Manley, "The Conservative Coalition in Congress," *American Behavioral Scientist* 17 (1973): pp. 223–247; Mack C. Shelley, *The Permanent Majority: The Conservative Coalition in the United States Congress* (Tuscaloosa: University of Alabama Press, 1983).

[13]David W. Brady and Charles S. Bullock III, "Coalition Politics in the House of Representatives," in Lawrence Dodd and Bruce I. Oppenheimer, eds., *Congress Reconsidered,* 2nd ed. (Washington, DC: CQ Press, 1981), p. 201. According to Brady and Bullock the coalition began to operate in 1937, but the forces that produced this cooperation had existed for some time.

[14]Joseph Martin, *My First Fifty Years in Politics* (New York: McGraw-Hill, 1960), p. 84.

Rayburn control the initial assignments of Democrats to committees.[15] In short, Rayburn possessed few of the leadership tools that Cannon had wielded so effectively to control the agenda and legislative results of the House.[16] Yet legislators almost universally viewed him as a powerful Speaker. How could this be so?

Rayburn did retain significant, if limited, formal powers and the discretion to recognize whom he wanted on the House floor. He also controlled the leadership organization, which kept him well informed on most issues. Rayburn could dominate the final scheduling of legislation, and he often used his position to trade favors with other members — both Republicans and Democrats.[17] Favors such as campaigning for a fellow Democrat, postponing a vote to mollify a freshman Republican, and supporting a new dam for a marginal-seat member allowed the Speaker to build up positive "balances" in his exchanges with legions of representatives (including those in the minority). As a result of past favors, Rayburn could request assistance on a specific issue from various legislators who would be hard-pressed to rebuff him.[18] In addition, Rayburn's work ethic, his absolute integrity, and his total dedication to the House provided strong foundations for his politicking on given legislation items.

More generally, however, Rayburn was influential because for most of his speakership he reflected the overall moderate-conservative policy leanings of the House during the 1950s. Although he had his differences with President Eisenhower, whom he regarded as a political amateur, Rayburn did not back the activist agenda that growing numbers of Northern Democrats favored. Rather, as a key conduit of information between the White House and the Congress (along with Senate Majority Leader Lyndon Johnson) he operated at the hub of an informal House oligarchy of party leaders and committee chairmen. In the end, however, these tough-minded committee leaders could dominate policymaking from their separate, formal power bases. Rayburn had neither the desire nor the authority to move the House very far beyond its comfortably moderate, limited-government course of the 1950s.

---

[15]Traditionally, Democratic members of the House Ways and Means Committee had served as the party's "committee on committees." In 1975, this power was transferred to the Steering and Policy Committee, where party leaders possessed much more influence on appointments.

[16]For a brief summary of the tools of powerful leadership, see Robert L. Peabody, *Leadership in Congress* (Boston: Little, Brown, 1976), pp. 41–47. See also, Ronald M. Peters, Jr., *The American Speakership* (Baltimore: Johns Hopkins University Press, 1990).

[17]Peters, *The American Speakership*, pp. 42–46; see also, Lewis L. Gould and Nancy Beck Young, "The Speaker and the Presidents: Sam Rayburn, the White House and the Legislative Process, 1941–1961," in *Masters of the House*, pp. 181–221.

[18]These tactics were similar to those used by former Ways and Means Chair Representative Wilbur Mills (D-Ark.), as detailed by John Manley, "Wilbur Mills: A Study in Congressional Influence," *American Political Science Review* 63 (June 1969): pp. 442–464. Mills served as Ways and Means chair from 1958 through 1974.

The congressional leadership began to undergo significant changes between 1958 and 1961; the fragility of Rayburn's leadership (and that of Lyndon Johnson, in the Senate), which was based on personality and favor trading, came under tremendous pressure with the large Democratic gains in the 1958 congressional elections and the party's 1960 capture of the presidency. In one of his last major actions as Speaker (before his death later in 1961), Rayburn put into motion the twenty-year process of recentralizing leadership powers in the House by wresting control of the Rules Committee from the Conservative Coalition. The committee's four Republicans and two Southern Democrats had been able to thwart the preferences of six regular Democrats, but the Speaker proposed adding three members — two Democrats and one Republican — to the panel; this would allow the leadership to increase its influence on the committee's important decisions as to how the House would structure its consideration of legislation.[19] Building an informal coalition among all 129 Northern Democrats, 30 (of 32) "border-state" Democrats, 36 (of 98) Southern Democrats, and 22 (of 170) Republicans, Rayburn, who disliked confrontation, won what he called "the worst fight of my life" by the narrow margin of 217-212.[20]

Typical of Rayburn's reverence for the House and his respect for his colleagues, the Speaker opted for a moderate course of reform in which "no member was unseated, nor was party discipline applied. . . . The enlargement resolution, as the Speaker himself said . . . was 'the way to embarrass nobody if they didn't want to be embarrassed.'"[21] Even so, Rayburn understood the stakes at hand; a Democratic president and a Democratic Congress might well be prevented from pushing forward their policies if the Rules Committee remained as an obstacle. Although the expansion of the Rules Committee applied only to the 87th Congress, the obstructionism of this body declined immediately, if not completely, and by the mid-1970s the panel had swung around to serve House leaders in structuring debates and scheduling votes on the floor.[22]

The Conservative Coalition continued to appear with great frequency in congressional voting alignments during the 1960s and 1970s, but the Demo-

---

[19]Ironically, one of the Democrats added to the Rules Committee, an Alabama Representative, did not always support the leadership's positions. But the principle of leadership control of this important committee had been established. See Charles Jones, "Joseph G. Cannon and Howard W. Smith: An Essay on The Limits of Leadership in The House of Representatives," *Journal of Politics* 30 (August 1968): 617–648.

[20]Two superb sources detail this important decision: Milton C. Cummings, Jr., and Robert L. Peabody, "The Decision to Enlarge the Committee on Rules: An Analysis of the 1961 Vote," in Robert L. Peabody and Nelson W. Polsby, eds., *New Perspectives on the House of Representatives* (Chicago: Rand McNally, 1963), pp. 167–194; and D. B. Hardeman and Donald C. Bacon, *Rayburn: A Biography* (Lanham, MD: Madison Books, 1984), pp. 447–466.

[21]Cummings and Peabody, "The Decision to Enlarge the Committee on Rules," p. 193.

[22]Bruce I. Oppenheimer, "The Rules Committee: New Arm of Leadership in a Decentralized House," in Lawrence Dodd and Bruce I. Oppenheimer, eds., *Congress Reconsidered* (New York: Praeger, 1977), pp. 96–116.

cratic leadership in the House gradually strengthened itself (this process moved slowly and was frequently obscured by the simultaneous decentralizing trends of stronger individual member enterprises and greater fragmentation within the committee system). However, neither of the two Speakers who followed Rayburn — Representatives John McCormack (D-Mass., 1961–1969) and Carl Albert (D-Okla., 1969–1977) — proved forceful or effective in countering the decentralizing forces that dominated the House in the late 1960s and the 1970s.

Slowly, members of the Democratic Caucus came to see that their leaders needed more authority to run the House. Echoing Woodrow Wilson's 1885 conclusions, political scientist Charles Jones observed that "*somebody must be trusted,* in order that when things go wrong it may be quite plain who should be punished."[23] From their base in the Democratic Study Group (one of the first informal groups on Capitol Hill) from the late 1950s on, liberals continually prodded the Democratic Caucus to reduce the autonomy of full committee chairs and increase the authority of the leadership and the full caucus, which the Northern Democrats increasingly dominated. More and more, majority-party House Democrats chose to trust themselves, as the caucus, or their leaders, as their direct agents.[24] In particular, the Democratic Caucus gave the Speaker the power to appoint members of the Rules Committee, thus making the committee a loyal "arm of the Leadership."[25] Next, the Caucus moved the committee assignment responsibility to the party leadership–dominated Steering and Policy Committee and thus greatly enhanced the leaders' roles in this process. Finally, to coordinate policy making within the fragmented committee system, the Speaker was granted broad powers to refer bills to multiple committees, often in a well-defined sequence that imposed deadlines on committee action.[26]

During his decade-long tenure as Speaker (1977–1986), Representative Thomas P. (Tip) O'Neill (D-Mass.) and his lieutenants created a new leadership style within a House that had encouraged more individual participation from virtually all members, but especially those of the majority party.[27] In this democratized context leaders became service providers, more than ever, to their colleagues; by offering meaningful support to incumbents, by keeping all the Democratic legislators well informed, and by granting any number of

---

[23]Quoted in Charles Jones, "Somebody Must Be Trusted: An Essay on Leadership of the U.S. Congress," in Norman J. Ornstein, *Congress in Change* (New York: Praeger, 1975), p. 266, Wilson's emphasis.

[24]For a good summary of this trend, see Barbara Sinclair, *Majority Leadership in the U.S. House* (Baltimore: Johns Hopkins University Press, 1983), pp. 2ff.

[25]Oppenheimer, "The Rules Committee," p. 1977.

[26]See Gary Young and Joseph Cooper, "Multiple Referral and the Transformation of House Decision Making," in Lawrence C. Dodd and Bruce I. Oppenheimer, eds., *Congress Reconsidered,* 5th ed. (Washington, DC: CQ Press, 1995), pp. 211–236.

[27]The following discussion draws on Sinclair, *Majority Leadership in the U.S. House,* pp. 28–29, as well as Sinclair, "Tip O'Neill and Contemporary House Leadership," in *Masters of the House,* pp. 289–318.

particular favors, the leadership demonstrated its responsiveness. At the same time, the Democratic leaders greatly increased their ability to structure the decision-making process through their formal powers to schedule bills and dominate the Rules Committee. Collectively, congressional Democrats were willing to allow their leadership considerable leeway here, as long as its actions did not conflict with clear membership preferences. Finally, the leaders consciously adopted an inclusive strategy, bringing large numbers of members into the leadership during the late 1970s, both in permanent positions (for example, as whips) and in ad hoc capacities (such as task force heads and members).

Even as subcommittees proliferated, individual enterprises grew, and new norms encouraged the participation of all members in the late 1970s, party leaders slowly gained more leverage and influence. Underlying the surface fragmentation was a growing willingness among most Democrats to accept a strengthened leadership that would allow Jim Wright to become, in 1987–1989, one of the House's most powerful Speakers. At the same time, the Republicans grew increasingly united and vocal in their protests against both the Democrats' policy positions and their use of procedures to limit meaningful minority participation within the House.[28] By acting as aggressive, effective partisans, the House Democrats simultaneously offered Republicans a model of strong leadership and a clear target for the opposition's efforts to gain control of the House.

Caucus-Based Centralization: The Democratic Model, 1981–1994

The notions of party leadership, partisanship, and party voting overlap within the Congress. Party leaders often structure votes and other decisions to take advantage of party majorities, but they must also take into account the preferences of their followers. Overall, the postreform Congress has become a highly partisan place, particularly in the House. In assessing the strength of political parties within the Congress, political scientists frequently analyze changes in two different but related measures of partisanship on roll-call votes.[29] From 1983 on, there is no question that both the proportion of party-

---

[28]The Republican position was thoroughly articulated in a paper issued by Representatives Richard T. Armey (R-Tex.), Jennifer Dunn (R-Wash.), and Christopher Shays (R-Conn.), "It's Long Enough: The Decline of Popular Government under Forty Years of Single Party Control of the U.S. House of Representatives" (Washington, DC: House Republican Conference, 1994).

[29]Most, though not all, important votes are recorded. If twenty-five House members or one-fifth of the senators present request a roll-call vote, the chamber goes on the record. This was not always the case; through the 1960s, many key issues were decided on "unrecorded teller" votes, in which Representatives would signify their vote by lining up and walking past vote counters on the "aye" or "nay" side of a given proposal. In the early 1970s, the House ceased this practice and installed an electronic voting system. The number of roll-call votes rose from an average of 175 annually in the 1960s to more than 600 per year in the 1970s. Subsequently, the average declined to about 450 in the 1980s. Virtually all major decisions are still on the record, however. In the Senate, the patterns have been similar, although the rise has been more gradual and the number of roll-call votes has averaged one hundred to two hundred fewer per year since the late 1970s.

TABLE 7-2
Party Unity Average Scores

Average Scores for Each Party in Both Chambers of Congress					
Year	Democrats	Republicans	Year	Democrats	Republicans
1961	71%	72%	1980	68%	70%
1962	69	68	1981	69	76
1963	71	72	1982	72	71
1964	67	69	1983	76	74
1965	69	70	1984	74	72
1966	61	67	1985	79	75
1967	66	71	1986	78	71
1968	57	63	1987	81	74
1969	62	62	1988	79	73
1970	57	59	1989	81	73
1971	62	66	1990	81	74
1972	57	64	1991	81	78
1973	68	68	1992	79	79
1974	63	62	1993	85	84
1975	69	70	1994	83	83
1976	65	66	1995	91	80
1977	67	70	1996	87	80
1978	64	67	1997	82	88
1979	69	72	1998	83	86

Sources: Congressional Quarterly Weekly Report, December 31, 1994, p. 3658; December 21, 1996, p. 346; and January 9, 1999, p. 92.

based votes and the level of party loyalty on these votes have increased considerably (see Tables 7–2 and 7–3). This increased partisanship has grown in large part because many contemporary Southern Democrats — those who hail from urban areas and districts with high percentages of African-American voters — tend to vote a lot like their Northern Democratic colleagues, and voting patterns of the growing number of Southern Republicans closely approximate those of their fellow GOP legislators. As traditionally conservative Southern Democrats have declined in numbers and impact, the Conservative Coalition has become a less active and less powerful force within the House. But the divisions between the parties have increased.

The party-voting scores of Southern Democrats have risen steadily, from an average 53 percent party unity score in the 94th Congress (1975–1976) to an average of 78 percent in the 100th through 103rd Congresses (1987–1994).[30] Although Southern Democrats remain more conservative than their Northern counterparts, the differences have shrunk considerably, from an approximately

[30]Figures from Norman Ornstein, Thomas Mann, and Michael Malbin, *Vital Statistics on Congress, 1993–1994* (Washington, DC: CQ Press, 1993), pp. 201–202, and *Congressional Quarterly Weekly Report,* December 31, 1994, p. 3659. See also David W. Rohde, *Parties and Leaders in the Post-Reform House* (Chicago: University of Chicago Press, 1991), p. 57.

TABLE 7-3
Proportion of Partisan Roll Calls

How Often a Majority of Democrats Voted against a Majority of Republicans											
Year	House	Senate	Year	House	Senate	Year	House	Senate	Year	House	Senate
1954	38%	47%	1966	41%	50%	1978	33%	45%	1989	55%	35%
1955	41	30	1967	36	35	1979	47	47	1990	49	54
1956	44	53	1968	35	32	1980	38	46	1991	55	49
1957	59	36	1969	31	36	1981	37	48	1992	64	53
1958	40	44	1970	27	35	1982	36	43	1993	65	67
1959	55	48	1971	38	42	1983	56	44	1994	62	52
1960	53	37	1972	27	36	1984	47	40	1995	73	69
1961	50	62	1973	42	40	1985	61	50	1996	56	62
1962	46	41	1974	29	44	1986	57	52	1997	50	50
1963	49	47	1975	48	48	1987	64	41	1998	56	56
1964	55	36	1976	36	37	1988	47	42			
1965	52	42	1977	42	42						

Source: Congressional Quarterly Weekly Report, December 31, 1994, p. 3659, December 21, 1996, p. 3462; and January 9, 1999, p. 93.

25 percent party-voting divergence in the ninetieth, ninety-first, and ninety-second Congresses (1967–1972) to a mere 9 percent gap in the 100th Congress. Rohde observes, "in 1971–2, the *average* southern Democrat supported his or her party less than half the time on those votes that divided party majorities. From that point on, southern unity began a gradual increase to almost 80 percent in recent years."[31]

Partisanship in voting does not necessarily flow from a stronger, more centralized party leadership; intense partisanship depends as much on electoral patterns as any set of revised practices within the Democratic Caucus or the House as a whole. In the 1980s, partisanship increased (more party-line votes, more unity on those votes), and party leaders gained more tools for leadership and more experience in employing these instruments (restrictive rules, suspensions of the rules, sequential referrals of legislation to committees). These two developments come together within the Democratic Caucus, where an increasingly homogenous membership can communicate its wishes to the leadership.[32]

Bearing in mind Fenno's conclusion that we get the kind of Congress that the members give us,[33] we got a postreform Congress in which, from the early

---

[31]Rohde, *Parties and Leaders in the Post-Reform House*, p. 55, Rohde's emphasis.

[32]For an extended discussion of strong legislative leadership in parties that are relatively weak outside the legislature, see Barbara Sinclair, *Legislators, Leaders, and Lawmaking: The U.S. House of Representatives in the Postreform Era* (Baltimore: Johns Hopkins University Press, 1995), especially pp. 300–306.

[33]Richard F. Fenno, Jr., "If, as Ralph Nader Says, Congress Is the 'Broken Branch,' How Come We Love Our Congressmen So Much?" in Norman Ornstein, ed., *Congress in Change* (New York: Praeger, 1975), p. 287.

1980s on, the Democratic Caucus empowered its leaders to act aggressively as its agents. This was accomplished in two related ways: (1) through an initial set of decisions at the beginning of each Congress and (2) through continuing conversations between party leaders and the Democratic membership, both in groups and one on one.

At the outset of a new Congress, in January of each odd-numbered year, members of the legislative parties select their respective leaders. In the postreform era, House Democrats elected the Speaker, the majority leader, and chief majority whip[34] and voted to approve all full-committee chairs, as well as each of the thirteen appropriations subcommittee chairs. After 1994, these selections continued, albeit for minority leadership positions and "ranking minority member" slots on committees. In short, the membership has a biennial opportunity to defeat any top party or committee leader who has lost the caucus' confidence. Between 1975 and 1993, Democrats unseated six committee chairs, eased another one out of his position, and, equally important, delivered numerous warnings through negative votes on many other committee heads.[35] For the party and committee leaders, this process is sometimes unnerving, but it is highly valuable in that these individuals receive the explicit endorsement of their peers. In an era when party leaders enjoy great formal powers, such as the Speaker's Rules Committee appointments, his chairmanship of the Policy and Steering Committee, and his domination over legislative scheduling, this endorsement by the party's legislators has given Democratic leaders wide latitude in setting agendas and providing specific assistance to individual members. Yet the grant of authority remains — as Speaker Wright discovered in 1989 — contingent on the continuing support of a firm caucus majority.

In the Rayburn era, after briefly coming together to select its top leadership, the Democratic Caucus would virtually disappear, meeting only rarely. The caucus within the postreform Congress remains much more active, both formally and informally. Not only are there regularly scheduled meetings but, more important, the caucus exists within the minds of leaders and backbenchers alike as an active force inside the House. In various circumstances leaders or the rank and file may choose to request a caucus meeting to reach a party position on a major issue (for example, calling for Reagan administration compliance with Strategic Arms Limitation Talks agreement provisions in 1987). More generally, leaders are continually gauging caucus support for legislative initiatives and procedural maneuvers.

The active Democratic Caucus both empowered and restrained the party's leaders. By the early 1990s, a fairly large core group of leaders emerged as the day-to-day directors of House business. The traditional leaders — the Speaker, the majority leader, and the whip — were joined by three chief deputy whips, along with the caucus chair and vice chair. In addition, congressional scholar Barbara Sinclair notes, "as the leadership has become more central to the

---

[34]The whip was appointed until a 1985 rules change mandated election by the caucus.

[35]Leroy N. Rieselbach, *Congressional Politics,* 2nd ed. (Boulder, CO: Westview Press, 1995), p. 93.

legislative process, members' desires for *representation* in the leadership have intensified."[36] Indeed, when Speaker Foley split the chief deputy whip's office into three positions, he appointed a woman (Barbara Kennelly, Conn.), a Southerner (Butler Derrick, S.C.), and an African American (John Lewis, Ga.), and in 1993 he added a fourth slot for Bill Richardson (N.M.), a Latino. Beyond these attempts to include more factions within the party leadership, this trend toward representation is important in that committees have historically served as the principal agents of representation. Given the emphasis on an expanded, inclusive leadership, however, the centrifugal forces of representation have grown stronger within the House's bastion of centralization.

The core leadership, aided by a formidable staff, serves as information source, sounding board, strategic and tactical decisionmaker, and, under divided government, interbranch negotiator. Nevertheless, given its highly inclusive style of operation, even an expanded core leadership could not maintain adequate communication lines with more than 250 House Democrats, so the Democrats established a much more extended leadership apparatus, which included almost half of the party's 256 legislators in the 103rd Congress. Of special note has been the systematic expansion of the whip system, which acts as a conduit for information between members and leaders and as an organization for mobilizing votes on the House floor.

In the 103rd Congress (1993–1995), the whip system included the majority whip, four deputy whips, a floor whip, an "ex-officio whip" (Representative Joe Moakley, Rules Committee chair), eleven deputy whips, two "whip task force" chairs, fifty-six leadership-appointed at-large whips, and eighteen assistant whips elected by members of regional zones. The whip system alone included ninety-two Democratic members, well over a third of the party's ranks in the House. But the expansion in the ranks of Democratic leaders did not stop with the whip system. Rules Committee members clearly occupied leadership slots, as did the chair of the Budget Committee and a host of ad hoc task force heads appointed by the majority leader to organize party efforts on specific legislative initiatives.[37] In addition, the chairmanship of the Democratic Congressional Campaign Committee (DCCC) represented an important leadership position.

Without question, the Democratic Caucus has sanctioned the development of a strong House leadership; in large part, this derives from the increased ideological homogeneity of the Democratic membership. Nonetheless, substantial limitations on leadership have remained in the 1990s; despite consistently high levels of partisan voting and active, inclusive leadership efforts, party-based policies did not flow smoothly from the House, most notably on such significant issues as free trade and health care.

---

[36]Barbara Sinclair, "House Majority Leadership in an Era of Divided Control," in Lawrence C. Dodd and Bruce I. Oppenheimer, eds., *Congress Reconsidered*, 5th ed. (Washington, DC: CQ Press, 1995), p. 243, emphasis added.

[37]On task forces, see Sinclair, *Majority Leadership in the U.S. House.*

At first with great hesitancy, and later with vigor and conviction, House Democrats acted to strengthen their party leadership, from the 1961 vote on wresting control of the Rules Committee away from the Conservative Coalition to their willingness in 1987–1988 to follow Speaker Jim Wright's lead to refashioning American foreign and military policy in Nicaragua. The Democratic majority came to structure the context of decision making in the House, which meant that the minority Republicans became less and less able to influence outcomes.[38] The movement toward strong party leadership in a weak-party era illustrates the trends toward more ideological cohesiveness within parties in the House, as well as in members' cost-benefit calculations, which increasingly led them to encourage leaders' latitude in structuring decisions.[39] Strong party leadership remained contingent on these calculations by the members and on the ideological divisions between the two parties, however, and Democratic leaders became more and more dependent on manipulating the agenda and structuring floor votes through the aggressive use of the Rules Committee.[40] Many, if not most, Republicans found themselves holding no stake in the institution of the House; with little remorse they would seek to tear down the House that the Democratic majority had constructed.

Postreform Politics in the Republican Mold

With the stunning results of the 1994 elections, Republicans gained control of the House after forty years as the minority. We shall explore in some detail the strong, centralized leadership adopted by the GOP. First, however, let us examine how the party operated as a minority within the contemporary House.

THE DILEMMA OF OPPOSITION   With the exception of a modest number of Northeastern Republicans (sometimes called Gypsy Moths), the generally conservative Republicans have maintained reasonably high levels of party voting (see Table 7–2). As members of a long-standing minority in the House, Republicans found themselves holding little authority, which freed them to pursue a variety of strategies in seeking to affect policy outcomes.[41] Simple hard-boiled opposition always served as one alternative, of course, but historically, many Republicans have opted to cooperate with the Democratic majority, hoping to affect policies in committee or by providing key votes on the floor. The Rayburn-era House presented frequent opportunities for committees' ranking minority

---

[38]On the theory of partisan control, see Gary W. Cox and Matthew McCubbins, *Legislative Leviathan* (Berkeley: University of California Press, 1993); for a Republican analysis of Democratic control of the House, see Representatives Armey, Dunn, and Shays, "It's Long Enough."

[39]Barbara Sinclair, "The Emergence of Strong Leadership in the 1980s House of Representatives," *Journal of Politics* 54 (August 1992): pp. 657–684.

[40]Rohde, *Parties and Leaders in the Post-Reform House,* p. 174.

[41]See Jones, "Somebody Must Be Trusted."

members to become important forces in shaping congressional policies. For example, in the 1950s and 1960s, Appropriations Committee chair Clarence Cannon (D-Mo.) consulted not just regularly, but almost continuously, with ranking minority member John Taber (R-N.Y.) in reaching agreements on spending bills.[42]

In the 1970s and 1980s, House Republicans found themselves in increasingly difficult straits. First, they often were expected to support the policies of a Republican president, even though their minority status denied them any effective means to implement the executive agendas articulated by Nixon, Reagan, and Bush. Second, Democratic majorities, especially after 1982, acted in highly partisan ways within committees and on the House floor. Republicans could do little in the face of the Rules Committee decisions to structure floor debates and votes, and the Speaker's control of scheduling allowed them little voice in decision making on either policies or procedures. A strong Democratic leadership and an increasingly unified set of Democratic members meant that House Republicans enjoyed few opportunities to influence outcomes.

In step with its generally conservative membership and often in reaction to the strengthened, sometimes arrogant, Democratic leadership, the House minority frequently chose confrontational strategies through the 1980s and into the 1990s. Indeed, the well-publicized actions of Representatives Newt Gingrich (R-Ga.), Robert Walker (R-Pa.), and Richard Armey (R-Tex.), among many others, heightened tensions in the increasingly partisan House. Gingrich enlisted other young, activist Representatives to join him in the Conservative Opportunity Society, an informal grouping that functioned simultaneously as in-House think tank and guerrilla base in challenging the established powers of both parties.[43]

Two decisions — one imposed by the Democrats, the other taken by the Republican conference — demonstrated the growing strength of the confrontational elements within the GOP. On May 1, 1985, following an extended and highly partisan process, the House opted in a partisan vote to give a contested seat to an Indiana Democratic incumbent, even though the state had certified the Republican challenger as the winner of the November election. Every Republican House member marched out of the chamber in protest; even the most moderate, least confrontational Republicans found this decision too much to swallow. Representative Vin Weber (R-Minn.), a Gingrich ally, observed that "it was essential to Newt and his success to drive home the point that after [thirty] years . . . something corrupting had happened to Democratic rule and it was just not in our interest to be in bed with the Democrats."[44]

---

[42]Richard F. Fenno, Jr., *The Power of the Purse* (Boston: Little, Brown, 1966).

[43]For a pre-Republican majority view of the party as minority, see William F. Connelly, Jr., and John F. Pitney, Jr., *Congress' Permanent Minority?* (Lanham, MD: Littlefield, Adams), 1994.

[44]Quoted in Dan Balz and Charles R. Babcock, "How Newt Climbed the Hill," *Washington Post National Weekly Edition*, January 9–15, 1995, p. 11.

The second decision came from within the Republican conference four years later. President Bush tapped House Minority Whip Dick Cheney (R-Wyo.) to become secretary of defense. The ensuing leadership contest pitted Gingrich against veteran Representative Edward Madigan (R-Ill.). Buoyed by the early support of some frustrated moderates such as Nancy Johnson (R-Conn.), Gingrich won the whip post by an 89-87 count. By the narrowest of margins, the Republican conference had decided to move in a confrontational direction.

In the early 1990s, Republicans sought to link the unpopularity of the Congress with its Democratic leadership, especially in the House. In a comprehensive broadside, Representatives Richard Armey (R-Tex.), Jennifer Dunn (R-Wash.), and Christopher Shays (R-Conn.) published the extensive attack on an unresponsive and allegedly corrupt Democratic House. They concluded, for example, that "forty years of single party control of the House of Representatives has created a *corrupt institution isolated from public sentiment. . . .* the ruling party has collectively used [its] powers to partisan ends. It has unleashed its investigatory power on enemies in the other party, while turning a blind eye and a deaf ear to equal or worse violations by some of its own. It has used its power over support institutions [such as the House Post Office] to give jobs to its supporters and to cover up scandals within them."[45]

In sum, members of the Republican House minority chose to oppose with increasing aggressiveness and hostility, as they sought to link an unpopular postreform Congress with its Democratic leadership. Given that Republicans became the majority and that no Republican incumbent lost his or her seat in the 1994 midterm elections, the conclusion can be drawn that they succeeded, at least in the short term. Over the longer haul, the increasing levels of partisan hostility and attacks on the House itself have reduced the possibility of civil discourse and serious deliberation on Capitol Hill.

THE REPUBLICANS ORGANIZE THE HOUSE, 1994   In the wake of the 1994 sweep, which gave Republicans a gain of fifty-two seats and a 230-205 margin in the House,[46] the Republican conference approved rules for the party and the chamber that centralized leadership authority more firmly than at any time since the overthrow of Speaker Cannon. Building on the examples and structures provided by congressional Democrats in the postreform era, the Republican membership empowered Speaker Newt Gingrich to dominate the reconfiguration of many House practices and procedures, as well as giving him great power in selecting committee chairs and making committee appointments.

More than any party leader since Cannon, Gingrich received a sweeping grant of authority from his party colleagues. Moreover, the House Republicans demonstrated overwhelming unity throughout the highly publicized first one

---

[45]Armey, Dunn, and Shays, "It's Long Enough," p. 131.

[46]Democrats actually won 204 seats, but Bernard Sanders (Ind.-Vt.) caucused with them. By late 1995, the defections of Democratic Representatives raised the Republicans' ranks to 234.

hundred days, in which they passed nine of ten items in their so-called Contract with America. The House cast 302 recorded votes in its first three months, and Republican levels of party unity reached near unanimity on all but a few issues such as term limits. On Contract items, 141 of 230 House Republicans voted with the party 100 percent of the time, and of seventy-three GOP freshmen, fifty-three compiled perfect records and seventy-one voted with the party at least 94 percent of the time.[47] This unity came in part from the momentum of capturing the House and having an agenda that had been developed through polling and focus groups, as well as in long discussions among Republicans for more than a decade; Gingrich was also credited for his skillful handling of both the seventy-three first-term members and the moderate wing of the party within the House. Indeed, "Gingrich has sought to encourage, rather than suppress the activist tendencies of the freshmen" by providing key committee appointments to the Appropriations, Budget, and Ways and Means Committees, as well as meeting with a different group of Republican freshmen every week.[48] Moderate Representative Sherwood Boehlert (R-N.Y.) observed that Gingrich proved a good listener, as "he challenges the moderates to unite, talk things over and come up with a plan."[49]

Beyond the Contract and a policy vision of a smaller national government, Gingrich's 1995 backing in the conference derived in large part from two perceptions: (1) Many junior members concluded that they owed their elections to him because of financial support, a nationalized election, and, for a lot of them, personal campaign visits; and (2) almost all House Republicans understood that they would not have won control in 1994 save for Gingrich's persistence and majority-building activities over the previous decade.

The first few months of the 104th Congress gave the impression that the Congress, at least in the House of Representatives, had become a parliamentary body; that is, the majority party could move its agenda through the legislature on its own schedule, essentially ignoring the minority Democrats. Indeed, Speaker Gingrich's ideal as a party leader was Benjamin Disraeli, the Tory leader who not only controlled the House of Commons, but who created his own majority through the rough and tumble of electoral politics.[50] Given the enthusiasm, homogeneity, and tactical advantages of the GOP majority, if the House alone could have decided which bills, in what form, would become law, the unified Republicans[51] would have passed substantive legislation that

---

[47]Donna Cassatta, "Republicans Bask in Success in Rousing Performance," *Congressional Quarterly Weekly Report,* April 8, 1995, p. 990.

[48]Carroll J. Doherty, "Time and Tax Cuts Will Test GOP Freshman Solidarity," *Congressional Quarterly Weekly Report,* April 1, 1995, p. 916. See also, James G. Gimpel, *Fulfilling the Contract* (Boston: Allyn & Bacon, 1996).

[49]Cassatta, "Republicans Bask in Success of Rousing Performance," p. 990.

[50]Ronald M. Peters, "The Republican Speakership" (paper presented at the 1996 American Political Science Association meetings, Chicago), p. 9.

[51]On party votes (Table 7–2), House Republicans supported the party position more than nine times out of ten in 1995, the highest figure in the post–World War II House.

truly would have been revolutionary — going beyond the Contract to eliminate several Cabinet Department positions and to enact far-reaching restrictions on federal regulations.

But the U.S. House is not a parliamentary body, nor was Speaker Gingrich a prime minister. The Republican majority had to contend with the constitutional constraints embodied in a Democratic president and a Senate that often requires a supermajority (sixty votes to break a filibuster) to work its will (see below and Chapter 8).[52] As 1995 wore on, the euphoria of the first 100 days gradually changed to exhaustion brought on by endless negotiations over the unresolved budget issues and a series of continuing resolutions to fund the government for short periods of time (from a few days to a few weeks, during the fall of 1995).[53] As with the strengthened Democratic leadership of the 1980s, the Republican version of enhanced party leadership remained constrained by the preferences of the party's membership. As one GOP House member put it, "We tried to do too much, and there was no exit strategy when the government shut down. And we had a whiner [Gingrich] for a spokesman."[54]

The narrow Republican majorities of the Gingrich Speakership (230-204 in the 104th Congress, 228-206 in the 105th, both with one independent) allowed the Republican leader little leeway. Even when party voting reached historically high levels, they found themselves at a great disadvantage in dealing with a generally united Democratic party in the House, a politically astute Democrat in the White House and a Senate Republican majority that could not overcome Democratic filibusters. For House Republicans, former Gingrich aide Tony Blankley noted, "There is no point in declaring war when you've got a squad and you need a battalion."[55] Although moderate Republicans could and did hold the majority hostage to their demands, on occasion, it was the die-hard conservatives, who had provided the margin of the GOP's (and Gingrich's) initial 1994 victory, that caused the lion's share of trouble for the leadership. Indeed, as congressional scholar Dan Palazzalo concluded, Gingrich's military allusions did not fit the partisan situation, in that "political parties aren't armies. They're fractious organizations."[56]

The House Republicans demonstrated their factiousness by dumping Gingrich, mounting a major challenge to Majority Leader Armey, and deposing Conference Chairman Representative John Boehner (R-Ohio), a Gingrich

---

[52]On the limitations imposed by constitutional constraints and Senate Rules, see Keith Krehbiel, *Pivotal Politics* (Chicago: University of Chicago Press, 1998).

[53]This is a complex and difficult story, best told, perhaps, in Elizabeth Drew's dense, insider account, *Showdown: The Struggle Between the Gingrich Congress and the Clinton White House* (New York: Touchstone, 1996).

[54]Quoted in Richard E. Cohen, "On the Brink," *National Journal,* February 22, 1997, p. 368.

[55]Katherine Q. Seelye, "Gingrich Draws Fire from the Right," *New York Times,* October 25, 1998, A22.

[56]Dan Palazzalo, quoted in Seelye, "Gingrich Draws Fire from the Right," p. A22.

loyalist. But with the 1998 elections, the fallout from intense interparty struggles during the leadership contests, and Speaker-designate Livingston's resignation, Republicans could scarcely hope for productive policy making in the 106th Congress. Rather, they would need to deal with the president that they had impeached in December 1998, and a Democratic Minority Leader (Representative Richard Gepardt D-Mo.) who put aside his presidential ambitions in order to recapture (or try to) the House for his party in the 2000 elections.

The Senate: Partisanship without Strong Leadership

Historically, the Senate has not encouraged strong partisanship or strong party leadership as much as the House. Writing in 1993, political scientist Steven Smith concluded that "although party cohesiveness and polarization ebb and flow, creating variation in the conditions associated with strong party leadership, only for a brief period in the past forty years has a Senate party been so strong that it could win most votes without help from the other party."[57] This assertion rings true, yet the job of Senate party leaders has changed considerably over the years. Unlike their House counterparts, Senate leaders have not seen their positions consistently strengthened in the postreform Congress. When partisanship has become sharply defining, it has most often occurred in a specific context, as with the Republicans' continuing opposition to Democratic proposals on health care and other initiatives in the last few months of 1994; this unity was built largely on the anticipation of capturing the chamber rather than any coherent program that brought individual Republican senators together.

Each Senate party elects a floor leader and a whip, as well as chairs of committees on policy, committee assignments, and campaigns.[58] Although Republicans have historically distributed these jobs more widely than have Democrats, the fact is that, aside from the majority and minority leader positions, no one slot is especially important. Undeniably, Senate leaders possess many fewer weapons than do their House counterparts. Rather than controlling the chamber's schedule, the majority leader endlessly negotiates and renegotiates the order of business. The minority leader serves as his chief sparring partner in these sessions,[59] and each leader must represent the interests of his own party's members. Nor do Senate party caucuses provide broad grants of authority to their respective leaders; rather, the fundamental expectation of party leaders is

---

[57]Steven S. Smith, "Forces of Change in Senate Party Leadership and Organization," in Dodd and Oppenheimer, *Congress Reconsidered,* 5th ed., p. 265.

[58]Roger Davidson and Walter Oleszek, *Congress and Its Members,* 4th ed. (Washington, DC: CQ Press, 1994), p. 192.

[59]A brief period of viewing C-SPAN II's coverage of the Senate will flesh out this description. Majority Leader Trent Lott (R-Miss.) and Minority Leader Tom Daschle (D-S.D.), along with a handful of other interested senators, often converse at length about how the schedule will proceed. Nothing is resolved until all actors are satisfied with the arrangements.

TABLE 7-4
Senate and House Party Unity Scores: 1969-1972; 1989-1992; and 1995-1998

Chamber and Party	1969-1972 Unity*	1989-1992 Unity*	1995-1998 Unity*
House Democrats (all)	71%	86%	81%
House Southern Democrats	48	78	74
House Republicans	74	80	88
Senate Democrats (all)	73	81	76
Senate Southern Democrats	51	72	90
Senate Republicans	73	81	87

*Four-year averages. Scores reflect the percentage of occasions that members vote with a majority of their fellow partisans on votes in which most (>.50 percent) Democrats vote against most (>50 percent) Republicans.

Source: Norman J. Ornstein, Thomas E. Mann, and Michael J. Malbin, eds., *Vital Statistics on Congress, 1997–1998* (Washington, DC: CQ Press/AEI, 1998), pp. 211–212; and *CQ Weekly,* January 9, 1999, pp. 79–81, 93–94.

to serve "the *personal* political needs of party colleagues."[60] Former Senator Fred Harris, writing in 1993, argued that party conferences (or caucuses) have grown in strength within the Senate of the 1980s and 1990s, but that these groupings have largely allowed individual senators, all with their own agendas, to influence leaders who continually seek consensus.[61]

Partisan voting levels have risen in the Senate, although not as much as in the House. Comparing the first four years of the Nixon administration to the four years of the Bush presidency, Senate partisanship, although very similar to the House in the earlier era, did not keep pace (see Table 7–4). Moreover, increasing levels of partisan voting do not necessarily result from strong party leadership. As in the House, the Senate Democratic party has become more homogeneous, as Southern senators act more like their Northern peers and as Republicans win higher proportions of Southern seats. In addition, many of the votes in the Bush era came on fiscal and budgetary matters, which provided the Democrats with very little incentive to help a Republican administration.

Even though their authority is close to nil, their power modest at best, and their influence open to question, contemporary Senate leaders work extraordinarily hard just to keep the chamber from bogging down entirely. Former Majority Leader Robert Byrd has labeled the responsibilities of the floor leader as essentially those of a "slave" to his fellow senators.[62] A leader spends countless hours on the Senate floor seeking to reconcile the interests and egos of one hundred separate lords and ladies, each of whom jealously guards his or

---

[60]Smith, "Forces of Change in Senate Party Leadership and Organization," p. 262. Emphasis added.

[61]Fred R. Harris, *Deadlock or Decision: The U.S. Senate and the Rise of National Politics* (New York: Oxford University Press, 1993), pp. 184ff.

[62]Quoted in Roger H. Davidson, "Senate Leaders: Janitors for an Untidy Chamber?" in Lawrence Dodd and Bruce Oppenheimer, eds., *Congress Reconsidered,* 3rd ed. (Washington, DC: CQ Press, 1985), p. 225.

her own prerogatives. Overall, the contemporary Senate demands of its top leaders at least five overlapping tasks:

1. Managing the affairs of their respective parties

2. Scheduling Senate business in accord with members' wishes

3. Monitoring floor deliberations, including the crafting of unanimous consent agreements that govern debates/votes

4. Serving as a conduit between the Senate and the White House (and the House) in managing an increasing number of interbranch/interchamber agreements (e.g., on budgets)

5. Representing the party and the Senate to the media[63]

Compared to their House counterparts, leaders in the postreform Senate spend much more time on management tasks (1–3 above) and much less on the formulation of policy alternatives. In addition, since the 1950s to 1960s, Senate floor leaders have changed their relationships with presidents and the media in ways that have not enhanced their power.

One of the major tools of floor leaders such as Republican Everett Dirksen (1959–1969) and Democrat Lyndon Johnson (1953–1960) was their regular access to the president, especially through unpublicized phone contacts or informal meetings. Dirksen and Johnson both maintained excellent relationships with President Eisenhower, and when Johnson became president in 1963, relations between him and Dirksen, the Minority Leader, reached new levels of intimacy. One senator concluded that Dirksen and Johnson were so close that "they understood, they knew, what was going on in each other's mind."[64] In fact, Dirksen often knew more about Johnson's thinking than did Majority Leader Mike Mansfield. This worked to Dirksen's great advantage in the early years of LBJ's presidency; later, Dirksen remained close to Johnson, but as their efforts increasingly focused on the Vietnam War, his ties ultimately diminished his authority among his fellow Republicans.

If Dirksen gained strength from his links to a series of presidents, he also demonstrated the value of taking his partisan opposition to the press. Wonderfully quotable and witty, Dirksen understood that he could hold his small (thirty-six or fewer senators from 1959 to 1969) Republican minority together in part by focusing attention on himself. Twenty years later, Senators Robert Dole (R-Kans.) and George Mitchell (D-Maine) won their respective floor

---

[63]This list comes from Roger H. Davidson, "Senate Leaders," p. 236. Steven Smith, writing in 1993, eight years after Davidson's article, depicts leaders' responsibilities in terms of more partisan expectations of the members; although many of these relate to individual reelection campaigns and other personal needs, there exists at least the possibility of substance-oriented leadership. See Smith, "Forces of Change in Senate Party Leadership and Organization."

[64]Senator Joseph Pearson (R-Kans.), quoted in Burdett A. Loomis, "Everett McKinley Dirksen: The Consummate Minority Leader," in Richard S. Baker and Roger H. Davidson, eds., *First Among Equals* (Washington, DC: CQ Press, 1990), p. 252.

leader roles in part because of their communications skills, but neither Dole, Mitchell, nor any of the post-Dirksen leaders benefited from strong, personal ties with any of the post-Johnson presidents. In fact, Dole as Majority Leader maintained a healthy distance from the Reagan White House, and Mitchell (leader between 1989 and 1994) often served as a tough-minded partisan adversary to President Bush. Both these performances came at the behest of their party colleagues in the Senate, who wanted Dole to remain relatively independent and Mitchell to provide a partisan counterpoint to the executive branch. In the post-1994 Republican era, neither Majority Leader Lott nor Minority Leader Daschle has cultivated strong personal links to the White House.

In the end, regardless of their ties to presidents or the attention accorded them by the media, Senate leaders must operate under rules that do not allow them much control over the pace of floor debate or the content of amendments offered by individual senators.[65] Unlike the House, the Senate is not a majoritarian body. A determined minority of forty-one senators can stop the body in its tracks through the filibuster, and a single member can often hold it hostage by rejecting a request for a unanimous consent agreement that governs the conduct of floor debate on a given issue. Unlike their House counterparts, Senate leaders cannot easily structure votes or schedules, nor can they routinely set time limits for debate. Rather, leaders must cajole their colleagues, privately and publicly; compromise with them; and provide consideration for a hundred different schedules, preferences, and egos.

Still, there is little question that the Senate has grown more partisan since the 1970s, under Democratic and Republican regimes alike. This trend is illustrated in the patterns of partisan voting, which culminated in historically high levels during the 104th Congress. Most notably, during the second session (1996) of the 104th, Senate Republicans compiled a higher party unity score (89 percent loyalty on all party votes) than did their House colleagues (87 percent), and the 89 percent figure represented the highest level of partisan voting by either party in the Senate for more than forty years.[66] Thus, even in a year that produced substantial legislative compromises between the Congress and President Clinton, Senate voting patterns reflected a historic level of partisanship. In part this occurred because Republican Majority Leader Dole was in the process of successfully seeking the Republican nomination for president. But the partisanship did not wane with Dole's resignation from the Senate and the choice of Trent Lott to succeed him as floor leader.

Although Lott quickly proved himself a skillful deal-maker, he also has reflected a style of leadership that was honed in the House, first as a staffer to

---

[65]See Steven Smith, *The American Congress* (Boston: Houghton Mifflin, 1995), pp. 232ff, for an excellent extended example of the problems inherent in making the Senate move with even moderate speed on a major issue.

[66]Figures drawn from *Vital Statistics on Congress, 1995–1996,* Norman J. Ornstein, Thomas E. Mann, and Michael J. Malbin, eds. (Washington, DC: CQ Press/AEI, 1995), 213–214; *Congressional Quarterly Weekly Report,* December 21, 1996, p. 3461.

Representative William Colmer (D-Miss.), then as a backbencher (1973–1980), and subsequently as minority whip, a position he captured after only four terms in office. Giving up his House leadership position, Lott won his Senate seat in 1988. Immediately after winning reelection in 1994, he successfully challenged Senator Alan Simpson (R-Wyo.), the sitting minority whip. Lott has structured the Senate leadership in a more collegial, participatory way than did Dole, who often tended to keep his own counsel as floor leader.[67] A collegial approach promotes party loyalty, noted Senator Connie Mack (R-Fla.), who observed that relying on the "Conference becomes a means to that end."[68] Led by Majority Leader Lott, Republican senators, while defending their individual rights within the institution, have moved to mute some of the intense individualism that has characterized the Senate of the past twenty years.

Still, during the 1999 impeachment trial, Majority Leader Lott and Minority Leader Daschle demonstrated consistent levels of consultation and collegiality that differed sharply from the party leaders' relations — or lack thereof — in the House. Senator John Breaux observed, "Daschle and Lott speak more in one day than Gephardt and Gingrich speak in one year."[69]

Rarely, however, can Senate leaders take full credit for making their institution run even passably well. Rather, a functioning Senate, no matter how messy and inefficient, requires that its leaders act more as facilitators than as aggressive commanders. I n the final analysis, the notion of Senate leadership remains largely a contradiction in terms within an institution that continues to serve its individual members.

PARTY AND THE LIMITS OF CENTRALIZATION IN THE POSTREFORM CONGRESS

The very individualism of the Senate provides one clear set of limitations on the potential for strong, centralized leadership within the Congress. In the House, however, party leadership has grown extremely strong, as evidenced by partisan voting levels, the extended whip system, and the formidable powers that leaders possess to control appointments, schedules, and legislative procedures. Although Republicans, in the wake of their forty years in the minority, granted Speaker Gingrich extraordinary powers over committee appointments, legislative schedules, and policy agendas, the leadership remains beholden to the party conference, just as Democratic leaders served as agents of their caucus.

---

[67]Donna Cassatta, "Lott's Task: Balance the Demands of His Chamber and His Party," *Congressional Quarterly Weekly Report,* March 8, 1997, pp. 567–571.

[68]Quoted in Richard E. Cohen, "The Senate Broker," *National Journal,* December 21, 1996, p. 2733.

[69]Frank Bruni, "Senate Leaders Forge New Ties in Trial's Fires," *New York Times,* February 7, 1999, p. 29.

And on numerous issues neither party, in or out of the Congress, can generate well-articulated positions.

In 1993, for example, many House Democrats found it impossible to vote for President Clinton's initial budget, which was actively supported by their leaders. Only grudgingly were enough Democrats rounded up, arms sore from extensive twisting, to pass the budget agreement. In that case, at least, Clinton could rely on Democratic House leaders to act on his behalf in seeking out the 218 Democrats, among them Representative Margolies-Mezvinsky (see Chapter 1), essential for the budget package's success.

Conversely, Democratic party leaders found themselves profoundly split over the North American Free Trade Agreement (NAFTA) in 1993, which President Clinton vigorously supported. While Speaker Tom Foley maintained a low profile, Majority Leader Richard Gephardt (D-Mo.) and Chief Whip David Bonoir (D-Mich.), who both hail from the industrial "Rust Belt," led the opposition to NAFTA despite the position of their party's first president in more than a decade. Why the split? The answer is straightforward: Democrats in the House were deeply divided, to the point that a majority would vote against the agreement. This opposition stemmed not from internal House politics, but from the profound hostility toward NAFTA among many key party constituencies, none more important than organized labor.

The House Democratic Caucus handled this division by treading gingerly around it, as did the whip organization. Deputy Whip John Lewis (D-Ga.) reported, "In the regular whip meetings, we just don't talk about it."[70] Unlike votes on abortion or the death penalty, where party may take a back seat to moral considerations, the NAFTA debate focused on crucial long-term policy issues of utmost importance to the Democrats. The extent to which the majority party could not follow its own president illustrates the limits to centralized leadership within the contemporary House. Constituency pressures, contributors' concerns, and the entreaties of organized interests demonstrated the continuing power of local forces on House members both as individuals and as a bloc within their caucus. At the same time, partisan divisions on a single, emotional issue such as NAFTA rarely lead to irreconcilable splits. As one House Democrat put it, "I don't think Gephardt or Bonoir are suffering any consequences for not supporting it. The administration needs Gephardt and Bonoir for a great many things. Plus, Gephardt and Bonoir represent the majority of Democrats in the House [in terms of NAFTA votes]."[71] Indeed, in the 106th Congress, "fast-track" trade legislation (see Chapter 3) remained off the president's agenda, largely because of Democratic opposition.

Much the same thing occurred among House Republicans during the 1995 debate on term limits. Although almost 80 percent of the GOP House contin-

---

[70]John Lewis, quoted in Robin Toner, "Divided Sentiments, Divided Loyalties," *New York Times,* November 16, 1993, p. A9.

[71]Toner, "Divided Sentiments."

gent voted in favor of the least restrictive proposal, Representative Henry Hyde (R-Ill.), Judiciary Committee chairman, led the cross-partisan block that vigorously opposed any form of limitation. Neither party's leadership has been able to construct agreement where there was none; not since Speaker Cannon had a leader possessed adequate powers to succeed at such a task, and in the end Cannon's procedural majority fell apart when he pushed too hard on substantive issues that divided the Republican backbenchers.

Nevertheless, given the high levels of partisan voting in the contemporary Congress, it is tempting to see the congressional party, especially the House majority, as dominating the legislative process — at least on many of the most salient issues. When legislative parties consist of homogeneous groups of partisans (e.g., mostly conservative Republicans and liberal Democrats), and the gap between them is wide, it makes sense that individual legislators, at least in the House, are willing to give up some individual power in order to give the larger group — the legislative party — more power. Both Democratic and Republican rank-and-file members have voted to restrain, and even replace, their leaders. At the same time leaders have great incentives to hold party majorities together, to the extent that those majorities reflect their members' policy preferences.[72]

Leadership in the contemporary U.S. Congress is surely stronger than it was between the 1920s and the 1970s, but many real constraints remain firmly in place, especially in the highly individualistic Senate. In the House, strong centralized leadership is possible, even likely, and partiship has risen sharply in the postreform era. Nevertheless, such leadership remains based on power willingly but not unreservedly granted by an attentive collection of activist members.[73]

---

[72]There is extensive theoretical literature about the importance of parties, their capacity to organize the legislative chamber, and their ultimate impact on policy outcomes. See, among others, John H. Aldrich and David W. Rohde, "The Transition to Republican Rule in the House: Implications for Theories of Congressional Politics," *Political Science Quarterly* 112: pp. 541–567; and "The Consequences of Party Organization in the House" (paper presented at "Congress and the President in a Partisan Era," Texas A&M University, February 5–6, 1999).

[73]Rohde, *Parties and Leaders in the Post-Reform House,* chap. 6.

Eight

PRESIDENTIAL-CONGRESSIONAL RELATIONS: FOCUS, AUTHORITY, AND NEGOTIATION

I t is January 1999. President Clinton has spent a year in the shadow of the Monica Lewinsky scandal, and the House has voted to impeach him, albeit on a largely partisan vote. The Senate is embarking upon a trial of the president. Both the House and the Senate retain their narrow Republican majorities as President Clinton heads into the last two years of his term of office — the lame-duck period for every two-term chief executive. If there were ever a time that the U.S. Congress should tower over the president in terms of setting the agenda and dominating the policy debate, this should be it. Right? Wrong.

The resilient Bill Clinton remained strong in the polls, at least in terms of job approval. Equally important, the public expressed an *increasing* amount of confidence in him to address the nation's ills, while simultaneously expressing a *declining* level of faith in the Congress's capacity to address significant issues. On January 4, 1995, the first day of the first Gingrich-led Republican Congress, the public gave the "Republicans in Congress" a 54-to-30 percent edge over President Clinton in response to the question: "Who do you trust to handle the nation's main problems?" Four years later, when the president delivered his State of the Union message — even as his trial proceeded in the Senate — the public's response to this question was completely reversed: 50 percent favored the president, while only 32 percent placed more trust in the congressional Republicans.[1]

As the impeachment process has demonstrated, the politics of the separation of powers is alive (if not necessarily well), but Clinton's remarkable performance in office demonstrates how, even under the most adverse circumstances,

---

[1]Andrew Taylor, "A Manifesto for 2000," *CQ Weekly,* January 23, 1999, p. 174. Not only did trust in Clinton rise between 1995 and 1999, but it did so in a straight line. Likewise, the Republicans consistently lost ground.

the politics of Capitol Hill are affected by the actions, position, and authority of the resident of 1600 Pennsylvania Avenue.

In his systematic study of presidential leadership of Congress, political scientist George Edwards concludes that "the president is not the ruler of the American state but a vital centralizing force, providing direction and energy for the nation's policy making."[2] The Congress, with its potential for fragmentation and individualism, can ordinarily benefit from focus and direction. Although in 1995 the Speakership of Newt Gingrich offered a historic alternative to strong presidential leadership, in twentieth-century American politics it has been the president whose position has provided the best chance of generating a coherent vision of where the nation should be headed. Convincing the Congress to act on this vision is quite another matter, however.

Setting the agenda is only one aspect of the president's ability to direct the actions of a fragmented Congress. Legislators must also work within a policy-making process that has increasingly given broad authority to the Executive Office of the President. With the growth of programs, regulations, and spending since the New Deal, the institution of the presidency has held the responsibility for making sure that prospective legislation, specific appropriations, and budget decisions compose a roughly coherent whole. The centralized authority for making these decisions has become formalized within the Office of Management and Budget (OMB), a part of the Executive Office of the President.[3] In going about its business, Congress must regularly peer over its collective shoulder, beyond Capitol Hill, to the White House. No matter who occupies 1600 Pennsylvania Avenue or which party organizes the proceedings on Capitol Hill, legislative actions are shaped by the chief executive's preferences and the authority for program and budget review held by OMB.

Ronald Reagan's performance as president demonstrates the potential for central coordination of the policy making process. Immediately after winning the presidency in 1980, President Reagan placed a large tax cut on the legislative agenda, and he lobbied consistently for its passage.[4] The Congress had little choice but to act on this initiative, although there was much politicking and position-taking on the exact nature of the reductions. In the end, the president won much of what he desired, even though most legislators did not agree with Reagan's "supply-side" economics assumptions. His large-scale tax cut proposals dominated the agenda, and lawmakers came under withering pressure to pass the legislation. The executive's agenda-setting power can also work to keep items from receiving serious legislative consideration. Along these lines, President Reagan simply refused to consider reauthorization of clean air legis-

---

[2]George Edwards, *At the Margins* (New Haven, CT: Yale University Press, 1989), p. 234.

[3]See Richard E. Neustadt, "Presidency and Legislation: The Growth of Central Clearance," *American Political Science Review* 48 (1954): pp. 641ff; John Hart, *The Presidential Branch,* 2nd ed. (Chatham, NJ: Chatham House, 1995).

[4]This story is well told in former OMB director David Stockman's *The Triumph of Politics* (New York: Harper & Row, 1986).

lation, which the Congress was scheduled to address in 1982. Given his opposition to this legislation, the Congress kept the 1977 provisions intact through his tenure and waited until 1989–1990 to negotiate with a more receptive Bush administration on a revised clean air bill.[5]

The results of the 1980 election and Ronald Reagan's unwavering commitment to lower taxes combined to generate major congressional action — the deep 1981 tax cut. Conversely, the White House's steadfast opposition to revised clean air regulations and the president's willingness to veto any meaningful legislation meant that Congress could accomplish little until Reagan left office.

The president's ability to dominate the agenda is scarcely his only weapon in his attempts to control the policy processes and outcomes. Using Ronald Reagan's presidency as an example again, at least as systematic as his agenda efforts were his administration's operations, centralized in the OMB, to oversee the status of legislation and increase control over regulations issued throughout the government. With its power to review all executive-branch regulations and thus ensure their compliance with presidential priorities, the OMB sometimes thwarted the legislative intent of laws, directing executive agencies to carry out specific policies.[6]

In the post–Franklin Roosevelt era of large-scale government, presidents cannot always get their way, but their wishes, as expressed in policy agendas or control of the regulatory process, must still be taken into account.[7] Nonetheless, even as the presidency has consistently grown in size and power, Congress has remained — both constitutionally and politically — central to national policy making. Political scientist Mark Peterson points out, "both presidents and the public must learn to recognize Congress as the executive's legislative partner." As in any partnership, the actors play distinctive roles; Peterson argues that presidents "should exploit the vantage point of their lofty position to bring coherence to policy making by functioning as agenda *focusers*. . . . Ideas for the nation's agenda will have originated in Congress and elsewhere in the nation. . . . Rather than attempting to be the government and the repository of all solutions for all problems, presidents would identify the problems, challenge others to respond, and work with other participants in the process to craft possible policy solutions."[8]

Reagan's determined support of a tax cut and his consistent opposition to renewed clean air legislation illustrate two ways in which the president can

---

[5]See Richard E. Cohen, *Washington at Work* (New York: Macmillan, 1992), chap. 3; Gary C. Bryner, *Blue Skies, Green Politics* (Washington, DC: CQ Press, 1993), pp. 86–93.

[6]James P. Pfiffner, "The President and the Post-Reform Congress," in Roger H. Davidson, ed., *The Postreform Congress* (New York: St. Martin's, 1992), pp. 216–217.

[7]Paul Light, *The President's Agenda,* rev. ed (Baltimore: Johns Hopkins University Press, 1991).

[8]Mark Peterson, *Legislating Together* (Cambridge, MA: Harvard University Press, 1990), p. 295. Emphasis added.

focus congressional attention. On the tax cut, his strong emphasis essentially required the Congress to respond to his initial proposal. Both in terms of modifying his proposal and addressing the issue with great speed, the Congress reacted directly to Reagan's focusing efforts. On the other hand, his unwillingness to consider further clean air legislation gave the Congress the freedom to explore potential courses of action during the 1980s. Thus, when President George Bush signaled his willingness to negotiate seriously on clean air in 1989, the Congress could move with reasonable speed toward a productive legislative partnership, in that it had hashed out many disagreements during extensive deliberations over the 1981–1989 period.[9]

When the president focuses attention on a given issue, especially in the form of specific proposals, he ordinarily acts to centralize the legislative process. Party leaders and the press pay special attention to major presidential initiatives, particularly when the White House maintains continuing and well-coordinated pressure. All things being equal, legislators of the president's party would like to support his proposals. In the absence of presidential leadership, senators and representatives enjoy more latitude, and the congressional fragmentation of constituencies, committees, and interests is more likely to dominate the policy-making process.

In the end, presidents can hope to exercise no more than partial and temporary influence over legislative actions and outcomes. Presidents such as Franklin Roosevelt, Lyndon Johnson, and Ronald Reagan won great victories, but all suffered serious setbacks. Others, such as Dwight Eisenhower, sought to exercise influence largely in private ways. Nonetheless, even the weakest post–World War II president, Republican Gerald Ford, who rose from serving as an unelected vice president to face a hostile, activist Democratic Congress in the wake of Richard Nixon's resignation, exercised considerable power. In his 1974–1976 tenure, he set much of the legislative agenda through his budget-writing authority, and he regularly exercised his constitutional weapon of the veto, thereby affecting legislative consideration of controversial matters.

This chapter emphasizes various elements of presidential-congressional relations, ranging from constitutional roles to the centralization of policymaking that derives from deficit-based budget policies. In addition, the impact of divided government (when the presidency and the Congress are controlled by opposing parties) is explored, in that this has been the most common political context in the United States since 1969. Finally, we consider the temporary nature of any president's capacity to provide focus and direction to the necessarily messy business of writing laws. The president can dominate parts of the process of agenda setting, but many issues emerge without his prompting. The president may win numerous legislative victories and suffer his share of defeats, but many bills pass with little presidential expression of interest. And although the OMB can monitor regulation writing, it has neither the staff nor

---

[9]See Cohen, *Washington at Work*; Bryner, *Blue Skies, Green Politics*.

the authority to control the entire process. In short, the modern presidency, no matter its size and reach, cannot dominate either the policy debates or the outcomes of all policy initiatives. As Bill Clinton discovered in facing an energized Republican majority on Capitol Hill, presidents must confront and negotiate with a Congress that can both originate and pass policies of its own creation, as well as being able to oversee the administration's execution of the laws.

THE PRESIDENT AS CHIEF LEGISLATOR

As a rule, no member of Congress is as important a legislator as is the chief executive, although in 1995 Speaker Newt Gingrich surely tested the absolute nature of such a proposition. Whether in setting the congressional agenda, twisting a lawmaker's arm to support a favored measure, or threatening to veto an unsatisfactory bill, the president can affect the legislative process more forcefully, and in more ways, than the most influential senator or representative. But does this mean that he gets what he wants? Hardly. A generation of research in presidential-congressional relations has demonstrated that neither partner can overwhelm the other. Rather, as Richard Neustadt observed in 1960 and Charles Jones confirmed more than thirty years later, the separate institutions of the Congress and the presidency must both share and compete for power.[10]

The Constitution offers only modest guidance in defining presidential–congressional relations. For example, Article I gives the Congress the power to declare war, but in the post–World War II era, presidents have committed American troops to three warlike conflicts (in Korea, Vietnam, and the Persian Gulf) without any formal declaration of war. Congress did agree to the actions through legislation and appropriations, but its attempt through the 1973 War Powers Act to wrest effective control from the executive branch of most decisions to commit troops has proved notably unsuccessful.[11] Likewise, the presidential power to veto legislation is a potent formal weapon, but one that is often most effective when used sparingly. Gerald Ford, for example, regularly employed the veto during his two-plus years as president, but largely as a defensive tool against the overwhelmingly Democratic Ninety-fourth Congress.[12] More creative use of veto power is available to most presidents. By making credible threats to veto unacceptable bills, presidents can enhance their capability to shape legislation, thus turning a negative power into a positive tool to influence policymaking on Capitol Hill.

---

[10]Richard Neustadt, *Presidential Power* (New York: Wiley, 1960); Charles O. Jones, *The Presidency in a Separated System* (Washington, DC: Brookings Institution, 1994).

[11]Pfiffner, "The President and the Post-Reform Congress," p. 233. More generally, see Louis Fisher, *Presidential War Power* (Lawrence: University Press of Kansas, 1995).

[12]Richard Watson, *Presidential Vetoes and Public Policy* (Lawrence: University Press of Kansas, 1993), p. 35.

Regardless of the executive's formal, constitutional powers, much of the president's ability to affect legislation results from the policy-making context, which comprises principally the president's electoral base, his popularity in the country, and the partisan balance within the Congress. A president who is woefully unpopular (such as Truman), who is confronted with large, opposing-party majorities in both houses of Congress (such as Ford), or who is elected with a modest percentage of the vote (as with Clinton's 43 percent in 1992) will have a difficult time winning a string of major legislative victories.

Agenda Setting and the Prospects for Presidential Influence

The core of the president's legislative strength lies in his ability to influence national policy agenda issues in both ordinary and extraordinary ways. The most consistent and predictable impact of the presidency comes through the centralization of the annual budget and the executive's capacity to monitor and pull together disparate proposals that bubble up within dozens of separate bureaucratic units. Indeed, the governmental agenda is ordinarily full; that is, there are always many issues, initiatives, and problems for presidents and legislators to consider. As Charles Jones observes, "Since it is not possible to treat all issues at once, members of Congress and others anxiously await the designation of priorities. These presidential choices are typically from a list that is familiar to other policy actors. Nonetheless, a designator is important, even if he is a Republican having to work with a Democratic Congress. As in any organization, there is a need for someone in authority to say: 'Let's start here.'"[13]

Aside from designating certain issues as priorities in the course of normal policy making, almost all presidents offer up some major initiatives that depart markedly from past policies. These proposals — Nixon's welfare reforms, Carter's energy plans, Reagan's tax cuts, Clinton's health care proposals — would require large-scale changes in existing policies and would disrupt well-established policy subsystems made up of congressional committees, interest groups, and bureaucratic units.[14] The president can push only a limited number of major items on to the legislative agenda; Presidents Carter and Clinton both found it difficult to move ahead on a wide range of substantial issues, especially when some of those issues, such as the North American Free Trade Agreement for Clinton, were inherited from the preceding administration. Even so, through the annual State of the Union message and other public pronouncements, presidents can consistently orient the discourse within both the Congress and the public at large.[15]

---

[13]Jones, *The Presidency in a Separated System*, p. 181.

[14]See Frank R. Baumgartner and Bryan D. Jones, *Agendas and Instability in American Politics* (Chicago: University of Chicago Press, 1993); Paul R. Schulman, *Large-Side Policy Making* (New York: Elsevier, 1980).

[15]See Jeffrey Cohen, "Presidential Rhetoric and the Public Agenda," *American Journal of Political Science* 39 (February 1995): pp. 87–107.

Ordinarily, the president can focus the attention of the press and the public on a few key issues; on occasion, as with Franklin Roosevelt and Lyndon Johnson, the context permits a broad agenda of large-scale changes. But even for these energetic, forceful leaders who enjoyed the favorable circumstances of large Democratic congressional majorities, the windows of opportunity for focusing legislative attention were relatively brief.[16] Regardless of political circumstances, presidents are well advised to set the agenda on major issues early in their terms — either "move it or lose it."[17] Delay is the enemy of change, and as an institution the Congress encourages delay at every turn in a legislative process that requires a succession of majorities — in committees, in both chambers, and often on conference committee reports. Moreover, presidents begin their terms of office with election victories that provide them with substantial amounts of political capital. Rarely do they increase this store of assets; rather, the longer they wait to introduce key pieces of legislation, the lower the chance of passage.[18]

Even Bill Clinton, a president elected with 43 percent of the popular vote in an era of $200 billion annual budget deficits, could move comprehensive health care reform on to the congressional agenda. But he failed to achieve his policy goal. Leading the 535 legislative horses to the trough does not mean that Clinton or any other president can make them drink. In the final years of his presidency, Clinton did not have the political clout to move major items through the legislative process, even though his skills at legislating had surely grown over his two terms as president. At the same time, despite much congressional opposition, he could prosecute a military action against Serbia in 1999.

In the end, both presidential and congressional dreams of major change produced only limited movement. In the wake of the budget battles in the 104th Congress, "Clinton and the Democrats had to adjust to the New Republican agenda, [while] Republicans had to compromise and learn that the president has substantial power through the veto and public opinion."[19] Despite a budget in balance by 1998, the presidential power to set the agenda through the budget remained sorely constrained. In his 2000 Budget message, laid out in early 1999, Clinton offered an array of modest, relatively inexpensive programs, many centered on education. But an aggressive agenda was simply not in the cards. Rather, "saving" Social Security dominated budget proposals. Regardless of which party controls the Congress, presidents and legislators alike will adopt "strategies of protection" for favored programs, and spending

---

[16]See James L. Sundquist, *Politics and Policy* (Washington, DC: Brookings Institution, 1968); Arthur Schlesinger, Jr., *The Cycles of American History* (Boston: Houghton Mifflin, 1986).

[17]Light, *The President's Agenda,* p. 218.

[18]Paul C. Light, "Passing Nonincremental Policy: Presidential Influence in Congress, Kennedy to Carter," *Congress and the Presidency* 9 (Winter 1981–1982): p. 78.

[19]James Thurber, "Centralization, Devolution, and Turf Protection in the Congressional Budget Process," in Lawrence Dodd and Bruce Oppenheimer, eds., *Congress Reconsidered,* 6th ed. (Washington, DC: CQ Press, 1997), p. 338.

on new initiatives will be difficult to pass,[20] especially in light of the electorate's endorsement of the pragmatism practiced by both branches of government in the late 1990s.

Legislating and the Contexts of Presidential Influence

No matter how successful presidents are in focusing public, media, and congressional attention on a major initiative, they and their aides must continue to participate in the process of lawmaking. The decentralized Congress — whether in its fragmented, contentious mode of the 1970s, its committee-based, conservative mode of the 1950s and early 1960s, or its more partisan mode of the 1980s and 1990s — has imposed great limitations on the ability of presidents to achieve their objectives. Indeed, even a renowned "focuser" like Ronald Reagan, who was widely admired for his single-minded emphasis on tax cuts in 1981, subsequently produced a series of budgets that the Congress felt free to ignore, labeling them "dead on arrival" on Capitol Hill.[21]

In the wake of extended scholarly debates over the nature of presidential influence on Congress, a rough consensus has emerged, which paints presidential power within the legislative process as an important force, but subject to many limitations. At at minimum, some restrictions include those of the "pure context" of a separation-of-powers system; such constitutional restraints are magnified by relatively weak political party organizations and electorally independent, well-staffed legislators who need little help from either presidents or parties to remain in office.[22]

No president can change the Senate rules that provide great advantages to those who would delay legislation through extended debate (the filibuster); likewise, informal congressional practices, such as the Senate's reliance on unanimous consent agreements (see Chapter 9) to conduct much of its business, are beyond the executive's control. In addition, there are other key elements of the policymaking context that further restrain executive actions. Aside from a second-term president's ineligibility to run for reelection (thus being labeled a "lame duck"), these include the president's margin of victory in his previous election, the partisan balance of congressional seats, and the president's standing with the public.[23] Although they do not determine legislative outcomes, these elements do shape the content and scope of executive initiatives, as well as the strategies the president constructs for winning congressional majorities.

---

[20]Thurber, "Centralization, Devolution, and Turf Protection," p. 341.

[21]Allen Schick, *The Federal Budget* (Washington, DC: Brookings Institution, 1995), p. 58.

[22]Peterson, *Legislating Together,* pp. 102ff.

[23]Somewhat strangely, Peterson labels these elements as "malleable" context (*Legislating Together,* pp. 118ff), but of the three, only the president's popularity can change between elections, and ordinarily not as a direct result of his actions.

TABLE 8-1
Electoral, Partisan, and Popularity Context for Newly Elected Presidents, 1960-1992

President	Year Elected, Percentage of Vote	Initial Party Balance House	Senate	Popularity after First Year (percent)
Kennedy	1960, 49%	262D–175R*	64D–36R	79%
Johnson	1964, 61	295D–140R	68D–32R	69
Nixon	1968, 43	243D–192R	58D–42R	67
Carter	1976, 50	292D–143R	61D–39R	59
Reagan	1980, 51	243D–192R	46D–54R	49
Bush	1988, 54	260D–175R	55D–45R	75
Clinton	1992, 43	258D–176R†	57D–43R	49

*Includes one extra member for Alaska and Hawaii.

†Representative Bernard Sanders (Vt.) elected as Independent.

Sources: Vital Statistics on American Politics; Vital Statistics on Congress, 1993–1994; New York Times, September 18, 1994, pp. 54–55. Copyright © The New York Times Company, Inc. Reprinted by permission.

Consider, for example, the range of different circumstances faced by presidents from the 1960s to the 1990s as they worked with their first Congresses (see Table 8–1). Lyndon Johnson's prospects differed dramatically from those of George Bush, for example. With overwhelming Democratic majorities in each house and a backlog of social programs, many of which had been fully aired in the Congress, Lyndon Johnson could seek passage of dozens of significant pieces of legislation in the Eighty-ninth Congress (1965–1966), literally changing the role of government in society with Medicare, civil rights bills, federal aid to education, and environmental initiatives, along with other elements that made up his Great Society vision.[24] Moreover, Johnson had enough fiscal flexibility that he could actually produce a balanced budget, albeit with a number of gimmicks, during his last year in office.

In contrast, George Bush was hemmed in by Democratic majorities in both House and Senate, a more modest electoral victory, and the prospect of annual $200 billion budget deficits for many years to come. As president, Bush could reach agreement with the Democrats on Capitol Hill on major environmental and deficit reduction legislation, but his role was as a partner to an assertive Congress. Indeed, to address rising deficits, the Democrat-controlled Congress framed a package of legislation that essentially forced Bush to accept a modest tax increase, which broke his "no new taxes" election pledge and split the Republican party.[25]

---

[24]For a recent perspective by a Johnson loyalist, see Joseph Califano, *The Triumph and Tragedy of Lyndon Johnson* (New York: Simon & Schuster, 1991).

[25]See Jones, *The Presidency in a Separated System,* pp. 266–268; Barbara Sinclair, "Governing Unheroically (and Sometimes Unappetizingly): Bush and the 101st Congress," in Colin Campbell and Bert Rockman, *The Bush Presidency: First Appraisals* (Chatham, NJ: Chatham House, 1991), p. 175.

More generally, Congress's partisan balance and the president's overall political strength shape his capacity to focus legislative attention, both in setting the agenda and in helping to move legislation through the labyrinth of Capitol Hill. Even in difficult circumstances, the president remains a key centralizing force, in that (1) his agenda items require congressional attention (if not agreement) and (2) he alone commands the position from which authoritative negotiations with legislators can take place. Legislating in the decentralized context of the U.S. Congress necessarily includes focusing attention and deal making, and only the president can serve as both chief focuser and key deal-maker.

The initial years of the Carter and Reagan presidencies illustrate the differences in focusing and deal-making skills. Carter sent a large number of proposals to Capitol Hill, 60 percent with accompanying messages that "suggested in each case that they were of the *highest priority* to the administration."[26] If everything is important, nothing is, and the president found himself lacking the political capital (to say nothing of the political skills) to make the deals essential to passing many of his true priorities, most notably comprehensive energy legislation. Conversely, the Reagan administration's focus on its 1981 tax cut proposals represented a textbook example of direction, only to be followed by a combination of firmness and flexibility in negotiations with members of Congress that outflanked as savvy a legislative veteran as Ways and Means Committee chair Dan Rostenkowski (D-Ill.), even though Democrats retained formal control of the House.

Legislating: Presidential Tools in a Retail Politics Era

> *My vote cannot be bought, but it can be rented.*

> Representative John Breaux (D-La.), 1981

> *I don't have bottom lines. You can't afford them in this business. I mean, we deal with the possible. That's what we have to be guided by: What can we get? What can you do? And as long as it's better than what we have, that's the bottom line.*

> Senator John Breaux (D-La.), 1994

Despite the rise in congressional partisanship during the 1980s and 1990s, most major legislative initiatives require "cross-partisan" majorities.[27] Given the narrow Republican margins in the recent Congresses, virtually all major legislation requires constructing majorities across party lines. Although there may not be extensive bipartisan cooperation, some legislators from the opposing party ordinarily join with the bulk of the president's partisans to forge a temporary majority. Cross-party majorities have long been important; for example, North-

---

[26]Peterson, *Legislating Together*, p. 256. Emphasis added.

[27]See Jones, *The Presidency in a Separated System.*

ern, moderate Republicans would sometimes join liberal Democrats in the 1950s and 1960s to provide the margin of victory for urban initiatives. In 1961, for example, a handful of Republicans gave the Kennedy administration and Speaker Sam Rayburn their crucial victory in expanding the House Rules Committee, thus wresting control from the conservative coalition.

Charles Jones notes that more recent Congresses, with increased fragmentation, individualism, and "greater openness in participation [have encouraged] more cross partisanship in lawmaking."[28] Presidents can no longer rely on a handful of party leaders (such as Speaker Sam Rayburn in the 1950s) or key committee chairs (such as Ways and Means chair Wilbur Mills in the 1960s) to inform them about what is legislatively possible. Rather, presidents and their agents, including executive-branch liaison staff; congressional leaders, both formal and informal; and even key interest group contacts, must build majorities from the ground up, one vote at a time. It was thus crucial to Ronald Reagan that he could negotiate with Representative John Breaux about Louisiana's oil and gas interests in 1981 as he sought to push through spending cuts. It was not essential that Breaux buy into the entire Reagan program. Rather, the president could "rent" the congressman for a few important votes in return for protecting a handful of key Louisiana interests.

As a rule, presidents can neither dictate the final content of legislation nor bargain fecklessly for votes to produce congressional majorities. Often they must attach their support to items already on the legislative agenda, and only when victory is within shouting distance in the Congress can they affect the outcome through bargaining with individual representatives and senators; presidents possess their greatest advantages on such close votes, when they can pressure, bargain with, and cajole fence-sitting lawmakers.

The Presidential Record

Political scientists and pundits have long attempted to measure rates of presidential success in winning congressional support for their proposals. On occasion, as with the outpouring of legislation in 1964–1966 under Lyndon Johnson, the evidence of presidential impact is overwhelming. Most of the time, however, the results are mixed and often depend on how success is measured. Until 1975, *Congressional Quarterly* generated a so-called box score of presidential success, but this measure was flawed and ultimately discontinued.[29] Subsequently, scholars have relied both on other broad measures such as overall success rates and more specific indicators such as the key votes for a given congress. In addition, many scholars have either constructed their own sets of important votes and attempts at presidential influence or relied on

---

[28]Jones, *The Presidency in a Separated System,* p. 270.

[29]For a discussion of this measure and others, see George Edwards, *At the Margins,* p. 16ff.

historical evidence that indicates those issues on which presidents sought to influence outcomes.[30]

All-encompassing measures of success rates rarely provide much insight into presidential influence. This is illustrated by two examples of *Congressional Quarterly*'s scoring of presidential success rates: In 1981, Ronald Reagan achieved 82 percent support on issues on which he took a position; in 1994, Bill Clinton obtained an 86 percent rating.[31] No sensible analysis of these two presidents and these two years would have found Clinton to have done better than Reagan. Indeed, Clinton not only lost his major initiative, health care, but found himself stymied by Senate Republicans for much of 1994 in that many major bills were never even brought to a vote. Moreover, in his sixth year as president, with a Congress controlled by the opposing party, Bill Clinton achieved a 51 percent success rate on legislation on which he took a position. Ronald Reagan and Richard Nixon, in similar circumstances, won 56 percent and 60 percent of the time, respectively.[32]

Perhaps the greatest problem in pinning down presidential influence is the task of disentangling context from presidential impact. The recent Republican presidents who faced Democratic congressional majorities — Nixon, Ford, Reagan, and Bush — won 61.5 percent of the votes on which they took a position; Democrats from Kennedy to Clinton (1993–1994) won 81.5 percent, a margin of 20 percent over the Republicans. Were Democratic presidents more skillful? Hardly, but they did enjoy party control in Congress.

It is more useful to view congressional contexts as offering presidents varying options as they pursue their legislative agendas. Should their lists be long or should they be short, emphasizing only a few key issues? Peterson notes that "large agendas invite problems," yet "as LBJ powerfully demonstrated, extremely ambitious, diverse, and sizable programmatic agendas can be guided through the legislative labyrinth."[33] In the end, a skillful president can offer centralized guidance for a coherent set of proposals, but the congressional context of committees, individual entrepreneurs, and wavering support by some party leaders renders questionable any consistent attempts at strong executive leadership.

Moreover, in the post–Twenty-Second Amendment era, second-term presidents face especially difficult circumstances. Even after winning landslide reelection victories, they have proved unwilling (Eisenhower and Reagan) or unable (Nixon) to produce a significant record of legislative successes. Faced with Republican majorities in Congress, tight budget limitations, and the mem-

---

[30]See Edwards, *At the Margins;* Jones, *The Presidency in a Separated System,* chap. 7; and Peterson, *Legislating Together,* especially appendix B, which offers an excellent review of quantitative research.

[31]*Congressional Quarterly Weekly Report,* December 31, 1994, p. 3654.

[32]David Hosansky, "Clinton's Biggest Prize Was a Frustrated GOP," *Congressional Quarterly Weekly Report,* January 9, 1999, p. 76.

[33]Peterson, *Legislating Together,* pp. 220–221.

ories of a spotty first-term record, President Clinton proved no more willing or able than his predecessors to place a formidable policy agenda before the Congress. Indeed, relations between the Congress and the president may well be defined not by current executive initiatives but by the budgetary constraints imposed by decades of past spending decisions, such as the funding of the interstate highway system and the adoption of Medicare.

BUDGETARY POLITICS:
CENTRALIZATION THROUGH CONSTRAINT

> *When Congress consents to the Executive making the budget it will have surrendered the most important part of a representative government.*
>
> **Former Speaker of the House Joseph Cannon, 1919**

One of the president's most significant powers in setting the national policy agenda has been the capacity to propose an annual budget. Since 1921, the Bureau of the Budget (renamed the Office of Management and Budget [OMB] in 1971) has monitored government spending and produced increasingly large compilations of proposed expenditures. The Congress, of course, retains the power of the purse — the appropriations authority — but the president and his budgetary staff provide both the overarching thrust of proposed spending (for example, by proposing new programs) and the myriad details of where federal monies will be spent.

As federal responsibilities and spending increased from the 1930s through the early 1970s, executive budget officials came to play an important role in shaping policy initiatives, large and small, old and new.[34] The president and Congress generally agreed on the expansion of executive authority as the scope and complexity of public policy grew steadily. Budget scholar Howard Shuman concludes that "in almost every case the delegation [of congressional authority] resulted in the aggrandizement of the executive at the expense of the Congress, but *this was done willingly, even joyously, and had few narrow or partisan or siege-mentality overtones*."[35]

By the late 1960s, however, the Congress and the president had begun to engage in budget wars, as spending levels and priorities began to be vigorously contested.[36] Party leaders and increasing numbers of back bench legislators wanted to exercise some control over spending, and Republican President Richard M. Nixon had sought to gain more control over spending levels and priorities through the use of the veto and his willingness to impound funds

---

[34]Lance T. LeLoup, *Budgetary Politics,* 3rd ed. (Brunswick, OH: Kings' Court, 1986), pp. 6ff.

[35]Howard E. Shuman, *Politics and the Budget,* 3rd ed. (Englewood Cliffs, NJ: Prentice-Hall, 1992), p. 213. Emphasis added.

[36]Allen Schick, *Congress and Money* (Washington, DC: Urban Institute Press, 1980), chap. 2.

(refuse to spend them) that the Congress had appropriated. As a Democratically controlled Congress grew frustrated with both an aggressive Republican president and its own incapacity to control overall levels of spending, the stage was set for major reform of the budget process. And, as luck would have it, the Congress confronted a president who had been grievously wounded by the Watergate affair. Indeed, Nixon would resign from office less than two months after the 1974 Congressional Budget and Impoundment Control Act was passed.

Although largely an attack on the executive, the 1974 legislation sought to rationalize budgetary policy making (to control overall expenditures and increase capacities to set priorities) and to strengthen the budget-related capacities of the Congress. By both accident and design, the reforms have paradoxically led to members' greater participation in budgetary politics and, simultaneously, to increased centralization of the ultimate budget decisions.

By setting a supposedly firm timetable for action and by requiring the Congress to address total levels of spending early in the process, the 1974 reforms sought to allow Congress greater control over the levels and composition of federal spending. To accomplish these goals, the Congress needed more resources and some organizational changes; thus, both houses created budget committees, and the nonpartisan Congressional Budget Office (CBO) was established. CBO provides the legislative branch an independent capacity to analyze the mountains of budget-related data and to make the projections for future revenue and spending patterns that are the heart of contemporary fiscal politics. The new committees increased the number of legislators who played a major role in budgetary politics; the well-respected CBO offered leaders, committees, and even individual members the opportunity to pose alternative budget scenarios to those offered by the executive branch's OMB. In a sense, budgetary politics became more open and democratic in the aftermath of the 1974 reforms. Various factions ranging from conservative Republicans to the generally liberal Congressional Black Caucus could propose their own budgetary priorities, even if they had little chance of winning congressional approval.[37]

In fact, the adoption of the budget reforms, especially when combined with the major tax cuts of 1981, conspired to "fiscalize" congressional politics during the 1980s.[38] With annual deficits escalating, budgetary restraints required that key legislators — budget committee members and party leaders, in particular — consider overall patterns of spending. Shepsle concludes, "The most significant consequence of the Budget Act has been that Congress has had little time to consider anything else. . . . The fiscalization of politics has dimin-

---

[37]Barbara Sinclair, *Legislators, Leaders and Lawmaking: The U.S. House of Representatives in the Postreform Era* (Baltimore: Johns Hopkins University Press, 1995), p. 143.

[38]Kenneth Shepsle uses this term in "The Changing Textbook Congress," in John E. Chubb and Paul E. Peterson, eds., *Can the Government Govern?* (Washington, DC: Brookings Institution, 1989), pp. 259ff.

ished the stature of standing committees, encouraged members to become generalists rather than specialists, ceded political advantage to those in party leadership positions, and put a premium on coordination among policy areas."[39]

The centralization of budgetary politics in the Congress was mirrored by a similar trend in the executive branch, where the OMB, under former Representative David Stockman, came to dominate policy decisions in the Reagan administration.[40] Facing the administration and the OMB were top party leaders in Congress, who controlled access to the floor and who could put together comprehensive fiscal packages (including initial budget resolutions, budget reconciliation agreements, and continuing and supplementary appropriations bills). Both the executive and legislative leaders developed a new model of policy making during their successful 1983 efforts to "save" the social security system.[41] In this instance, a nine-member "gang" of executive and legislative leaders (a subset of a larger bipartisan commission) reached agreement on a set of benefit reductions and rate increases; leadership representatives from both legislative parties in both chambers hammered out compromise positions that were offered on an all-or-nothing basis to their respective party members.

Throughout the 1980s, variations on this model dominated budgetary decisions, as leaders annually struggled to produce agreements acceptable both to the administration and to congressional majorities in each house. Although the memberships of the House and Senate played little role in reaching budget deals, they could — and sometimes did — upset their leaders' applecarts by defeating the entire package. Indeed, as top legislators and presidential envoys met to negotiate, both sides had to bear in mind their constituents. Congressional leaders knew they had to convince majorities of their followers to approve their actions, whereas the president's constituents were the voters whom he would eventually face. Thus, for chief executives and congressional leaders alike, there remain real limits to the exercise of centralized power.

Among legislators, this was forcefully brought home in 1985, when junior Republican senators and conservative Democrats forced the issue of deficit reduction after top-level "budget summitry" broke down. The Congress agreed to a reduction package proposed by Senators Phil Gramm (R-Tex.), Warren Rudman (R-N.H.), and Ernest Hollings (D-S.C.), which they attached to a "must-pass" bill to raise the debt ceiling (without which the federal government would be forced to shut down).[42] To oversimplify a most complicated set of maneuvers, congressional leaders realized that the Gramm-Rudman-

---

[39]Shepsle, "The Changing Textbook Congress," pp. 261–262.

[40]Stockman, *The Triumph of Politics;* William Greider, "The Education of David Stockman," *Atlantic Monthly,* December 1981.

[41]See Paul Light, *Artful Work* (New York: Random House, 1985); Richard E. Neustadt and Ernest R. May, *Thinking in Time* (New York: Free Press, 1986), chap. 2.

[42]For more extensive discussion, see Shuman, *Politics and the Budget,* 3rd ed., pp. 286ff.

Hollings formula of annual, automatic cuts in the absence of real deficit reduction would obtain majority support in both houses. After some modifications, the proposal became law and thus framed subsequent budgetary politics. The centralized powers of congressional leaders had been severely limited by insurgent budget-cutters.

Despite some judicial setbacks and legislative modifications, the Gramm-Rudman-Hollings principle of holding down spending through automatic cuts in the absence of legislation remained dominant for several years. Then in 1990, President Bush reluctantly agreed to provisions in the Budget Enforcement Act that contradicted his "no new taxes" pledge of the 1988 campaign. The agreement, hammered out in lengthy, secret negotiations between top administration officials and congressional leaders, also effectively killed the Gramm-Rudman-Hollings experiment in automatic deficit reduction. This ad hoc, highly centralized process required a handful of legislative leaders to represent the entire Congress; neither rank-and-file members, committee chairs, nor Appropriations Committee members were involved. The negotiators did reach a bipartisan agreement with meaningful deficit reductions, but congressional Democrats insisted that a majority of Republicans in each house support it before they would go along. With less than a month before the 1990 congressional elections, legislators found it hard to swallow even modest tax increases and spending reductions that were concentrated in the last years of the five-year plan. House Republicans opposed the package 105-71, and Democrats followed suit, 149-108. The budget summit agreement, cobbled together by top Bush administration officials and most congressional leaders (then–Republican Whip Newt Gingrich was a notable exception), failed overwhelmingly. The legislative troops had taken the only action available to them — opposition to a pact they had no hand in writing.

After more partisan jousting, in which the Bush administration made further modest concessions on tax increases, the Budget Enforcement Act was passed, only a few days before the elections and with relatively little Republican support. In the House, for example, only 47 of 173 minority members voted for the bill. The highly centralized, highly political negotiations did produce some real deficit reduction, but also resulted in some significant political damage to President Bush. Most members of Congress had little impact on the most important piece of legislation passed during the 101st Congress. When the entire budget became the focus of a policy decision, the fragmentation of the House and the individualism of the Senate necessarily gave way to private negotiations by a handful of top legislative leaders. Nevertheless, as James Thurber argues, there remains a lot of decentralization in contemporary budget making.[43] He notes that even disciplined parties have problems building solid coalitions. In 1996, for example, Republicans added funds to buy off some potential opponents to cutting domestic programs. Powerful constituencies

---

[43]Thurber, "Centralization, Devolution, and Turf Protection."

(agriculture, defense) retain substantial clout. With budget surpluses becoming the norm, a new politics of budgets is likely to emerge. (See Chapters 3 and 10.)

POLICY, POWER, AND DIVIDED GOVERNMENT

The politics of the 1990 Budget Enforcement Act provides an apt illustration of decision-making under divided government, the dominant pattern over the 1969–1993 period, when Republican presidents (save Carter, 1977–1981) faced Democratic Congressional majorities (save the Senate, 1918–1987). In 1990, a Republican president and a Democratic Congress could, however haltingly, produce a substantial policy change. At the same time, disagreements between the president and GOP legislators and between Democratic congressional leaders and many Democratic back-benchers did not generate great confidence in either the content of the legislation or the process of lawmaking. Moreover, there were few clear lines of accountability as voters sought to reward or penalize those responsible for the legislation. Unfortunately for George Bush, the president offered a clearer target in 1992 than did most senators and Representatives seeking reelection.[44] Nonetheless, Congressional Democrats found themselves in the electorate's sights in 1994.

Political scientist David Mayhew has demonstrated that divided government has not prevented the federal government from enacting major legislation on important public policy topics.[45] Divided government, particularly since the early 1980s, has required congressional negotiation with the White House, whether on budget issues, clean air, or Social Security reform. Negotiation encourages centralization, in that only a handful of leaders can effectively represent the legislature. More generally, Mayhew has raised systematic questions about the nature of American policy making, a process that has been increasingly viewed as being centered in the presidency.[46] Despite the growth of the so-called imperial presidency in the 1960s and early 1970s, the president remains enmeshed in a system of shared powers, even in foreign and military affairs, where chief executives retain wider latitude.[47] From time to time, certain presidents may take advantage of circumstances (such as party majorities and crises) to extend their influence, but congressional reaction is rarely long in coming, as legislative leaders seek to assert their institutional prerogatives. Although Lyndon Johnson pushed the Eighty-ninth Congress mercilessly to pass Democratic domestic programs and to support the growing American

---

[44]Congressional turnover, especially with 110 new members in the House, was high in comparison with recent elections, but few defeats could be linked directly to budget positions.

[45]David Mayhew, *Divided We Govern* (New Haven, CT: Yale University Press, 1991).

[46]See, for example, Arthur M. Schlesinger, Jr., *The Imperial Presidency* (Boston: Houghton Mifflin, 1973).

[47]See Barbara Hinckley, *Less than Meets the Eye* (Chicago: University of Chicago Press, 1995).

involvement in Vietnam, he correctly recognized that his window of opportunity for great change would probably close with the 1966 election.[48] Richard Nixon, operating without Republican majorities in either chamber, recognized the need for extraordinary administrative actions, such as impounding huge amounts of appropriated funds, placing key loyalists in departmental slots, and encouraging clandestine operations, that would bypass normal congressional participation in many policy decisions.

In surveying presidential-congressional relations, Charles Jones concludes that "understanding the production of laws requires analysis of law-making" and that the "system is now, *and always has been,* one of 'separated institutions sharing powers' as Neustadt puts it [originally in 1960]."[49] Indeed, within the context of an extended period of split-party control of government, Jones reformulates Neustadt's observation as "separated institutions competing for shares of power."[50] The 104th Congress, with its Republican majorities, offered renewed support for such a conclusion. Speaker Newt Gingrich clearly succeeded at establishing the policy agenda and, early on, dominated the legislative process. But a bicameral system, with its separation of powers, denies the likelihood of congressional dominance, save through overwhelming majorities. Rather, as John Bader concludes, congressional leadership must ordinarily strive to maintain "a balance . . . between heavy-handed leadership and fragmenting anarchy,"[51] as it struggles against the relatively unified executive branch.

In the Republican congressional era (1995–   ), after a difficult, even disastrous, first year, President Clinton learned to take advantage of the constitutional system and the modest divisions among congressional Republicans to win both political and policy points. If the Bush and early Clinton administrations were marked by high-profile, comprehensive budget summits in 1990 and 1993, the post-1995 Clinton strategy has been to move toward Republican positions on some major issues, such as welfare reform and "saving" Medicare, while articulating a number of modest policy initiatives of his own. In the end, former Clinton Chief of Staff (and former Representative) Leon Panetta argues that we should not expect consistent bipartisanship across a wide range of concerns, especially given the partisan dominance of congressional organization in the modern era. He observes that

> institutional power in both House and Senate resides with the parties [that]
> rely on activists and interest groups that tend to bunch on the left and
> right. . . . [Moreover,] the legislative process allows centrist coalitions little

---

[48]See Jeff Fishel, *Party and Opposition* (New York: David McKay, 1973); Sundquist, *Politics and Policy.*

[49]Jones, *The Presidency in a Separated System,* p. 207. Emphasis added.

[50]Ibid., p. 207.

[51]John Bader, *Taking the Initiative: Leadership Agendas in Congress and the Contract with America* (Washington, DC: Georgetown University Press, 1996), 222–223.

power or time to coalesce for action. . . . Once party discipline descends on an issue, it leaves little room for representatives to gather at the center without the risk of angering the party leadership.[52]

How then — beyond pure political opportunism — can we explain the 1996 set of compromises on difficult issues like welfare and an increase in the minimum wage? Panetta argues that we should not expect any "ongoing governing coalition at the center, but one that can be created on each individual issues."[53] The president, with his capacity to focus on issues and occasionally twist arms, along with a willingness to move toward his opponents' positions, can make divided government work, although not (save in wartime, perhaps) on a continuing bipartisan basis. Rather, as political scientists Peterson and Jones suggest, we might well look for issue-by-issue construction of cross-party majorities that depend more on particular cooperation than general agreement. More colorfully, Representative Barney Frank anticipated a particular style of governance in an era of divided, yet partisan, government, coupled with severe budget constraints:

> There's a certain kind of boxing match that's called a "waltz." The fighters beat each other silly for a while, then decide, "We've been slugging each other long enough — let's just hang on till the end of the fight and get paid." I think we're going to govern in a fairly boring fashion.[54]

As we shall see in Chapter 10, Congressman Frank was half right. Much of governing in the post-1998 era has, indeed, looked like an awkward "waltz" — a series of minor pieces of legislation punctuated by large budget packages ($600 billion in 1998). At the same time, the impeachment battle between Republicans on Capitol Hill, especially in the House, and President Clinton has scarcely qualified as a waltz. Rather, the president's very survival was at stake. What remains unresolved (and probably unresolvable) is whether impeachment was a principled struggle over constitutional issues or a partisan drive by frustrated Republican legislators against an executive they had never respected or (even) viewed as legitimate.[55]

[52]Leon E. Panetta, "The True Balance of Power," *New York Times*, February 2, 1997, p. 11, section 4.

[53]Panetta, "The True Balance of Power."

[54]Barney Frank quoted in Joe Klein, "The Hug," *New Yorker*, December 16, 1996, p. 56.

[55]Among the voluminous recountings of this struggle, Joe Klein's "The Town That Ate Itself" (*New Yorker*, November 23, 1998, pp. 78–99) is particularly lucid.

Nine

THE LEGISLATIVE PROCESS AND THE RULES OF THE GAME

E ach January the president comes before the assembled members of the House and Senate to present his State of the Union message, as mandated, roughly speaking, by the U.S. Constitution. Like much of American politics, the State of the Union has evolved over time as formal requirements and procedures have been modified by informal norms of behavior. Ordinarily, it is a mix of politics and policy, all with a generous measure of performance thrown in. Even when the president's message will surely be greeted skeptically, as with the Democrats' approach to the Reagan speeches of the 1980s, the night ordinarily combines congressional formalities with considerable good will, as legislators bask in the annual spectacle of democratic politics.

In 1999, however, President Clinton and his congressional audience faced an almost surreal situation. The representatives who had voted for impeachment in December 1998, and the senators who were about to begin the process of judgment filed into the House chamber to listen to an address by the president who was under mortal attack by at least half of the legislators. Although some Republicans absented themselves, most, including their leaders, sat through all seventy-seven minutes of the speech. Clinton's speech elicited modest, if infrequent, applause from almost all GOP lawmakers, while Democrats found lots to cheer about. Hence, there was a strange, unbalanced feel to the audience response. But that was nothing in comparison to the behavior of Majority Leader Dick Armey (R-Tex.) and Majority Whip Tom DeLay (R-Tex.), who sat stone-faced (or whispering to each other) throughout the speech. Only once or twice — as when Rosa Parks, the hero of the 1955 Montgomery bus boycott, was introduced — did they applaud. Otherwise, they sat still — mutedly demonstrating their complete disdain for the president of the United States.

Party leaders have often been fierce opponents of sitting presidents, but in the television age, at least, no such gesture of disrespect previously had been directed at both the individual and the office. A few years earlier, Representative DeLay had gotten into a scuffle with Representative Downey (D-N.Y.), and Representative Armey had once labeled Representative Barney Frank (D-Mass.), an acknowledged homosexual, "Barney Fag," and then apologized, arguing that the usage had been accidental. Their behavior within the context of the State of the Union message, however, may have reached new depths in the decline of civility in the Congress. Political opposition had transformed into bitter, personal enmity — knowingly presented to a television audience that extended well beyond the American people.

From universities to corporations to legislative bodies, all institutions operate under parallel sets of expectations, one established by formal rules and structures, the other resulting from informal arrangements that have grown up over an extended period of time. Legislatures rely heavily on the different kinds of order that are imposed by formal procedures and implicit understandings. Watching Congress on C-SPAN, one immediately observes the elaborate courtesies that legislators ordinarily extend to each other, even when they are engaged in fierce battles over a particular bill. Courtesy is one of many important, if informal, rules of the game that most members observe, although perhaps less so in the contemporary Congress than thirty or forty years ago. In addition, procedural constraints and time limitations that characterize the way the House does business appear largely absent in the Senate, where debate meanders forward at a snail's pace as senators speak ad infinitum to an almost empty chamber about a series of often unrelated issues.

The House and the Senate operate under separate sets of formal rules, and each chamber fosters its own legislators' so-called folkways[1] — expectations about behavior that influence actions on Capitol Hill. For example, courtesy and hard work are encouraged, and insolence and sloth are discouraged (if not eliminated). Folkways are especially important in Congress, where all members are technically equal in that they have won elections from similar constituencies and each can cast a single vote. In such an organization, power relationships are often delicate and unstated, expressed through agreed-upon norms rather than in explicit procedures.

Overall, formal rules play a more important role in the House, whereas norms are more important in the Senate. This makes sense, because the larger House must rely on procedures in order to reach decisions in a timely, less-than-chaotic manner. Members of the smaller Senate depend much more on informal agreements reached among all senators.[2]

This chapter first discusses the ways in which formal rules affect the legislative process and then considers the evolution and impact of congressional folkways. Neither chamber can function effectively without a blend of formal and informal strictures, but the mixes of procedures and norms differ greatly on the different sides of the Capitol.

---

[1]Donald Matthews first employed the "folkways" notion in his groundbreaking *U.S. Senators and Their World* (New York: Vintage, 1960).

[2]See Ross K. Baker, *House and Senate,* 2nd ed. (New York: Norton, 1995), pp. 71–73.

RULES, PROCEDURE, AND THE LEGISLATIVE PROCESS

If you let me write procedure and I let you write substance,
I'll screw you every time.

Representative John Dingell (D–Mich.)

Although the Congress is a thoroughly rule-oriented institution, only a few of its procedures are mandated by the Constitution; these include the requirement that each chamber maintain a journal, that half the membership constitutes a quorum, that tax bills must originate in the House of Representatives, and that the two chambers can override a presidential veto by a two-thirds vote in each body.[3] Beyond these basics and the more expansive constitutional limitations on the entire federal government, the House and Senate have been free to establish their own distinct sets of rules. The House rules currently run to more than seven hundred pages, but the Senate makes do with about one hundred pages.[4]

After being introduced by individual legislators, bills are referred to committees by the Speaker or the Senate's presiding officer, who consult when necessary with the parliamentarians of the respective chambers. As appointees of the majority party, the parliamentarians work closely with the leadership. In the Democratic House of the 1980s and 1990s, a steadily growing number of bills were referred to multiple committees (almost one in five by the 1991–1992 period).[5] With the 104th Congress, majority Republicans refashioned House committee jurisdictions, which reduced the need for such referrals.[6]

No more than one bill in ten eventually becomes law, and the vast majority of bills never make it out of committee. Many proposals are introduced with no hope of passage or are duplicates of other bills. Senators and representatives may simply want to claim credit for offering a bill, especially when they recognize that constituents or interest groups are keeping tabs on their actions. More generally, the legislative process is one of winnowing desirable or politically popular proposals from those that have little merit or chance for passage. At the same time, the House remains a majoritarian body whose rules encourage dispatch, assuming that consistent voting majorities can be mobilized. The individualistic Senate, however, makes it more difficult for majorities to work their will.

The House

PATHS OF LEGISLATION   All bills are not created equal, nor do they move along the same path toward final passage. Minor bills appear on the House Con-

---

[3]Steven S. Smith, *The American Congress* (Boston: Houghton Mifflin, 1995), pp. 25–26.

[4]Smith, *The American Congress,* p. 43.

[5]Gary Young and Joseph Cooper, "Multiple Referral and the Transformation of House Decision Making," in Lawrence Dodd and Bruce I. Oppenheimer, eds., *Congress Reconsidered,* 5th ed. (Washington, DC: CQ Press, 1993), p. 214.

[6]The Speaker can refer a bill to multiple committees, but he or she designates a lead committee and sets deadlines (see Chapter 5).

sent Calendar and are considered on the first and third Mondays of each month; other legislation can take the shortcut of being considered under a suspension-of-the-rules procedure, which requires a two-thirds affirmative House vote and cannot routinely exceed $100 million in expenditures.[7] Within the Democratic postreform House of the 1980s, more than a third of all legislation was essentially symbolic, commemorating events such as Black History Month and National Peach Week.[8] Although these noncontroversial bills were routinely passed, they did consume a growing amount of legislative resources, and the Republicans essentially eliminated them after winning control of Congress in 1994.

Major legislation moves to the floor from House committees in two ways. Budget and appropriations measures are entitled to a privileged status that allows them to be brought to the floor at almost any time; most other important legislation must go before the Rules Committee to receive a rule that will govern debate and amendments. In addition, budget resolutions and large-scale, or omnibus, spending packages also obtain rules that set out constraints on deliberation and waive procedural points of order;[9] otherwise, the politics of delay could dominate and chaos might well reign on the House floor.

In national service legislation and changes in student loan mechanisms, the relevant bills took different paths in gaining legislative approval (see Figure 9–1). After being introduced at the behest of the administration, both proposals went to the House Education and Labor Committee, but national service proceeded as a stand-alone bill, whereas student aid policy was incorporated into the overall budget bill. The politics of the two pieces of legislation were not dissimilar, despite their distinct routes to passage. Each proposal could have been defeated on its merits, but the student aid changes could also have been derailed within the highly partisan process that culminated in the August 5, 1993, vote to approve the budget package (see Chapter 1).

ORGANIZING HOUSE FLOOR ACTION   Given the ample staff resources of individual members, the proliferation of subcommittees (at least through the 1980s), and the growth of special interest caucuses, Democratic leaders struggled to control legislation that reached the floor of the postreform House. As Barbara Sinclair summarizes,

> The 1970s reformers, most of them liberal Democrats, were motivated by concerns about both policy and participation. The changes they instituted would . . . produce better . . . policy and provide greater opportunities for the rank and file to participate in the legislative process. By the late 1970s many had concluded that unrestrained participation, particularly on the House floor, hindered rather than facilitated . . . good public policy. And in the more

---

[7]Roger Davidson and Walter Oleszek, *Congress and Its Members,* 4th ed. (Washington, DC: CQ Press, 1994), pp. 330–331.

[8]Roger Davidson, "The Emergence of the Postreform Congress," in Roger Davidson, ed., *The Postreform Congress* (New York: St. Martin's, 1992), p. 17.

[9]Allen Schick, *The Federal Budget* (Washington, DC: Brookings Institution, 1995), p. 79.

FIGURE 9-1
Two Regular Order Versions of the Legislative Process

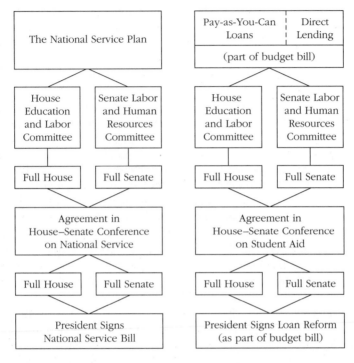

Source: Adapted from Steven Waldman, *The Bill* (New York: Viking, 1995), p. xv.

hostile political climate of the 1980s [that is, divided government], the policy costs of unrestrained and uncoordinated legislative activism rose further.[10]

Most troubling to party and committee leaders was a sharp increase in amendments offered on the House floor both by members of committees that processed the legislation and by other backbenchers.[11]

The House Democratic leaders adopted various tactics to regain control of the floor, including an increased reliance on suspension-of-the-rules votes, but the most important procedural changes came in their use of the Rules Committee.[12] This committee dictates both the flow of major, nonprivileged legislation onto the House floor and the procedural limitations that apply once it gets

[10]Barbara Sinclair, "House Majority Leadership in an Era of Legislative Constraint," in Davidson, *The Postreform Congress,* p. 92. More generally, see Barbara Sinclair, *Unorthodox Lawmaking* (Washington, DC: CQ Press 1997).

[11]For a detailed analysis, see Steven S. Smith, *Call to Order* (Washington, DC: Brookings Institution, 1989).

[12]Where not otherwise noted, the following discussion is drawn from Walter Oleszek, *Congressional Procedures and the Policy Process,* 3rd ed. (Washington, DC: CQ Press, 1989), pp. 119 ff. Suspension of the rules allows bills to be considered in a expedited manner, subject to passage by a two-thirds vote.

there. Although the Rules Committee has at times proven to be an obstacle to the Speaker's control of business on the House floor, since the mid-1970s it has become a reliable "arm of the leadership."[13] Given the Speaker's power to appoint (and remove) Rules Committee members, the panel has served the leadership by reporting out rules that structure floor action according to the leadership's wishes. Moreover, it has resolved disagreements among committees with overlapping jurisdictions as to which bill or combination of bills will be used as the legislation to be considered on the floor.

More importantly, however, the Rules Committee sets time limits for floor debate and establishes which amendments, if any, can be offered. As floor action grew more partisan during the 1980s, Democratic leaders relied heavily on restrictive rules to maintain control of the legislative process, as well as to structure substantive decision making to favor their own policy positions (see Table 9–1). Although some of these rules simply imposed a deadline for amendments, in the 103rd Congress, 45 of 104 rules "barred all amendments [closed rules] or allowed only specific proposals" that the Democratic leadership approved.[14] Only thirty-one rules were open to any amendment from the floor. Some rules even extended the Democrats' procedural control of the House deep into substantive concerns. The Rules Committee employed two specific types of rules that directly affected policy results:

1. The king-of-the-hill rule, first devised in 1982, waived various precedents and procedures in allowing a series of votes on several major policy amendments, each offered as an entire substitute an original proposal. This rule "gave ultimate victory to the last one approved, even if one of the earlier options had gotten more 'yea' votes."[15]

TABLE 9-1

Restrictions on Amendments in the Democratic House, 1977-1994

Congress	Open Rules	Restrictive Rules	Percent Restrictive
95th (1977–78)	179	32	15
96th (1979–80)	161	53	25
97th (1981–82)	90	30	25
98th (1983–84)	105	50	32
99th (1985–86)	65	50	43
100th (1987–88)	66	57	46
101st (1989–90)	47	57	55
102nd (1991–92)	37	72	66
103rd (1993–94)	31	73	70

Source: Congressional Quarterly Weekly Report, November 19, 1994, p. 3321.

[13]See, in particular, Bruce I. Oppenheimer, "The Rules Committee: New Arm of Leadership in a Decentralized House," in Lawrence Dodd and Bruce I. Oppenheimer, eds., *Congress Reconsidered* (New York: Praeger, 1977), pp. 96–116.

[14]Pat Towell, "GOP's Drive for a More Open House . . . Reflects Pragmatism and Resentment," *Congressional Quarterly Weekly Report,* November 19, 1994, p. 3321.

[15]Towell, "GOP's Drive for a More Open House," p. 3320.

.   **2.** The self-executing rule "stipulates a two-for-one procedure: adoption
        of the rule simultaneously enacts another measure, amendment, or
        both."[16] Long employed for technical purposes in considering Senate
        legislation, in the 1980s this ploy was used to enact policies without
        requiring a direct vote on the issue.

Through these procedures the Democratic leadership could use the Rules
Committee to provide members with the chance to vote in favor of policies
they knew would not become law (the initial king-of-the-hill substitutes) and
to approve policies without requiring a recorded vote (self-executing rules).

   In sum, within a majoritarian institution, the majority-party Democratic
members invested in their leadership, the Rules Committee included, the power
to structure legislation so that it would have the best chance of winning, often
in a highly partisan vote. The only recourse available to Republicans and dissident Democrats was to defeat the rule on the House floor; on occasion this
occurred, but ordinarily the Democratic leadership could depend on holding its
troops together on the procedural vote to approve the rule. With little effect and
growing frustration, the Republican minority of the postreform era argued that
the Democratic leadership acted unfairly in constructing rules that restricted the
introduction of potentially embarrassing amendments and manipulated the voting process through king-of-the-hill and self-executing procedures.

   One additional consequence of the Democrats' practices was to foster sentiments within the minority Republicans that they had little stake in maintaining comity and civility within the chamber. The Democrats' reliance on formal
rules may well have undermined the informal bonds that held the House
together.

   RULES AND PROCEDURES IN THE REPUBLICAN ERA   After forty years in the
House minority, Republicans pledged that they would not rely on House procedures to dominate the legislative process. Rather, bills would come to the
floor with fewer restrictions on amending activity, and the body would be
given a chance for up-or-down votes on amendments offered by members of
both the majority and the minority. Running counter to this promise was the
hectic schedule of the contract in 1995, with requirements of voting three hundred times in ninety-three days. Unsurprisingly, the House Rules Committee
claimed that their data (somewhat different from Table 9–1) showed that 65
percent of all rules for floor amendments were open (or mostly so) in the first
year of the 104th Congress, compared to 44 percent in the 103rd. Democrats
complained that, although rules might have been more open, the Republican
leadership enforced tight time restrictions on legislation that served the same

---

[16]Oleszek, *Congressional Procedures and the Policy Process,* p. 129.

[17]Kristin Kanthak and Elizabeth M. Martin, "House Republicans and Restrictive Rules: A New
   Regime?" (paper presented at the American Political Science Association meetings, San Francisco,
   August 29–September 1, 1996), pp. 4–7.

purpose — to restrict debate and amending activity. One study concluded that the Republicans did follow through on their promise of greater openness, in that, compared to the 103rd Congress, there was more debate, more amendments offered, and more amendments passed in the first, highly partisan, session of the 104th Congress.[17] Inevitably, Republicans relied on a substantial number of restrictive rules, as well as adopting self-executing rules to adopt substantive policies without a separate vote. The Republican majority did eschew the "king-of-the-hill" rule, and overall did bring a measure of greater openness to the House floor, even in the raucous, exhausting first months of the 104th Congress.

Early on, the Republican leadership demonstrated how a well-disciplined majority can dominate the House. When push came to shove in the initial one hundred days, Speaker Gingrich could call upon his party majority to support him on both procedures and substance (see Chapter 7 for a more extended discussion). At the same time, the 100 days' emphasis on speed demonstrated graphically that any benefits of legislative efficiency came accompanied by a set of costs in deliberation.[18] With the partisan shoe on the other foot, Democratic Minority Leader Richard Gephardt (D-Mo.) complained that the Republicans' intense focus on one hundred days' accomplishments "caused all of them to jerk stuff through the procedure much faster than it should have been. There hasn't been enough committee considerations or floor consideration."[19] Ultimately, however, the process within a single chamber cannot dominate, and the Senate retained its status as a slower, more leisurely institution that offered both moderate Republicans and Democrats many chances to refashion the House's speedy legislative work. Moreover, after the Contract with America sprint, the House slowed down substantially. In the end, the House voted more, held longer sessions, but passed less legislation, although the latter conclusion is deceptive, given the decline in symbolic commemorative bills.

As Table 9–2 illustrates, the first session of the 104th Congress (1995) was an aberration, in that the Congress met longer and, in terms of legislation, accomplished less than in any other recent year. With the exception of 1995, the Republican Congress of the late 1990s looks a lot like the Democratic body of the early 1990s. Aside from a long-term trend toward the introduction of less legislation, the statistical Congress appears relatively constant. Informally, however, the institutional norms of comity may have been tested as thoroughly as at any time since the era of Speaker Cannon in the House and isolationist filibusters in the Senate.

---

[18]See James A. Thurber, "Guest Observer," *Roll Call,* March 2, 1995, p. 5; John Aldrich and David Rohde, "Theories of the Party in the Legislature and the Transition to Republican Rule in the House" (paper presented at the American Political Science Association meeting, Chicago, August 31–September 3, 1995), p. 13.

[19]Richard Gephardt quoted in Donna Cassatta, *Congressional Quarterly Weekly Report,* April 8, 1995, p. 990.

TABLE 9-2
Congress by the Numbers, 1989–1998

	101st Congress		102nd Congress		103rd Congress		104th Congress		105th Congress	
	1989	*1990*	*1991*	*1992*	*1993*	*1994*	*1995*	*1996*	*1997*	*1998*
Days in Session										
House	147	134	154	123	142	123	168	122	132	119
Senate	136	138	158	129	153	138	211	132	153	143
Time in Session (hours)										
House	749	939	939	857	982	905	1,525	919	1,004	999
Senate	1,003	1,250	1,201	1,091	1,270	1,244	1,839	1,037	1,093	1,095
Average Hours/Day										
House	5.1	7.0	6.1	7.0	6.9	7.4	9.1	7.5	7.6	8.4
Senate	7.4	9.1	7.6	8.5	8.3	9.0	8.7	7.9	7.1	7.7
Appropriations (in millions of dollars)										
House	$506	$537	$648	$694	$699	$685	$729	$672	$683	$709
Senate	$341	$374	$437	$450	$451	$443	$461	$427	$441	$461
Bills/Resolutions Introduced										
House	4,842	2,769	5,057	2,714	4,543	2,104	3,430	1,899	3,662	2,253
Senate	2,548	1,636	2,701	1,544	2,178	999	1,801	860	1,829	1,321
Recorded Votes										
House	379	536	444	488	615	507	885	455	640	547
Senate	312	326	280	270	395	329	613	306	298	314
Public Laws										
Enacted	**240**	**410**	**243**	**347**	**210**	**255**	**88**	**245**	**153**	**241**
Vetoes	10	11	3	10	0	0	9	6	13*	6*

*Does not include line-item vetoes.

Sources: Congressional Quarterly Weekly, January 9, 1999, p. 85, *Vital Statistics on Congress 1997–1998,* p. 147–148, PL105-55, 1997.

The Senate: Agreeing to Proceed

Although the Senate does have a set of formal rules, most often it operates under unanimous consent procedures that give tremendous leverage to a single senator in negotiating the conditions of debate. In the absence of an informal but binding agreement that structures debate, limits amendments, and imposes time limits, the Senate must labor under its formal rules, which opens the door to delay and gridlock through filibusters.

In many ways unanimous consent agreements resemble House rules, but they are hatched in very different ways. As opposed to the domination of the House process by partisan majorities in the chamber and the Rules Committee, Senate leaders must satisfy all of their interested colleagues from both parties in crafting a set of conditions for debating and amending legislation. Unanimous consent means precisely that: *All* senators must acquiesce to the provisions of the agreement. As with House rules, unanimous consent agreements can be complex, but the complexity tends to serve both the Senate as a whole and specific members rather than advancing the interests of the majority party.

CONGRESSIONAL FOLKWAYS:
THE INFORMAL RULES OF THE GAME

Looking back to the 1950s, the "textbook Congress" era seems positively quaint. Speaker Sam Rayburn could sincerely counsel incoming House members to "get along, go along." And Senate Majority Leader Lyndon Johnson would give each new senator a copy of journalist William S. White's *Citadel,* with its glorification of the chamber's "Inner Club," where "Senate types" of legislators informally dominated the institution. To be sure, Rayburn's advice was generally sound, and White's description roughly accurate. For all their formal leadership and committee structures, both bodies harbored well-accepted sets of norms — informal rules of the game — that governed the behavior of most, if not all, members.

In contrast, the Congress of the 1980s and 1990s has become a thoroughly contentious place. No contemporary Speaker could — or would — deliver Rayburn's fatherly advice, and there is no club of in-group senators that can dominate their chamber. Social ties in both House and Senate have weakened substantially since the 1950s, in part because more and more congressional actions are conducted in public by legislators whose workloads have increased steadily and who have spent rising amounts of time back in their districts. More generally, members of Congress may well reflect the declining levels of trust and civility within the public at large.[20]

The decline of comity scarcely means its elimination.[21] Viewers of C-SPAN can still observe the elaborate formalities and courtesies of the legislative process. But these niceties are often more perfunctory and forced than they were a generation or two ago. The social fabric that holds together congressional life has been frayed, sometimes to the breaking point. Although the partisan, often acidic, nature of debate has reduced civility in the postreform House, this chamber has never relied completely on informal ties to maintain order. The Senate, however, is a different story, with the lack of comity and the growth of partisanship combining to increase individual rancor and reduce the institution's capacity for deliberation.

The Senate of the 1950s: The Old Club Ties

In his classic study of the Senate, published in 1960, political scientist Donald Matthews approvingly quoted a senator as observing that each member "of the Senate has as much power as he has the sense to use. For this very reason he has to be careful to use it properly or else he will incur the wrath of his

---

[20]Eric Uslaner, *The Decline of Comity in Congress* (Ann Arbor: University of Michigan Press, 1994), esp. chap. 5.

[21]See, for example, Judd Choate "Changing Perspectives on Congressional Norms" (paper presented at American Political Science Association meeting, San Francisco, August 29–September 1, 1996).

colleagues."[22] Such restraint typified the unspoken limits imposed by the "folk-ways" that Matthews discovered in his research.

Six important norms governed Senate behavior, according to Matthews:[23]

▶ *Apprenticeship,* which included performing menial tasks (such as pre-siding over floor debate on routine matters), speaking only occasionally on the floor, and generally deferring to senior senators.

▶ *Legislative work,* which emphasized doing the unglamorous tasks that fill up most days, as opposed to seeking publicity for one's actions and statements.

▶ *Specialization,* which meant focusing virtually all of one's efforts on work within two or three of the ten-plus subcommittees and commit-tees that a member was assigned to.

▶ *Courtesy,* which "permitted competitors to cooperate"[24] by discouraging public, personal attacks, especially in floor debate, and encouraging elaborate compliments between senators of all political stripes (for example, "My good friend, the most distinguished senator from _____, has made an excellent point, but I must offer an alternative perspective . . .").

▶ *Institutional patriotism,* which translated into a willingness to defend the Senate, with a strong emotional commitment to the body and its members.

▶ *Reciprocity,* which was perhaps the single most important folkway, in that the bargaining among senators depended on the unstated premise that no individual would take advantage of the practice of performing mutual favors on a host of issues and procedures.

In the 1950s, most senators played by these informal rules of the game most of the time. There were notable exceptions, ranging from Senator Joe McCarthy's (R-Wis.) abuse of the investigative process in his hearings on com-munist penetration of the government to first-term Senator William Proxmire's (D-Wis.) conscious decision not to observe the chamber's norms.[25] But the institution was dominated by veteran legislators, including many Southern

---

[22]Quoted in Donald Matthews, *U.S. Senators and Their World,* p. 101. Matthews discusses at length the *men* in the Senate, and this quote makes the assumption of gender. The fact is that the Sen-ate of the 1950s was a white male institution, as it has always been. Senator Margaret Chase Smith (R-Maine) was the single exception in the 1950s.

[23]Matthews, *U.S. Senators and Their World,* pp. 92ff.

[24]Matthews, *U.S. Senators and Their World,* p. 99.

[25]Ralph K. Huitt, "The Outsider in the Senate," *American Political Science Review* (September 1961): pp. 566–575. It may be no coincidence that McCarthy and his successor Proxmire both hailed from Wisconsin. Although the state has elected its share of team players, it did send one of the ultimate nonconformists—Robert LaFollette—to the Senate, and its newest senator, Russ Feingold, based his campaign on his status as an outsider.

Democrats. White's almost reverential description of the "Senate type" captures the essence of respect for the chamber's folkways. Such a loyalist, White writes,

> makes the Institution his home in an almost literal sense, and certainly in a deeply emotional sense. His head swims with its history, its lore and the accounts of past personnel and deeds and purposes. . . . His concern for the preservation is so great that he distrusts anything out of the ordinary, . . . [and] the Senate type knows precisely how to treat his colleagues. . . .
>
> Indeed, it may be that [tolerance] is one of the keys to the qualities of the Senate type — tolerance toward his fellows, intolerance toward any who would in any way change the Senate, its customs or way of life.[26]

One effect of general adherence to the Senate's folkways was to reinforce the decentralized power of the committee system, where the norm of seniority, a well-established element of reciprocity, had been elevated to a governing principle for both parties in advancing members toward committee chairmanships. Relying on seniority meant that consecutive service on a committee was virtually the sole criterion for selecting a chair. This encouraged senators to build careers on given panels and defend the related programs and jurisdictions (the turf) against all challenges. At the core of the Senate, according to both supporters (such as White) and critics (such as Senator Joseph Clark, [D-Pa.]), was an "Inner Club" of senators who, along with the party leaders, pulled together the committee-based structure that dominated legislative process.[27] This was a tidy state of affairs for a relatively conservative, Southern-dominated Senate that had a limited policy agenda.

Even as Matthews was defining the Senate's folkways and White was celebrating them, the institution and its norms were evolving. Randall Ripley, for example, labels the 1937–1955 Senate as *decentralized* but sees the 1955–1961 period as one of transition to a more *individualistic* body, which it was from 1961 on.[28] Given their informality, norms are always susceptible to erosion, and the Senate was beginning to change, however imperceptibly, in the 1950s. Although the large, liberal Democratic "class of 1958" would increase pressure on some of the norms, such as apprenticeship, it was Lyndon Johnson, one of the pillars of the Inner Club, who initiated the slide toward individualism. In a bid to strengthen his own position, as minority leader in 1953, Johnson instituted a committee assignment rule that guaranteed every Democratic senator a seat on at least one major committee. He continued this practice as majority leader (1955–1960), and Republican leaders followed suit. The "Johnson rule" thus enhanced the individual standing of all incoming senators, while simultaneously placing each in the debt of the party leadership. Although this practice

---

[26]William S. White, *Citadel* (New York: Harper & Row, 1956), pp. 85ff.

[27]See Joseph S. Clark, *Congress: The Sapless Branch* (New York, Harper & Row, 1964).

[28]Randall Ripley, *Power in the Senate* (New York: St. Martin's, 1969), pp. 13ff.

did not demolish the apprenticeship norm, it did increase the expectations that every senator had something to contribute, even during their initial months of service.

Norm Change and the Individualistic Senate

In two distinct but related ways, power within the Senate changed dramatically between the late 1950s and the 1970s. First, liberal and mostly non-Southern Democrats rose to occupy key committee positions.[29] Second, the Senate became more thoroughly individualistic as various institutional norms evolved or, in the case of apprenticeship, simply disappeared.

Rohde, Ornstein, and Peabody divided Matthews' six folkways into two separate types:[30]

▶ *General benefit norms* including legislative work, courtesy, reciprocity, and institutional patriotism, which serve all members as well as the Senate as a whole.

▶ *Limited benefit norms* such as apprenticeship, which serve some senators at the expense of others.

Specialization falls into both categories. They found apprenticeship to have vanished by the early 1970s, while the remainder of the norms remained intact, though somewhat modified.

Even though most folkways were still in place, the demise of apprenticeship, along with a decline in specialization, signaled much greater individualism in the chamber. All one hundred senators were expected to participate in the process, and there was little time for learning the ropes through years of committee experience.

By 1984, Rohde and his colleagues noted that "the egalitarian trend that opened up the Senate and shared power more widely among its members still holds sway."[31] Moreover, they observed a decline in the other general benefit norms, as an increasing workload and greater ideological divisions had begun to undermine some of the traditional Senate comity. In particular, they noted Senator Jesse Helms' (R-N.C.) "frequent violations of courtesy and reciprocity."[32] Somewhat perversely, they interpreted the public criticisms of Helms by fellow conservative Republican senators such as Arizona's Barry Goldwater and Wyoming's Alan Simpson as indicating that "the behavior of Helms is

---

[29]See Ripley, *Power in the Senate,* David W. Rohde, Norman J. Ornstein, and Robert L. Peabody, "Political Change and the U.S. Senate, 1957–1974," in Glenn Parker, ed., *Studies of Congress* (Washington, DC: CQ Press, 1985), pp. 147–188; Barbara Sinclair, *The Transformation of the U.S. Senate* (Baltimore: Johns Hopkins University Press, 1989).

[30]Rohde, Ornstein, and Peabody, "Political Change and the Senate," p. 183.

[31]Rohde, Ornstein, and Peabody, "Political Change and the Senate," p. 183.

[32]Rohde, Ornstein, and Peabody, "Political Change and the Senate," p. 183.

viewed by colleagues as violations of expectations, which tells us that the norms are still intact."[33]

The juxtaposition of behavior and norms is, of course, one of the problems in assessing the importance of informal rules of the game. Sooner or later, if there are lots of violations of norms by Helms and others, we are justified in asking if the folkways have any effect in restraining behavior. Under the generally permissive majority leaderships of Senators Mike Mansfield (D-Mont., 1961–1976), Robert Byrd (D-W.V., 1977–1980 and 1987–1988), and Howard Baker (R-Tenn., 1981–1984) some legislators felt a growing freedom to flout or take advantage of the reciprocity and courtesy norms. Indeed, near the end of his tenure, a frustrated Baker "wondered aloud whether 'the principal job of the leadership is janitorial.'"[34]

In the end, behavior contradicting the traditional folkways will reformulate the accepted rules of the game. By the late 1980s, Matthews' set of norms, although still generally recognizable, had been so modified that they helped produce a very different Senate from that of the 1950s. As congressional scholar Barbara Sinclair has concluded, "Both in terms of expectations and behavior, the norms of apprenticeship, specialization and legislative work are defunct; reciprocity and institutional patriotism have undergone major changes; courtesy is still a Senate norm but is more frequently breached in practice."[35]

Obstructionism and the Partisan Impulse in the Contemporary Senate

The Senate has always provided great leeway to its members, and its processes have emphasized lengthy deliberation rather than speedy action. Indeed, "extended debate" (the filibuster) is probably the best-known single element of Senate procedure, as much as a result of Jimmy Stewart's performance in *Mr. Smith Goes to Washington* as of the speeches of LaFollette, the record-setting effort of Senator Strom Thurmond (R-S.C.) (more than twenty-four hours straight), or a well-organized Southern opposition to civil rights legislation in the 1950s and early 1960s.

In fact, filibusters were rarely undertaken in the decentralized but collegial Senate of the 1950s. They have become much more common in the contemporary chamber, as both individual members and organized factions have used the tactic to bring the chamber's business to a halt over minor issues and even for matters of convenience (such as a scheduling dispute). Despite the procedural importance of filibusters, their frequent use and even more frequent

---

[33]Rohde, Ornstein, and Peabody, "Political Change and the Senate," p. 183.

[34]Quoted in Roger Davidson, "Senate Leaders: Janitors for an Untidy Chamber," in Lawrence Dodd and Bruce I. Oppenheimer, eds., *Congress Reconsidered,* 3rd ed. (Washington, DC: CQ Press, 1985), p. 225.

[35]Barbara Sinclair, *The Transformation of the U.S. Senate* (Baltimore: Johns Hopkins University Press, 1989), p. 101.

threatened use demonstrate a pernicious side of the increasingly individualistic Senate. In 1982 Senator Russell Long (D-La.), whose service began in 1948, argued as a member in good standing of the Inner Club that "we've given far too much power to the impeders [of action]."[36] Congressional scholar Barbara Sinclair concludes that the Senate has created this situation "*not by changing its rules,* but by being *unwilling and unable* to prevent senators from fully exploiting the power those rules grant to each of them."[37] And informed rules of the game have not constrained actions by a Helms or former Senator Howard Metzenbaum, who often abused the Senate reliance on unanimous consent to conduct its business.

Again, we get the kind of Senate that the senators give us. In the 1950s the chamber's individualism was restrained by the general agreement on the folkways that constrained the individual behavior of most senators. Occasional mavericks such as Proxmire or aggressive committee chairman Estes Kefauver (D-Tenn.) could be regarded as lively exceptions to the prevailing norms. As Senator Joseph Biden (D-Del.) observed, "We end up with 100 Proxmires here. One . . . makes a real contribution. All you need is 30 of them to guarantee the place doesn't work."[38]

Given its informality and reliance on cordial, respectful relations among its members, the Senate is fractured by declining reciprocity and courtesy. Tending to the well-being of the entire chamber does not offer many rewards. Rather, as Sinclair bleakly reports, "Asked their prescription for being an effective senator, several staffers (not attached to senators particularly known for pushing their powers to the limit) responded that *the senator who does not care if he is liked can be very effective.*" There is perhaps no better indicator of how much the Senate has changed.[39]

Some observers, such as political scientist Ross Baker, see this interpretation of the Senate as a sort of snapshot in time, taken in the early 1980s and since modified. But given the vitriolic exchanges between senators in the Supreme Court confirmation hearings for Robert Bork (1987) and Clarence Thomas (1991), among other well-publicized disputes, his perspective seems unduly optimistic. Especially when combined with the frustrations inherent in addressing tough issues within a chamber that is so difficult to lead, it is no wonder that such noted senators as Nancy Kassebaum (R-Kans.), Warren Rudman (R-N.H.), David Boren (D-Okla.), Bill Bradley (D-N.J.), and Sam Nunn (D-Ga.) decided voluntarily in recent years to leave the body. It is thus ironic that the increasing overlay of partisanship (see Chapter 7) in the Senate has done little to curb rampant individualism. The polarized environment of the

---

[36]Quoted in Sinclair, *The Transformation of the U.S. Senate,* p. 125.

[37]Sinclair, *The Transformation of the U.S. Senate,* p. 125. Emphasis added.

[38]Uslaner, *The Decline of Comity in Congress,* pp. 24–25. Uslaner cites Senator Bob Packwood (R-Oreg.) as making a similar estimate of twenty-five or so senators who cannot be trusted to keep their word, thus threatening the key norm of reciprocity.

[39]Sinclair, *The Transformation of the U.S. Senate,* p. 204. Emphasis added.

post–1994 Republican era has often led to stalemate and acrimony, although the demise of strong party leadership in the House has offered a considerable opening for Senate Republicans and Majority Leader Trent Lott. Still, the combination of (a) partisan behavior, (b) individualism, and (c) the filibuster[40] has left the Senate in search of a "stable and satisfying role" in American politics.[41] Ironically, impeachment may have strengthened Lott's hand as Republican floor leader, in that he emerged from the process with an enhanced reputation, in part because he maintained a strong and effective relationship with Minority Leader Tom Daschle (D-S.D.).

The House Is Not a Home

Given its size and the related need for organization, informal rules of the game have never been quite as important in the House as in the Senate. Nonetheless, norms remain significant in this fragmented body, and all evidence points to a substantial "decline in comity" in the house.[42] The Rayburn-era House (late 1930s–1961) resembled the clubbish Senate in many ways. Apprenticeships were long, specialization was expected, and virtually all members assumed that courtesy and reciprocity would govern their relations.

The infusion of new members into the House — especially after the Democratic landslides of 1958, 1964, and 1974 and the widespread Republican victories of 1966, 1978, and 1980 — caused a twenty-year reevaluation of legislative folkways.[43] Although the data are sketchy, the trend is clear: Less than half the junior members completely accept the bedrock norms of courtesy and reciprocity. In addition, almost all these legislators reject the notions of apprenticeship and institutional patriotism.

Anecdotal evidence offers extensive support for these survey data. Members have scuffled in the House aisles, and others have had to be physically restrained from doing so. The level of verbal attacks has also escalated steadily since the early 1970s. Members who entered the House in the mid-1970s were more attuned to the chamber's folkways as newcomers than they were later as three-term veterans; in 1976, 63 percent of first-termers reported that "personal cordiality" was very important; four years later, only 37 percent of this group agreed.[44]

---

[40]Sarah Binder and Steven S. Smith, in *Politics or Principle: Filibustering in the United States Senate* (Washington, DC: Brookings Institution, 1997), conclude that filibusters have generally served partisan purposes, not those of principled advocates.

[41]Norman J. Ornstein, Robert L. Peabody, and David W. Rohde, "The U.S. Senate: Toward the 21st Century," in Lawrence Dodd and Bruce I. Oppenheimer, eds. *Congress Reconsidered*, 6th ed., (Washington, DC: CQ Press, 1997), p. 27. See also, Robert Dreyfuss, "Mississippi Waltz," *American Prospect* (March–April, 1999), pp. 18–25.

[42]See Uslaner, *The Decline of Comity in Congress*, chap. 2.

[43]The data here come from Burdett Loomis, *The New American Politician* (New York: Basic Books, 1988), p. 48; Herbert Asher, "The Learning of Legislative Norms," *American Political Science Review* 67 (June 1973): p. 503.

[44]Loomis, *The New American Politician*, p. 48.

A study of civility in the 104th and earlier Congresses, focusing on the House, found that by most measures the 104th Congress was the least civil in more than 40 years.[45] House members and reporters thought that incivility had risen steadily in past years, the study's data — based largely on *Congressional Record* scans — demonstrated only a sharp spike in the first session of the 104th Congress. Still, contentious rhetoric remains a part of House debates, and many members feel alienated from the institution in which they serve.

In sum, the bonds forged by the informal rules of the game have weakened in the House, much as they have in the Senate. Such a breakdown, both in behavior and the reported acceptance of norms, may have fewer obvious consequences in the House, but no one could confuse the 1950s House of Sam Rayburn and Republican leader Joseph Martin with the contemporary chamber of Speakers Jim Wright and Newt Gingrich (R-Ga.).[46] There can be little hope that folkways will soon contribute much toward producing a well-integrated, coherent, productive House of Representatives.

RULES AND NORMS, AND THE LEGISLATIVE ARENA

The tensions between centralizing and decentralizing elements on Capitol Hill come in many forms; congressional scholars have most often focused their attention on committees and parties as the major elements of such tensions, but the nature of the legislative process — both formal and informal — plays an important role. The postreform Congress has encouraged less comity, more individualism, and behavior that aggressively uses institutional rules for partisan or personal advantage. In the House this has meant the assertion of majority control of the process, whereas the Senate has encouraged almost unfettered individualism. These developments have affected the possibilities for integration and coherence within the Congress in very different ways, with the majoritarian House often facing a Senate that is hard-pressed to act quickly and effectively.

Most obvious, and most important, has been the deterioration of folkways that structured legislative life in the Congress of the 1950s. This is not to say that norms such as apprenticeship made good use of legislators and their skills. Quite the contrary. Junior members' grudging willingness to place their careers on hold for several years as they learned the ropes merely reflected the imposing ability of committee chairs and top party leaders to enforce norms and dominate the legislative process.

Beginning in the late 1950s, an informal grouping of legislators — the Democratic Study Group — brought younger members together to provide a voice for greater distribution of power in the House and an end to apprentice-

---

[45]Kathleen Hall Jamieson, *Civility in the House of Representatives* (Philadelphia: Annenberg Public Policy Center, 1997).

[46]See John Barry, *The Ambition and the Power* (New York: Viking, 1989).

ship. Equally important as a motivating factor for this change was the growing legislative workload that came with the enactment and oversight of the Great Society and Nixon administration domestic programs. Making and overseeing this raft of new policy virtually required that the Congress make use of all its members, not just a handful of top committee and party leaders.

As a representative institution, Congress reflects the society at large, albeit with some significant distortions. The decline of the key congressional norms of reciprocity, courtesy, and institutional loyalty that together produce comity derives from a parallel erosion of comity in the population as a whole. The very representativeness of Congress is crucial; Uslaner argues that "Congress is first and foremost an institution of interest representation. If the cause of the decline of comity in Congress is a waning of values in the larger society, then neither structural reform nor exhortation can restore the folkways of the 1950s and 1960s."[47]

Well-accepted folkways — reciprocity in particular — could sometimes overcome the representation of narrow interests, especially when compromises could be hammered out behind closed doors. Ironically, reforms that opened up the Congress to public scrutiny (such as more recorded votes, televised sessions, and open committee meetings) provided interests with greatly increased amounts of information as to how they were being treated within the legislative process. Moreover, junior legislators, freed from many of the constraints imposed by the folkways of the Rayburn era, could become much more active as independent operators on Capitol Hill. The "new apprenticeship" of the 1970s and 1980s encouraged members to take on key policy roles in caucuses, party task forces, and subcommittees very early in their careers.[48] Yet John Hibbing demonstrates that of all the components of a legislative career, the only element that changes dramatically over time is significant involvement in the legislative process.[49] It may well take substantial experience to become a major force in lawmaking, regardless of the norms regarding activity. By the mid-1980s, for example, members of the highly active "class of 1974" began to move into the formal positions in parties and committees that would allow them consistent impact on outcomes.[50]

Long careers based on the skillful use of incumbency and its resources may insulate members of Congress from their parties and the president, but many of these same lawmakers do eventually fill formal positions that grant them increased legislative opportunities. Indeed, given its ascension to majority status and its great increase in numbers, the Republican party in the House

---

[47]Uslaner, *The Decline of Comity in Congress,* p. 168.

[48]Christopher J. Deering, "The New Apprenticeship: Strategies of Effectiveness for New Members of the House" (paper presented at the American Political Science Association meeting, August 30–September 2, 1984).

[49]John Hibbing, *Congressional Careers* (Chapel Hill: University of North Carolina Press, 1991), chap. 5.

[50]Loomis, *The New American Politician,* chap. 5.

has relied heavily on junior members not only to cast important votes, but also to sit on key committees, chair important subcommittees, and head major task forces.[51] To take advantage of these possibilities for influence, however, legislators must move beyond merely representing interests to develop broad, majority-building proposals and strategies. With its majoritarian rules and structure, as expressed by centralized party leadership control of the Rules Committee, for example, the House has sometimes harnessed the energy of its junior members to build consistent partisan majorities. At the same time, many Republican representatives plan on leaving the House after a few terms, even if they remain in the majority. As Representative Joe Scarborough (R-Fla.) put it, "It's not fun. . . . If I didn't feel I was part of an important movement, I'd be home. . . . I can't imagine being in the back benches of the minority for more than two years."[52] On a Capitol Hill that discourages comity and rewards the representations of a series of specific interests, generating the succession of majorities needed to pass important legislation remains a difficult feat, especially when the well-entrenched individualism that is nurtured by the permissive rules and the evolving norms of the Senate meets the emotional partisanship that characterizes the House.[53]

---

[51]See Linda Killian, *The Freshmen* (New York: Westview Press, 1998).

[52]Joe Scarborough, quoted in Nicol C. Rae, *Conservative Reformers* (Armonk, NY: M. E. Sharpe, 1998, p. 199. See also Killian, *The Freshmen,* and Timothy J. Barnett, *Legislative Learning: The 104th Republicans in the House* (New York: Garland, 1999)

[53]See Fred R. Harris, *Deadlock or Decision* (New York: Oxford University Press, 1993), chap. 4. Harris argues that the nationalization of Senate politics has gone hand in hand with its growing individualism. In 1999, Senate leaders Lott and Daschle asserted that anonymous "holds" on legislation would no longer be granted. Senators could object to a bill, but they would have to agree to be identified as obstructing the legislative processes.

Ten

THE COMPETITIVE CONGRESS: CENTRIFUGAL FORCES IN A PARTISAN ERA

April 17, 1997. For those who think that irony has vanished from modern politics, the morning's proceedings in the House of Representatives offered a telling contradiction. Indeed, irony emerged intact, even triumphant. In the Rayburn Office Building, named for the Speaker who encouraged members to "get along" by "going along," a subcommittee of the Rules Committee opened hearings on comity in Congress. Academics, members, and staff gathered to explore how partisanship can coexist with civility, productive debate, and meaningful deliberation. After the first witnesses' opening statements, however, Representative David Dreier (R-Calif.) sheepishly announced that he and his fellow committee members must adjourn the hearing because of a pending vote on the House floor. For veterans of committee hearings, such disruptions are commonplace, the price of testifying before busy members of Congress. But that day's vote was unexpected, and unwelcome, in that it came during the one-minute speeches that precede the major legislative business of the day.

On the House floor, after a series of increasingly inflammatory and coordinated statements from both sides of the aisle, Representative John Lewis (D-Ga.) had called Speaker Newt Gingrich an admitted liar in the context of his settling a $300,000 judgment against him by the House.[1] Veteran Representative Gerald Solomon (R-N.Y.) requested that the sitting chair of the House "take down" (that is, strike) Lewis's words from the *Congressional Record;* approval of such a motion would mean that Lewis could not speak again in the day's debate without the assent of the entire House. More importantly, having one's words taken down represents a serious reprimand for a representative. On a party-line vote (save for a few Democratic defectors), the House did

---

[1]The House Committee on Official Conduct, often labeled the Ethics Committee, entered into an agreement with the Speaker that he pay $300,000 to the House to compensate the body for its extended investigation into the financing of several organizations that supported him. Republicans called the payment a "reimbursement," while Democrats described it as a fine. The ambiguity of the decision allowed each side to characterize the payment in different terms. Moreover, Gingrich's decision to settle part of the debt by accepting a loan guaranteed by former GOP presidential candidate Bob Dole generated criticism, both inside and outside the House. In the end, Gingrich did not avail himself of Dole's assistance.

strike Lewis's words, the business of the House proceeded, and after a delay the subcommittee's hearing on civility resumed. Few legislators or scholars held much hope that comity would bloom on Capitol Hill in the 1990s.

Partisanship in speech and action remain central to the House, yet throughout that year and into the 106th Congress, the Republicans could not muster partisan majorities to move any important legislation through the chamber — almost a complete reversal of the 1995 glory days of the Contract with America. Finally, in October 1998, Republian majorities capitulated to pressure from President Clinton and agreed to a comprehensive budget package that favored the White House. In the end, given its narrow, twenty-vote majority in the 105th Congress, House Republicans were held hostage by even a few potential defectors on any given vote.

Nor were things much better in the Senate. On the same day that Lewis's words were taken down, the Senate Rules Committee voted along party lines to reject a bipartisan staff report and to pursue a full-scale investigation of voter fraud in the 1996 election of Mary Landrieu (D-La.) over Republican candidate Woody Jenkins.[2] In both the House and Senate, partisanship and individualism held sway simultaneously as the Congress edged into a new era of Republican control within a context of divided government.

This is not to say that the Congress was incapable of action. In 1996, far-reaching telecommunications reform, begun in a Democratic Congress, won final, bipartisan support in the Republican 104th Congress. In 1997, the congressional Republicans joined with the Clinton administration and some, though scarcely all, Capitol Hill Democrats to endorse and subsequently pass a balanced budget agreement, and in 1998–1999, Congress passed by large majorities, bills that would combine dozens of existing programs for job training and K–12 education. Partisan bickering does not mean that the legislative process necessarily drags to a halt. Indeed, the 1999 "ed-flex" legislation was enacted just a month after President Clinton's impeachment trial had ended.

THE OXYMORONIC CONGRESS: INDIVIDUALISTIC PARTISANSHIP

Writing in 1997, three veteran congressional scholars concluded that, regardless of its partisan makeup, the Senate

> has become a more decentralized, more democratized chamber. Individual senators, from the most senior to the most junior, have benefited — but have also become frustrated. . . . Neither a great deliberative body nor an efficient processor of laws, the Senate, after years of change, is an institution in search of an identity. [At the same time,] partisan tension and ideo-

---

[2]Donna Cassatta, "GOP Conservatives Get Their Wish as Louisiana Probe Expanded," *Congressional Quarterly Weekly Report,* April 19, 1997, pp. 886–887.

logical division became a more regular part of the institution [in the 104th and 105th Congresses], itself contributing to the decision of prominent centrist legislators like Nancy Kassebaum (R-Kans.), Bill Bradley (D-N.J.), and Bennett Johnston (D-La.) to retire.[3]

In both House and Senate, the combining of individualism/fragmentation with partisanship has made for a Congress that encourages — simultaneously — both centrifugal (decentralizing) and centripetal (centralizing) forces. In the House of Representatives, committees have regained some of the strength that they had surrendered to the Republican party leadership in 1995, although party leaders retain much of their formal authority. In the Senate, party voting rates have hovered at almost 90 percent on votes that divide the parties, yet an individual senator, such as Jesse Helms, can impose lengthy delays on key issues that a clear majority favors, as he did on the ratification of the chemical weapons treaty in 1996–1997. As the so-called postreform Congress of the 1981–1994 period gives way to a series of narrow Republican majorities in the late 1990s, both House and Senate are undergoing "an identity crisis."[4] Do we have a Congress in which a majority party sets out a coherent agenda? Or do we have a new phase of divided government, in which a weakened president faces a Congress that, despite its partisanship, seems incapable of producing reliable majorities? Perhaps, the more things change, the more they remain — roughly speaking — the same, defined by the checks and balances that have dominated U.S. politics, and congressional decision-making, since the founding.

THE LIMITS OF PARTISAN POLICY MAKING: THE CONTRACT WITH AMERICA AND ITS AFTERMATH

Whether a unique combination of circumstance and chutzpa or an indication of a sea change in congressional thinking, the House Republicans' capacity to develop a ten-item Contract with America, find near unanimous support for it, and then move all the items through the House in the first ninety-three days of the 104th Congress was a remarkable achievement. Despite modest success in winning Senate and/or presidential approval for Contract items, the Republicans demonstrated the potential for issue-based, even ideological, accomplishment by a unified congressional party. As discussed in Chapter 7, the extent of centralization within the House Republican Conference in the first session of the 104th Congress surprised virtually all observers. As Capitol Hill reporter

---

[3]Norman J. Ornstein, Robert L. Peabody, and David W. Rohde, "The U.S. Senate: Toward the Twenty-First Century," in Lawrence Dodd and Bruce I. Oppenheimer, eds., *Congress Reconsidered,* 6th ed. (Washington, DC: CQ Press, 1997), p. 26.

[4]Ornstein, Peabody, and Rohde, "The U.S. Senate," p. 3.

Richard Cohen wrote in March 1995, about sixty days after Republicans assumed control of the Congress:

> Self-styled experts, from lobbyists to think-tank types, are best advised to toss out their old scripts and to start from scratch. The notion of a House that's balkanized into legislative fiefdoms and informal caucuses — realities that, among others, helped to sink President Clinton's health care proposals last year — has become antiquated. Instead, the House is driven by a Speaker who wields extraordinary power and by rank-and-file Members who are intent on proving to a skeptical public that they can change how Washington works.[5]

But party unity and ideological zeal count for only so much in a political system that historically has encouraged fragmentation and delay. To be sure, homogeneous parties in both House and Senate have increased partisanship in both chambers, and legislators have been willing — on a conditional, contingent basis — to surrender some powers to their leaders. In the end, however, if elections produce closely divided legislative bodies, homogeneous party memberships and strong leaders will be hard pressed to overcome the pressures exerted by constituents and organized interests, the traditional sources of centrifugal politics.[6]

The 1994 Elections, the Contract, and the First 100 Days of Republican Control of Congress

Despite its overwhelming, and well-publicized, adoption by Republican House candidates in September 1994, the Contract with America did not directly determine the stunning GOP triumph in November. Most voters remained unaware of or unswayed by its ten provisions, and many successful Republican candidates downplayed it in the final weeks of the campaign. Yet the Contract quickly proved an effective rallying point for Speaker Newt Gingrich, who acknowledged that "we cleverly picked popular things to do"[7] (see Table 10–1). Nevertheless, Gingrich, the seventy-three Republican freshmen, and the Republican leadership could claim that moving the Contract quickly through the House "demonstrat[ed] that campaigns and elections really matter."[8] That judgment can be challenged by the ultimate results, but the House Republicans did succeed in fulfilling the Contract's principal goals — (1) to offer clear differences between the two congressional parties and (2) to

---

[5]Richard E. Cohen, "The Transformers," *National Journal*, March 4, 1995, pp. 528–529.

[6]See Lawrence C. Dodd and Bruce I. Oppenheimer, "Congress and the Emerging Order: Conditional Party Government or Constructive Partisanship?" in Dodd and Oppenheimer, eds., *Congress Reconsidered*, 6th ed., pp. 390–413.

[7]Quoted in John F. Stacks, "100 Days of Attitude," *Time*, April 10, 1995, p. 34.

[8]David S. Broder, "Thanks for the 'Contract,'" *Washington Post National Weekly Edition*, April 17–23, 1995.

TABLE 10-1
The Contract with America

Item	Voted in House (1995 date)	Signed into Law (1995, 1996, 1997, or not passed)
Preface, Congressional Reforms	January 4–5, 17	1995*
1. Balanced Budget Amendment	January 26,	Not passed†
Line-Item Veto	February 6	1996
2. Crime Bills (various)	February 10	1996‡
3. Welfare Reform	March 24	1996
4. Families and Children (various)	April 5	1996
5. Middle-Class Tax Cut	April 5	1997
6. National Security (various, including missile defense, prohibition of U.S. troops under command of UN)	February 16	Not passed or vetoed
7. Social Security earnings limit rise	April 5	Passed
Repeal of 1993 tax on benefits		Not passed
8. Capital gain cuts	April 4	1997
Reduced unfunded mandates	April 4	Passed
9. Civil Law and Product Liability Reform	March 10	Not passed
10. Term Limits	March 29	Not passed†

*Many changes are internal to House; major legislation is Congressional Accountability Act that requires Congress to end exemptions to eleven workplace laws.

†Constitutional Amendment, does not require presidential approval.

‡Signed in various subsequent packages.

Source: Congressional Quarterly Weekly Report, various issues.

demonstrate their competence to govern by presenting workable ideas for solving major societal problems.[9]

Indeed, the 1994 elections mattered in terms of partisan politics and democratic accountability, and the nationalized campaign worked to centralize the power of Speaker Gingrich and the House Republicans. First, Gingrich's ability to funnel funds to challengers and open-seat candidates provided a solid base of backing within the new Republican class of seventy-three conservatives.

---

[9]John B. Bader, *Taking the Initiative* (Washington, DC: Georgetown University Press), p. 181ff. More generally, Bader provides a thorough, theoretically driven analysis of the contract in the broader context of congressional policy development. The GOP freshman class and the 104th Congress have stimulated a lot of research and writing. Judgments on the impact of the class (and the 104th Congress) vary, to an extent based on when the book was completed. Major works include: James Gimpel, *Fulfilling the Contract* (Boston: Allyn & Bacon, 1997); Richard F. Fenno, Jr., *Learning to Govern* (Washington, DC: Brookings Institution, 1997); C. Lawrence Evans and Walter J. Oleszek, *Congress Under Fire* (Boston: Houghton Mifflin, 1997); Elizabeth Drew, *Showdown* (New York: Touchstone, 1997); Douglas L. Koopman, *Hostile Takeover* (Lanham, MD: Rowan & Littlefield, 1996); David Maraniss and Michael Weisskopf, *Tell Newt to Shut Up* (New York, Touchstone, 1996); Nicol C. Rae, *Conservative Reformers* (Armonk, NY: M. E. Sharpe, 1998); Linda Killian, *The Freshmen* (Boulder, Westview Press, 1998); and Timothy J. Barnett, *Legislative Learning: The 104th Republicans in the House* (New York: Garland, 1999).

Second, the returning Republican incumbents almost unanimously gave him credit for building the first House Republican majority in forty years.

Nowhere were the differences between the Democratic 103rd Congress and the Republican 104th Congress more striking than in the relationships between party leaders and committee chairs. Speaker Gingrich did not have to face entrenched, independently powerful chairmen; rather, grateful Republicans gave him the authority to choose committee leaders, subject to Conference approval. In the end, the Republican chairs were veteran loyalists who almost uniformly worked hand in glove with the party leadership to hurry the Contract items through the legislative process. For example, in January, Judiciary Committee chair Henry Hyde (R-Ill.) cut off debate on a balanced budget plan while Democrats still had amendments to offer, and the House Government Reform Committee approved unfunded mandates legislation without holding any committee hearings.[10]

In fact, despite heavy workloads, committees largely carried the Republican leadership's water during the hundred-day push to enact the contract. When disagreements surfaced, there was little question of who held the reins of power. After the Government Reform Committee came to a bipartisan agreement on protecting children from intrusive federal surveys, "the leadership jettisoned the compromise" and substituted the original Contract language.[11] Overall, party leaders tended to dominate in their relationships with committee chairs during the consideration of Contract-based legislation in early 1995; the party's self-imposed deadlines denied committees the opportunity to deliberate thoroughly or rally particular interests to support a panel's position. The time constraints of passing the Contract advantaged the party leaders and reduced most committees to supporting roles in the first few months of the 104th Congress.

Beyond the extensive powers the Republican Conference granted Newt Gingrich as Speaker (see Chapter 7), the Contract with America enhanced the strength of the entire party leadership. The Contract and its hundred-day deadline for bringing items to a vote proved an ideal vehicle for channeling the "pent-up demand" of a long-frustrated Republican House minority.[12] At the same time, House Republicans harbored only modest ideological diversity, at least compared with their Democratic counterparts, and Gingrich maintained good relations with his party's moderates in the transition to majority status. Even with a unified party, Republican leaders discovered that to remain on schedule they needed to exploit the distinct procedural advantages enjoyed by the House majority. This posed a significant problem for the Republicans, both politically

---

[10]Janet Hook, "GOP's Race to Move 'Contract' Hits a Few Bumps in Road," *Congressional Quarterly Weekly Report,* January 14, 1995, p. 136.

[11]Donna Cassatta, "Republicans Bask in Success of Rousing Performance," *Congressional Quarterly Weekly Report,* April 8, 1995, p. 988.

[12]Former Representative Bill Frenzel (R-Minn.), quoted in Cassatta, "Republicans Bask in Success of Rousing Performance," p. 986.

and philosophically. Among their most bitter complaints against the Democratic leadership were legitimate claims that the Rules Committee systematically denied them the opportunity to offer meaningful amendments. Republican leaders promised that they would not resort to such procedural games to maintain control of floor action. Nevertheless, as time pressures mounted, Speaker Gingrich and Majority Leader Armey sought rules that protected Contract items from attack on the House floor. Representative Christopher Shays (R-Conn.) pointed out that "it just got more and more restrictive as we went along [through the 100 days]. We began to do what we had criticized Democrats for."[13]

The Republicans' ninety-three-day forced march in passing most of the Contract demonstrated their leadership's clear understanding that the House is a majoritarian body. With only modest lapses, GOP legislators provided consistent backing for a Speaker who acted more like a prime minister than a legislative leader. At least temporarily, the fragmenting elements of committees, caucuses, individual policy entrepreneurs, self-interested incumbents, and particularistic interest groups proved weaker than a legislative party buoyed by long-awaited electoral success and a willingness to invest great power in its leaders.

In the end, however, no speaker can be a prime minister, who combines both legislative and executive power. Given a bicameral legislature and a divided government, the Contract votes did not reflect an authoritative set of decisions, in that Senate modifications, conference committee negotiations, and presidential vetoes stood between the House Republicans and their agenda of policy change.

Newt Gingrich Meets James Madison

Even though nine of the original Contract items had won House passage, as did a series of legislative reforms, the Republican Revolution was scarcely complete. The Republican Senate was scarcely as radical as the House, and the White House remained in Democratic hands. Buttressing the "Civics 101" realities of Madisonian checks and balances were Senate Majority Leader Bob Dole and President Bill Clinton, who shared both a tendency toward compromise and a concern for how their actions would look to voters in the 1996 presidential campaign.[14] Despite all the attention accorded the particular items in the Contract, much of the success or failure of the House initiatives in 1995–1996 would come in the budget for fiscal year 1996, which was scheduled to go into effect on October 1, 1995.

In contrast to the highly partisan and programmatic nature of Speaker Gingrich's House of Representatives, the Republican Senate retained its individualistic nature, even as it became more partisan (see Chapter 7). Led by Majority

---

[13]Quoted in Jennifer Babson, "Armey Stood Guard over Contract," *Congressional Quarterly Weekly Report,* April 8, 1995, p. 987. For further elaboration of the Republican use of restrictive rules, see Chapter 9.

[14]Clinton was virtually assured renomination; Dole stood as the front-runner for the Republican nomination throughout 1995 and early 1996, before sewing it up by April 1996.

Leader Dole and Budget Committee chair Pete Domenici (R-N.M.), GOP senators generally favored a budget that emphasized deficit reduction and downplayed a major tax cut (which House Republicans called the "Crown Jewel" of
the Contract).[15] Overall, the House budget cut many more programs (280 vs.
100) and proposed greater tax relief ($353 billion vs. $170 billion that would
kick in only after the budget was balanced) than did the Senate proposal. In
the end, after fending off proposals to cut taxes sharply, the Senate voted,
mostly along party lines, for a budget that mandated tax cuts to be financed by
the savings from balancing the budget.[16] For the most part, the Senate had followed the House's footsteps on the FY1996 budget; at the same time, the Senate had demonstrated its preference for deficit reduction over large tax cuts.

Simultaneously, President Clinton still had to agree to any set of budget
figures, and he signaled his willingness to play hardball by vetoing the final
1995 rescission bill that included more cuts in education than he desired.[17] Perhaps as a precursor of things to come, an acceptable compromise to the
vetoed legislation did not clear the Congress for almost two months after Clinton's May veto, largely because various factions mounted a filibuster in the
Senate, much to the dismay of Majority Leader Dole.

The long delay demonstrated that the Madisonian checks and balances
remained in working order, as did the tortuous House-Senate conference over
the FY1996 budget numbers. Moreover, even as the budget worked its way
through the legislative process, the Republicans in both House and Senate
employed their new majorities to attack myriad federal programs, ranging from
the National Endowment for the Arts to enforcement of environmental laws. In
vote after vote, debate after debate, partisanship was the order of the day, and
Speaker Gingrich worked continuously to maintain his majority through negotiations with factions inside his own legislative party.

In particular, the Republican leadership found itself at loggerheads with
many of the members of its prized freshman class. As Majority Leader Richard
Armey observed, some zealous first-termers "have something they want to get
done and have a sense of urgency about it." Problems arise, he noted, because
"You never compromise on principle but you do on details." The freshmen,
however, "don't understand the practical need to bend a little here and there to
serve the principle."[18]

In November 1995 and January 1996, the deadlock between the Democratic president and the Republican Congress shut down large parts of the federal government, as President Clinton would not agree to various conditions
placed upon continuing resolutions that would have kept the government

---

[15]Drew, *Showdown* p. 207ff.

[16]Drew, *Showdown,* p. 212.

[17]Rescissions legislation is part of the budget process that produces cuts to meet current budget
year targets. Thus, as the FY1996 budget was taking shape, the 1995 rescissions bills were also
under consideration.

[18]Quoted in Killian, *The Freshman,* p. 31.

open. The conflict between the branches went to the heart of the constitutional system. The Republican suspicion of government, best expressed in the first-term Representatives' sense of an electoral mandate to slash programs, prompted veteran Senator Paul Sarbanes (D-Md.) to respond: "To make our Constitutional system work requires a certain amount of restraint and good judgment on the part of decision-makers. It must be an essential part of our system that one is not willing to subvert everything, in effect to bring the whole building crashing down, in order to get your way."[19] In essence, the House Republicans, dragging along their often-reluctant Senate counterparts, allowed themselves to be blamed for shutting down large parts of the federal government, even as the separation of powers operated — however inelegantly — more or less the way the Framers envisioned it.

Although Gingrich's star fell throughout 1996 and the House Republicans abandoned much of their absolutist approach to the Contract and the budget, it would be a mistake to underestimate the long-term impact of their actions. First, they did succeed in implementing some significant internal House reforms (see Chapter 9); second, several of the Contract's items did become law, most notably the 1996 welfare reform bill that Clinton signed (see Table 10-1); and third, both the particulars and the tone of the congressional debate turned toward the right. Most significant, perhaps, was the willingness of most members of Congress, regardless of party, to support balancing the budget by 2002 — sentiments that led directly to the May 1997 agreement to do exactly that.[20]

More generally, the 1997 budget deal illustrates the continuing importance of cross-partisan coalitions in the Congress, as so-called deficit hawks in both parties worked together to reach an agreement. Despite the growth of party-based voting patterns over the 1980s and 1990s, most major legislation obtains support across parties. Likewise, the 1997 budget agreement emphasizes the resilience of the committee system; although negotiations reflected the typically centralized pattern that has become familiar in the postreform Congress, the crucial details remain in the hands of the major committees, especially Ways and Means and Finance.[21]

Turning to electoral politics, the Republicans survived their confrontation with the administration to retain control of both the House and Senate in 1996.

---

[19]Quoted in Drew, *Showdown,* p. 336. Ironically, House Republicans made almost the exact same mistake in 1997 as they loaded partisan items on to a disaster aid bill, which Clinton vetoed.

[20]Embodied in 1997 legislation, President Clinton, most congressional Republicans, and a substantial number of Democratic legislators reached a compromise plan that was facilitated by favorable economic conditions and optimistic projections for federal revenues. Despite some skepticism, most observers and participants viewed the agreement as promising the real chance of balancing the budget. See various articles, *New York Times* and *Congressional Quarterly Weekly Report,* May–July, 1997.

[21]Once the budget deal was converted into legislation, the taxing and spending committees and their chairs became more important. On the role of Representative Bill Archer (R-Tex.), the Ways and Means chair, see Jerry Gray, "New Budget Pact Goes to Congress," *New York Times,* May 4, 1997, p. 1. See also, Daniel J. Palazzolo, *Done Deal?* (New York: Chatham House, 1999).

House Republicans may have felt betrayed as the contract became less relevant in the waning days of the 104th Congress, but 92 percent of them won reelection to the 105th Congress, a performance that offered the possibility of long-term GOP majority status on Capitol Hill. As Speaker Gingrich observed in 1996, "It takes two elections to make the revolution real."[22] Or maybe more.

Indeed, Gingrich's words seemed especially empty in the wake of the third election (1998) of the post-1994 Republican era, which saw the GOP's House majority whittled to a 223-211 margin. Any modest grouping of Republicans could threaten to break ranks to defeat a leadership initiative. In fact, such a threat doomed any hopes Gingrich had for remaining Speaker in the 106th Congress and led to his resignation from the Congress. After the six-week rise and fall of putative Speaker Robert Livingston (R-La.), the majority settled on the popular, low-key, and relatively unknown Dennis Hastert (R-Ill.) as Speaker for the 106th Congress. To an extent this choice recognized that even a unified Republican party would have a great deal of trouble in passing much of a policy agenda. At the same time, in the wake of the 1998 elections (and before the commencement of the 106th Congress in early January 1999), the House of Representatives embarked on the highly partisan impeachment of President Bill Clinton.

In many ways, the Clinton impeachment in the House and the subsequent Senate trial (January–February 1999) both marked the end of the Gingrich reign and reemphasized the partisanship that dominates life on Capitol Hill. Moreover, the impeachment episode frames the tensions between Republicans and Democrats, between House and Senate, between the president and Congress, and between the Congress and the public that define the nature of congressional politics in a highly competitive, highly contentious era. The following few pages do not offer any complete rendering of the Clinton impeachment and trial; rather, they lay out briefly how the politics of impeachment shed light on many aspects of the contemporary Congress.

THE CONGRESS AND IMPEACHMENT: OF PARTISANSHIP AND PRINCIPLE

Congressional scholars have consistently emphasized the importance of party within the Congress of the 1980s and 1990s,[23] and the impeachment proceed-

---

[22]Quoted in Drew, *Showdown*, p. 375.

[23]Among others, see David W. Rohde, *Parties and Leaders in the Postreform House* (Chicago: University of Chicago Press, 1991); several papers by John Aldrich and David Rhode, including, "The Consequences of Party Government in the House" (paper presented at "Congress and the President in a Partisan Era," Texas A&M University, February 5–6, 1999); Barbara Sinclair, *Legislators, Leaders, and Lawmaking* (Baltimore: Johns Hopkins, 1995), and Gary Cox and Matthew McCubbins, *Legislative Leviathan: Party Government in the House* (Berkeley: University of California Press, 1993).

ings did nothing to challenge this perspective. Virtually always in the House and often, if in more muted ways, in the Senate, party stood out as the core distinguishing characteristic between Clinton's accusers and his defenders. Not that *any* legislator defended the president's actions — especially his sexual relations with an intern, but also his subsequent perjury in a civil case. Rather, party came into play in terms of whether the president had committed an impeachable offense, and subsequently, in the Senate, of whether he was guilty, as charged, to the two impeachment articles.

Drawing heavily on Independent Counsel Kenneth Starr's investigation, his extensive record, and his recommendations, the House majority relied on a highly partisan Judiciary Committee to sort out the charges. Both Republicans and Democrats on the Judiciary Committee reflected the partisan extremes of their respective parties; there was little chance that they would reach some middle ground. Led by conservative (and historically fair-minded) Representative Henry Hyde (R-Ill.), the majority called no witnesses and expeditiously moved toward impeachment in the weeks following the 1998 election.

The partisan context of the impeachment decision was straightforward and reflected the fact that, on various measures, the Congress of the 1990s was highly partisan.[24] This context is well-illustrated by a comparison of the House of Representatives in the 93rd Congress (1973–1974) and 104th Congress (1995–1996). The latter House demonstrates much greater ideological compactness than the earlier one (see Figure 10–1). That is, Republicans and Democrats were both more tightly bunched, and more distinct, in the mid-1990s than they were in the period of the Nixon impeachment.[25] Not only were the groupings more compact, fewer House members approached the ideological center of the moment. As political scientist Terry Sullivan concludes, "The middle ground . . . disappears by the 104th Congress. Very few members in either party can bridge the gap between the ideological centers of the two parties. . . . No one scratches anyone's back anymore. Rather, they reserve scratching for the eyes."[26]

As Sullivan implies, congressional partisanship is not just a construct of voting patterns. It also includes an element of hostility than extends both across the aisle within the Congress, especially in the House, and across the branches of government, with many Republican members expressing extensive hostility toward the president. In particular, the consideration of impeachment on the House floor in late 1998 brought out levels of uncivil behavior that exceeded even the breakdown in comity that occurred in the first session of the 104th Congress (1995). Communications scholar Kathleen Hall Jamieson

---

[24]See, for example, the discussion by R. Lawrence Butler, "Conditional Party Government and Its Alternatives: Defining Party Power in the House" (paper presented at Midwest Political Science Association meeting, Chicago, April 15–17, 1999).

[25]Terry Sullivan, "Impeachment Practice in the Era of Lethal Conflict," *Congress and the Presidency* 25 (Autumn 1998), 117–129.

[26]Sullivan, "Impeachment Practice," p. 127.

FIGURE 10-1
The Partisan Contest for Impeachment in the House, 93rd and 104th Congresses
(1973-1974 and 1995-1996)

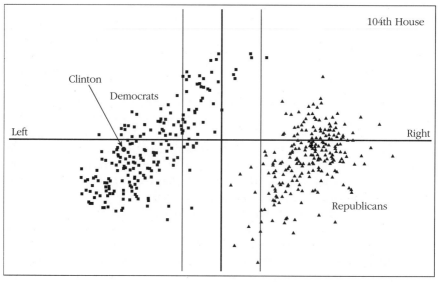

Source: Terry Sullivan, "Impeachment Practice in an Era of Lethal Conflict," *Congress and the Presidency* 25 (Autumn 1998), p. 126.

observes that some elements of the House debate were handled with decorum and thoughtful exchanges, but in general the impeachment resolution generated low levels of cooperation and substantial increases in vulgarity and name-calling.[27] Party-based hostilities returned to the House floor, sometimes exceeding the rancor of the tumultuous first few months of 1995.

At the beginning of the House impeachment proceedings, Judiciary Committee chairman Hyde observed that the process would have to be bipartisan, or else it would fail. Yet as the weeks ran on, there was little in the committee work that was not partisan. Each party in the House has grown more homogeneous, and the Judiciary Committee's composition exaggerated such a trend. In fact, the committee included virtually no Republican moderates; rather its roster was dominated by social conservatives, almost half of whom won their seats in 1994 or 1996.[28] Democrats were similarly left of center and disproportionately represented by minority members. If anyone thought there would be, or could be, effective deliberation within the Judiciary Committee, that person was sorely mistaken.

Nor would the partisanship and the absence of deliberation be any different on the House floor, where debate was limited and the two articles of impeachment (on one count of perjury and one of obstructing justice) were adopted on heavily party-line votes (228-206 and 221-212, respectively). Nevertheless, the House did reject two other articles, including one on abuse of power, which was soundly defeated. In the end, some Republicans broke ranks on these votes, but the key decisions were split along party lines, as only five Democrats voted for impeachment on the two articles that were adopted, while five and twelve Republicans, respectively, voted in opposition.

The partisanship of the House debate and the subsequent votes probably doomed any real chance of convicting President Clinton in the Senate. There were never any indications that twelve Democratic votes existed to combine with the fifty-five Republicans to convict the president on either count. Such a foreordained outcome contributed to a less vitriolic, far more civil process in the Senate. At the same time, the final votes did break down, for the most part, along party lines. In fact, the Senate Democrats, who voted unanimously against impeachment on both counts, acted more as a block than their Republican counterparts in the Senate or either House party.

In the end, partisanship did define the impeachment process, as manifested in terms of both voting and, especially in the House, the uncivil nature of the debate. Yet the Senate demonstrated that the proceedings could be partisan while remaining reasonably civil. Indeed, most legislators see strong parties and differences over issues as healthy, even as they decry the decline of comity in Congress.

---

[27]Kathleen Hall Jamieson, "Civility in the House of Representatives: The 105th Congress," report prepared by Annenberg Public Policy Center, University of Pennsylvania, March 1999.

[28]Don Carney, "Hyde Staying above Clinton Fray but Tries to Raise Panel Profile," *Congressional Quarterly Weekly Report,* March 7, 1998, p. 564.

THE POST-IMPEACHMENT CONGRESS:
THE STRUGGLE FOR CONTROL
AND THE LIMITS OF PARTY

If, as Aldrich and Rohde contend, the "condition" of party (as measured by the size and unity of the majority, especially in the House) defines congressional politics,[29] why are we also concerned about divided government, gridlock, and the rampant individualism of the U.S. Senate?[30] In part the answer is self-evident: That is, we do live in a system of checks and balances, where the president and the courts, to say nothing of the bureaucracy, have their say. Still, some of the limits on parties derive from the nature of congressional politics, both in permanent and transitory ways. Among the permanent limitations include the strength of individual lawmakers, both to win reelection and to use their substantial individual resources to affect the policy process.

A single Representative may not have much influence on his or her own, but 435 individuals, all with professional staffers, can move a host of issues, large and small. One brief example can illustrate this point. Representative Henry Waxman (D-Calif.) has proven himself one of the great "policy entrepreneurs" of the modern Congress. A formidable member of the majority for two decades, he has also demonstrated himself capable of affecting policies as a member of the minority party. In April 1999, for instance, he raised the issue of whether the federal government should allow tax breaks for corporations whose sponsorship benefited the International Olympic Committee (IOC), which was thoroughly enmeshed in a scandal over locating the 2002 Winter Olympics in Salt Lake City. Waxman saw an opportunity, and by merely raising the issue he inserted himself, as a member of the powerful Commerce Committee, into the debate. "We need to put pressure on for real reform," he noted.[31] Moreover, he framed the issue in such a way as to move discussion beyond partisanship. The ultimate impact of his actions remains up in the air, but Waxman clearly used his position as a member of Congress to press his case for reform of the IOC, an international body, but heavily dependent on U.S. revenues. Individual senators, of course, wield considerably more power than do their House colleagues, both due to their staff and to the extent that the Senate conducts its business by unanimous consent (see Chapter 9).

In the post-1994 era, however, the greatest limitation on even well-disciplined legislative parties has been the small size of the majorities. The elections of 1994, 1996, and 1998 produced an average majority of 227 for the Republicans in the House, against 207 Democrats (and one Democrat-leaning independent).

---

[29]John H. Aldrich and David W. Rohde, "Measuring Conditional Party Government," paper presented at Midwest Political Science Association meetings, April 23–5, 1998, Chicago.

[30]See David W. Brady and Craig Volden, *Revolving Gridlock* (Boulder: Westview, 1998).

[31]Alan Abrahamson, "Widening Olympic Scandal Takes to Hill Today," *Los Angeles Times,* April 14, 1998, p. D8.

A group of a dozen Republicans could threaten the majority's ability to move legislation. It's no wonder that the 1990s witnessed an *increase* in the number of special-interest caucuses within the Congress, even as the Republican leadership sought to discourage their existence and limit their activities.[32] Moreover, there is little on the horizon (however cloudy) to suggest that either Democrats or Republicans will win a sweeping majority in the House in the near future.

Two well-established trends indicate that a rough partisan balance is likely to remain for some time. First, the capacity of incumbent House members to win reelection remains one of the cornerstones of Congress in the modern era. After the relatively high turnovers of 1992 and 1994 (see Chapter 4), incumbent survival rates averaged more than 96 percent for the 1996 and 1998 elections. The price of entry to mount a competitive congressional campaign continues to rise, approaching $1 million for the 2000 elections. Second, and directly related to the first trend, most House members come from districts that are relatively homogeneous and do not necessarily tend toward being competitive. One look at the geography of representation in the House demonstrates the implications of this development (see Figure 10-2).[33] Districts in much of the South, substantial parts of the Midwest, and lots of the Mountain West are disproportionately represented by Republicans, often of a very conservative stripe. Conversely, Democrats clearly dominate in the East, on the West Coast, and in some other parts of the Midwest. The number of truly competitive House seats has stood at under fifty in 1996 and 1998, and in the latter year the actual number may have been as low as twenty.

Ironically, the small number of competitive races—the remainder of the "vanishing marginals" (see Chapter 4)—has not meant that less money is spent on congressional campaigning. Rather, the national parties have focused their attention and funding on a relatively small number of hotly contested seats.[34] In addition, both parties' congressional leaders in Congress have encouraged their colleagues to send excess campaign funds to the close races. In short, the campaigns for a small number of competitive House seats have become nationally important.

Still, no matter how much the parties' congressional campaign committees spend on a handful of close races, a narrow House majority of either party will remain beholden to a myriad of internal factions. Even if party discipline were perfect, a closely divided House would surely be matched to a similar Senate, where 60 votes are often required to take major actions, in light of the rules on extended debate (filibusters).

Even though parties have grown stronger inside the Congress and as forces within the electoral system, they will not be able to dominate congressional

---

[32]Susan Webb Hammond, *Congressional Caucuses in National Policy-Making* (Washington: Brookings Institution, 1997).

[33]John Maggs, "Divided We Stand," *National Journal,* March 20, 1999, pp. 748–751.

[34]Eliza Newlin Carney, "Winner Take All," *National Journal,* March 20, 1999, pp. 734–740.

FIGURE 10–2
The Geographic Base of Partisanship

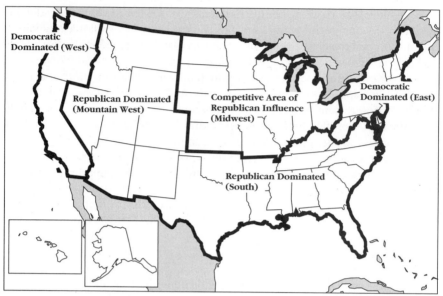

Source: Adapted from National Journal, March 29, 1999, p. 751

policy making unless one of them produces enough of a majority to survive the influences of small groupings of majority-party members who have their own policy preferences. In the 106th Congress, for example, moderate Republicans hold disproportionate power—not because of their positions or persuasiveness—but due to their capacity to join with Democrats to thwart the leanings of most GOP members. In fact, the region-based homogeneity of the parties, which might conventionally be seen as strengthening them, may serve to reduce their capacity to act effectively in an era of narrow partisan margins. Even if leaders wanted to compromise and deliberate in good faith, their members' constituencies may make such reconciliation difficult, if not impossible.

In the end, a Congress of strong, closely divided parties may be able to act only when they can produce large majorities, especially under the conditions of divided government. It may be up to the electorate to provide further direction to a highly partisan, yet simultaneously atomistic, Congress. The tension between centralization and decentralization remains a defining element of this, our most representative branch.

As with the Congress circa 1900, the contemporary Congress, for all its centralization of power in the House, retains much of its fragmentation. The extreme individualism of the Senate remains the most notable example of the staying power of centrifugal forces on Capitol Hill. Beyond the Senate, however, the unity of House Republicans continues to be tested by divisions on social issues, tax cuts, budget priorities, term limits, and the appropriate role of the federal government.

The very nature of representation demands that tensions among individual legislators eat away at strong, centralized party (or presidential) leadership. In the end, presidents and legislative leaders can do little to affect the fates of the lawmakers they seek to lead. On occasion, as in 1995 (or 1964–1966), members provide the votes and cede the authority that makes for strong leadership. But party leaders and presidents rarely capture the Congress for long, as legislators return to Maine, Kansas, or California to renew their personal contracts with the electorate. The very nature of representation — in Hanna Pitkin's words, "acting in the interest of the represented, in a manner responsive to them"[35] — means that the tensions between action and delay, between centralization and decentralization, will continue to define the nature of the contemporary Congress, even in a partisan age.

---

[35]Hanna F. Pitkin, *The Concept of Representation* (Berkeley: University of California Press, 1967).

INDEX